RECEIVED
OCT - - 2017
By

D0122711

VOICE LESSONS

ST. MARTIN'S PRESS NEW YORK

VOICE LESSONS

A SISTERS STORY

CARA MENTZEL

FOREWORD BY MY BIG SISTER,

IDINA MENZEL

 Printed in the United States of America. For information, address St. Martin's Press, 175 Fifth Avenue, New York, NY 10010.

www.stmartins.com

Photos courtesy of the Mentzel family

The Library of Congress Cataloging-in-Publication Data is available upon request.

ISBN 978-1-250-10524-0 (hardcover)
ISBN 978-1-250-10525-7 (ebook)

First Edition: October 2017

10 9 8 7 6 5 4 3 2 1

For Dina

Contents

Foreword *ix*

Prologue *1*

PART I. TWO GIRLS

Lesson 1: How to Breathe *9*

Lesson 2: How to Work Things Out—Or Not *25*

Lesson 3: How to Play a Part *36*

PART II. MOVING ON

Lesson 4: How to Measure a Year *57*

Lesson 5: How to Sing a Solo *86*

Lesson 6: How to Sing a Duet *105*

PART III. FLYING HIGH

Lesson 7: How to Fail *127*

Lesson 8: How to Love a Witch *139*

Lesson 9: How to *Want* to Win *155*

Lesson 10: How to Make Mistakes *164*

Lesson 11: How to Make Hello Dollies *174*

Lesson 12: How to Envy *185*

PART IV. LETTING GO

Lesson 13: How to Live *201*

Lesson 14: How to Make a Mark (or Marry One) *211*

Lesson 15: How to Jump *226*

Lesson 16: How to Let Go *238*

Acknowledgments *257*

Foreword

I am not the writer in the family. In fact, the last good metaphor I wrote was probably back in the fourth grade when my favorite teacher of all time, Mrs. Rosalind Pincus, rosy cheeked, always jolly, saw the blizzard outside our Baylis Elementary School windows and exclaimed, "Children! Oh children! Pick up your pencils and run to the window! I want you to write a poem about what you see!" I obediently grabbed my pencil and Bionic Woman spiral notebook and wrote the masterpiece entitled "The White Ghost." It proudly lives in the drawer at the bottom of my mother's armoire where every so often she pulls it out in an attempt to build my confidence when I need to write something of merit.

No, I'm not the writer in the family. So when an agent came to me asking if I would write a book about my life, I rudely laughed in her face. I have no desire to write about myself. I actually don't enjoy writing. Songwriting is excruciating for me, which is why I now make sure I collaborate with others *all* the time. I hate the pressure of completing a song. More than anything I dread the "morning after" feeling when I think I've written my first smash hit only to find it sucks or I ripped off some melody from a Beyoncé song. So the task of writing about my life? Not for me. Though, the writing gene did find my sister.

I told the agent that my sister, Cara, was a writer. She enthusiastically suggested that Cara write the book for me. "She can be your ghostwriter!" And I told her my sister isn't "ghosting" anything. A ghostwriter is some mysterious person who writes for people but doesn't get credit. There was no way I would allow that. My sister writing my story was not okay with me. It needed to be *our* story.

It just made sense. At their core, so many of the projects I've been involved with have explored the bond between women. Elsa and Anna. Elphaba and Glinda. Best friends. Sisters. Not always pretty, not always perfect. Yet these relationships, these amazing women, have shaped the way I see the world. There is an uncanny, inexplicable reason these projects keep finding me. And I am so grateful for that.

Years before anyone had heard of the film *Frozen*, Cara would send me these hysterical, beautiful little essays about the two of us. Just stuff that she was reminiscing about. I sent out some of her writing samples, encouraged the agent to check them out, and said, "You should let her write the book; not some biography, but a book about us as sisters."

Selfishly I thought this was a wonderful way to bond even more with Cara. She lives in Colorado. I live everywhere. Our lives are so busy, caught up in career and kids and trying to remember birthdays and spa treatments for our mother on Mother's Day. After all is said and done, how much quality time have we really spent together? How many details do we truly know about each other's day? I was excited about the idea of this book. Ha! I was excited about her writing it and me sticking my two cents in every so often to say "That's not how it happened" or "Wait, you should talk about the time . . ."

Years back, I had an idea for a moment in one of my concerts, to finish the haftorah I never had. It's a special prayer Jewish kids "perform" at their bar mitzvah ceremony. My parents let me quit Hebrew school when

I complained of an impatient teacher getting aggravated by my barrage of questions about God and how certain things in the Bible seemed sexist and unforgiving and not befitting a god whom I was praying to at night. So, having failed my grandparents and hearing for the next twenty years what a shame it was that I didn't sing my haftorah, I thought I would revisit it in my late thirties on stage. I had learned of a woman in the Bible named Devorah (also known as Deborah and Dvora). "The Triple Threat" I liked to call her. The poet, the judge, and general. And she sang too! When summoning her armies to battle, her husband—also a general, who would never go without her—would chant, "The rulers ceased in Israel until you Devorah arose. Awake, awake, Devorah, awake and sing your song." A few years earlier, I'd taken a trip to see my sister and baby nephew, Avery. When Cara went to put him down for his nap, I listened at the bedroom door and overheard her sing Avery to sleep. Cara never sang around me, or anyone for that matter. I was the singer in the family. I had some invisible claim to that. But just then she had the most hauntingly beautiful voice. It was sweet and pure and emotional. In that moment I felt as if I had stolen something from her. All these years. That voice was inside my sister and I didn't even know. By the time I wrote about Devorah, Cara was pushing through some hard times. She was busting her ass to finish her master's degree, provide for her children, and keep her writing dreams alive. She was my Devorah, the true warrior. She needed her chance to rise up and shine.

Nearly a decade later, in my blind enthusiasm for this book, I failed to realize that writing our story wasn't going to be all that simple. This whole book journeys through the lives of older and younger siblings and the shadow-dancing we do. I wanted this to be Cara's book. Cara's perspective. I didn't want to rob her of the purity of the accomplishment. I didn't want to steal her light.

It's funny. To me, Cara was always the old soul, the wiser, the younger sister with the older sister who looked to her for guidance. I called her first. Number one. When I felt like life was falling apart at the seams. She taught me so much about the kind of woman I wanted to be. In this book, she's not just telling our story, but she's speaking for all of us trying to figure out who we are. Who we want to be. Sisterhood is a complicated relationship. Anytime you love someone so much you are not sure where you start and where they begin. When is the right time to bask in their glow and when do you need to separate yourself and find your own stage? Sometimes it was hard to hear about those moments when I hurt her or let her down. And I know it was no fun for Cara to turn the spotlight on herself magnifying her innermost fears and thoughts. But every moment is authentic and true and if we can't look at the mistakes we have made we never evolve. In our version of snowy Arendelle, there are no "white ghosts" or ghostwriters, just siblings, each one deserving to be seen and heard. I forgive myself for being a young, scrawny little wicked witch-in-training who coerced my baby sister to drink from a dirt potion I concocted in our backyard. And as traumatizing as it sounds, Cara survived and lived to tell a pretty cool tale of two sisters from Long Island, lost in a perpetual search to find their true voices.

—Idina Menzel

Prologue

On a typical day, I wear a pair of Chuck Taylors, jeans, and a sweater long enough to cover my butt when I bend over in the classroom to pick up a stray glue stick. I teach elementary school students how to read while doing my best to steer clear of snot (theirs) and profanity (mine)—at least until after 3:00. At home I have two dogs, two boys, and a husband. At home I try to steer clear of farts (particularly in the kitchen), and anyone who's gonna give me shit for cussing.

I don't mean to be misleading; I clean up nicely, I just don't clean up often. And that's why being on the red carpet at the Oscars with Dee was such a shock; glamour is in short supply where I live.

My sister—I call her Dee—is Tony Award–winning Broadway star Idina Menzel. She starred in *Rent, Wicked,* and, most recently, *If/Then*. Moreover, she is the voice of Disney's Elsa, the powerful ice queen, in the blockbuster *Frozen*. She sings the infectious torch song "Let It Go," which set records on the *Billboard* charts and landed her on the cover of *Billboard* magazine. The one that had little girls singing into video cameras all over the globe, "Let it go . . . can't hold it back anymore" and "The cold never bothered me anyway" was the same one my elementary school students constantly sang in the hallways, pointing at me and whispering, "That's Elsa's sister."

When the song was nominated for an Academy Award, Dee was asked to perform it live at the ceremony. Singing at the Oscars was a contender for the grandest moment of her career to date, right up there with serenading President Obama and Barbra Streisand, and with winning a Tony Award. I was her date.

Dee has been on the stage as far back as my first memories, back when she was Mabel in the fourth-grade production of *The Pirates of Penzance* on a stage made out of Baylis Elementary School risers. But even more prominently, she's been on a pedestal in my mind. There are just two children in our family, and I'm the younger one. I've looked up to her for the same reasons so many little sisters and brothers look up to their older siblings—because she was three years better than me at everything: tennis, painting, calligraphy . . . even folding little boxes out of dollar bills with Grandpa Max. When it came to singing, though, she wasn't just better than *me,* she was better than anyone we knew.

Dee and I arrived on the red carpet to flashing cameras, screaming fans, and a demanding press corps that hounded the celebrities to glance in their direction. To our left, velvet ropes separated the celebrities from a thick line of journalists with large microphones awaiting interviews. To our right was a morphing mass of people—stars with their agents, managers, and spouses or dates. In the distance stood the entrance to The Dolby Theatre. I'd anticipated the frenzy, the glitz and the glamour, but it still felt bizarre to stand in the heart of it.

Dee looked beautiful, as beautiful as I was proud. Her dark brown hair was parted to the side, straight and sleek, her makeup understated—she doesn't need makeup to look beautiful. She has full heart-shaped lips, steep cheekbones once described by *The New York Times* "as distinctive as the New York skyline," and green eyes. She wore a dark green Vera Wang gown with a four-foot train. A gown her stylist described with words I assume are French but can neither define nor pronounce, words like *godet, degredes,* and *ruche.*

I followed Dee through the crowd. Every now and then she looked over her shoulder at me and reached her hand back, checking in with her eyes and the slightest dip of her chin—an expression that said, *You with me?* She was taking care of me, which I was used to. I extended my hand toward the borrowed million-dollar diamond ring she wore.

I reached forward, but the train of Dee's dress was just long enough to keep our hands a mere centimeter apart. I'd known that centimeter—if only metaphorically—for a long time. And I'd come to hate it. When people asked if we were close I always said yes—a true answer. Our love was as significant and near as my hand, never doubted, never absent.

But I've always wished we were closer. I've wished I knew what she did, what she felt on any given day. I've wished she called me for no reason at all, to chat, to check in, to tell me that she woke up that morning to find my four-year-old nephew playing the drums naked. I've wished I were a habit for her, that when she fiddled absentmindedly with her phone she always thought to call me. Instead, more often we've joined at the extremes, at the Tony Awards or Broadway openings. Events drenched in logistics—flights and hotels, timelines and schedules. Celebrations that afforded us really only mini-moments together—a photo op or a quick hug. Occasionally, we had slightly more time together at a family wedding or a baby's birth, but she lived in Manhattan and Los Angeles, and I lived in Colorado.

When we weren't together for celebrations, we were together when it was time to grieve—a divorce, a death. We sat next to each other at our grandmother's funeral, and took naps curled up in bed together when our respective marriages ended. In between those landmark events, our time was spent apart—not only because taking a flight to see each other was a pain in the ass, or because we both have busy lives full of daily responsibilities, but because sometimes she was hard to reach. Those lulls in our relationship were difficult for me. When I *needed* her she was always there, but I didn't want to need her in order to have her in my life. My sister and I shared love, but we often haven't shared our lives. I've wished we did.

On the red carpet Dee's tall, blond publicist cleared a lane for us through the crowd. Dee followed her and I followed Dee. As far as I could tell, the publicist's job that evening was to guide Dee through the crowd and tell her when to stop for photos and interviews. As Dee's date, my job was to stay with her, but also, in some instances, to step out of the way and wait; there would be interviews and photos she needed to do alone. It wasn't always clear to me when I should step up and take my place beside her and when I should step back, so I was self-conscious.

Dee, meanwhile, waved to fans and smiled graciously. She had mastered the art of what she called "Chin Down, Eyes Up."

"With our long noses, you have to tilt your chin down a bit, but look up at the camera," she explained. Dee had graced many red carpets before, at theater and movie openings and the Tony Awards. But this was the Oscars, or, as I like to call it, Hollywood Prom. I suspected that even Dee was a little unnerved; the red carpet at the Oscars was on another scale altogether. The Chimento diamonds around her neck were a testament to that.

I didn't want to be nervous. Nerves were inconvenient. When I'm nervous I have to go to the bathroom. I sweat. I put on a phony smile so my face starts to feel (and, I'm sure, look) like plastic.

I tried to talk myself out of being nervous. *Get a grip, Cara. Breathe. Breathe, but don't trip. But if you do trip, don't take anyone else down with you.* My composure teetered on four-inch Casadei heels. I knew the shoe designer only because Dee's publicist—or was it her stylist?—had asked me to memorize the names of the designers of everything I was wearing that evening, even my clutch—"clutch," a term I'd never used in my pre-Oscar life. My entire getup, with the exception of my thong, was borrowed, and that made me a walking advertisement. My clutch: Nancy Gonzalez. My diamonds: Forevermark (a name I loved because my husband's name is Mark). My dress: Vera Wang. I'm not too proud to admit that I had anxiously rehearsed these facts earlier in my

Four Seasons at Beverly Hills suite, in the privacy of my room's full-length mirror. Even though I wasn't Dee, I was told to be prepared for the question, "And who are *you* wearing, dahling?" The shameless *People* magazine lover in me wouldn't dare screw up the answer.

Dee gave a couple of interviews as I waited behind her in the adjacent crowd. I chatted with her two managers and her agent, people who have worked with my sister for many years and have taken good care of her. We hug—her entourage and I—whenever we see each other, but I'm still not clear exactly what their responsibilities are. I don't really know the difference between an agent and a manager, or how many of each someone in my sister's profession needs. I know their names, that Dee loves them, and that with them I felt more comfortable on the red carpet. In their company I was safe from the chaos and didn't have to stand awkwardly alone, waiting.

The people around me were checking their iPhones, probably to see how well *their* celebrity was trending on social media. I couldn't resist the urge to snap a few quick selfies, but mostly I tried to ignore my phone altogether, until I felt it vibrate and noticed a text from my teenage son. It read, "You just picked your butt on national television." Minutes earlier I'd pulled the back of my dress out from under my heel and apparently it was caught on camera; I thought I'd been subtle. Not so.

Striking another stiff, contrived pose, I felt more like a witness to the Hollywood hullabaloo than a participant. I had to remind myself I was *on* television, not watching it. But I *was* watching, too, and I was a good and practiced observer. I'd been watching Dee perform nearly my whole life. I was an audience of one listening to her sing in the bedroom next door. I sat in living rooms, auditoriums, gymnasiums, and theaters watching her perform in casual, amateur, and then professional productions, and joined a television audience of millions watching her sing on *The Late Show with David Letterman*. The image of Dee standing in the spotlight was long fixed in my mind.

When Dee resumed her walk up the red carpet, I followed carefully behind. It was only seconds before she reached back for me again. I read the expression on her face and it was familiar—concern. She didn't like that I was trailing behind her. I knew it. We'd had *that* conversation before. The one where she says she wants me to feel *more* special when I'm with her, not less. The one where I admit that I sometimes feel less significant when I'm with her and she admits it's hard to feel like her success sometimes hurts me. The one where Dee says that she has *me* on a pedestal, that I'm *her* hero, that her confidence in me is greater than my confidence in myself—and that drives her crazy. The one that ends with tears because our feelings are so knotted together, we don't know how to untie them.

That night, Dee was to perform a song from a story about sisters. An older sister, Elsa, who had special powers. A younger sister, Anna, who yearned to be closer to her. Two sisters who wanted to take care of each other and two sisters whose lives evolved in relationship to one another. I knew the story well. Dee and I had a similar story, and the irony wasn't lost on me.

PART I

TWO GIRLS

Lesson 1

HOW TO BREATHE

Dina—that's what I called her then—was nearly seven years old, and I was three. We sat facing each other across a couple of feet of dirt, surrounded by crunchy fall leaves. The weather had turned crisp as autumn inched its way toward winter, and Mom had dressed us in turtlenecks—red and pink, with jeans and loose pigtails, our hair fuzzy around our foreheads the way it always was after a good night's sleep. With imaginations as vivid as our shirts, we pretended we were witches making a potion.

"Pass me that pebble," Dina said. I hopped up and grabbed the pebble. When I gave her the stone she dropped it into the dirt in front of us. Then she scraped a thin layer of sand into her hand and let it fall onto the pile as if her closed fist were the narrow neck of an hourglass.

"Now all we need is a big spoon to mix it," she told me. I looked around and spotted a twig the length of a magic wand.

"I got it!" I shouted. I uncrossed my legs and bolted toward the twig, then returned with it.

"Perfect," she said. Her approval sent a happy wiggle through my belly.

She took the stick and moved it through the dirt in slow circles, her eyes fixed on the potion, my eyes fixed on her. She began to whisper, and her voice, a soothing spell, grew steadily louder.

"Ree-ma-ta-din, Ree-ma-ta-din," she chanted over and over, and then set the stick down beside her. She reached into the pile of dirt and scooped up a small handful.

"Here," she said, lifting her upturned palm to my chin, the dirt a tiny present. "Taste it." My eyes widened. But not because I was afraid. I wasn't worried. I *wanted* to eat it. I wanted to play my part, to please my big sister. I looked up at her, spellbound. I dabbed my tongue gently into her hand and tasted the dirt. I smiled.

I met Dina on August 12, 1974, the day I was born. She looked in my eyes and smiled, so I'm told. She kissed me. She held me on her little lap, close. She loved me.

Two weeks later I stopped breathing. My mother found me in my crib. I wasn't blue, just pale and silent and still—too still, no rise and fall of my chest. She lifted me and hit me on the back—nothing. Again harder, again nothing. She laid me on my back, opened my tiny mouth, and placed a single finger down my throat. She withdrew her finger and with it thick and slippery strands of clear mucus. I took a breath. I wailed.

I was barely eight pounds when I arrived at the hospital, coughing. Short quick coughs, one on top of the other, each one quieter than the one before it, until I was empty and silent. Suffocating. Waiting and waiting on that next breath. Then, a gasping squeal. Only to cry or begin the litany again.

The doctors and nurses strapped me to a table and took X-rays. They splayed me like a chicken from the butcher and took blood from every possible vein, even in my groin—Dad fainted. They put tubes down my throat, up my nose. And they jammed instruments down my airway.

But as Mom tells the story, sometimes the doctors and nurses didn't do anything. They ignored my cries, my choking, and she was the one, day and night, who cleared my throat and watched me suffer.

Mom was by my side constantly, rarely sleeping. Dad was between work, the hospital, and shuffling Dina, only three and half years old, to family or friends' homes. An uncle was probably pulling a quarter out of her ear.

There was more coughing. More gagging. More blood. More needles. My trachea, narrower than a standard pencil, was bloody, bruised, torn. And a sterile packaged scalpel waited, like a threat, on a sterile tray next to the sterile makeshift oxygen tent where I lay. Tracheotomy?

They told Mom and Dad I had a newborn cough.

I continued to cough and wail, a raspy, rattling cry. Day, night. Day and night.

They changed the diagnosis. I had cystic fibrosis. If I lived, it would probably be until I was twenty or twenty-one years old.

They changed the diagnosis again. No longer did I have cystic fibrosis. Instead, my mother was a "nervous" mother and I had a "nervous" cough. They urged her to take Valium. She refused.

"We're done here," Mom finally said to the doctors. "I'm not letting my daughter die here."

"You can't take her out of the hospital," they insisted. "We'll file an injunction."

"I don't give a shit," Mom replied.

There was a rescue mission. Our neighborhood had a rescue squad saddled with the task of ensuring neighborhood safety. In the name of safety, they agreed to shuttle me to a new hospital. Mom bundled me up. She walked down a hall past an army of giant egos. She walked down another hall. Entered the elevator. Entered the lobby. Walked out the doors and met three burly firefighters and their ambulance. She handed me to them and they helped her into the back. Dad pulled his car up next to them. He'd drive in tandem.

A nurse, a nun, at the new hospital met Mom and Dad at the entrance; Mom was holding me in her arms.

"Mrs. Mentzel," she said. "If Cara so much as yawns, we'll be there. I promise."

Mom and Dad cried. The nurse reached for me. "It's safe to sleep now," she said to them. "Your daughter is going to live."

I hadn't seen my sister in ten days. She'd barely seen Mom or Dad. A close family friend was probably fanning out a deck of cards in front of her, "Pick a card, any card," she'd be saying.

They had an accurate diagnosis within twenty-four hours. I had pertussis—whooping cough. Mom had it when I was born, but didn't know. There were twelve hundred cases in the New Jersey metro area that year.

I hadn't seen my sister in a month. Finally, I went home—we *all* went home. My sister and I were together again. She looked into my eyes and smiled, so I'm told. She kissed me. She held me in a rocking chair, close. She loved me.

Home had changed for my sister. Mom was on high alert. *Was Cara still breathing? Did Cara cough?* Mom hunted every germ in my surroundings and wouldn't let my sister have friends over. "Don't touch the baby," Mom would say. "Wash your hands first." "Be careful with your sister." "Can you go check on your sister?"

Back then I guess I was the center of attention, but not in the same way as other babies, who go home from the hospital and their older siblings have to step aside a bit. I was the center of attention because I was sick. Because fighting the whoop was all I knew, and even when it was gone it left me weak in its wake. My family was in a perpetual state of fear over losing me. And though I can't be certain, I suspect my sister also feared being left again.

It took nearly a year for me to fully recover. And by then illness was more familiar to me than health. I'd become Cara so little, Cara so weak.

Cara so fragile.

Cara who needs to be rescued.

But every new experience was an opportunity to tip the scales back toward health. By the time I was one, I'd played on a Florida beach with my big sister in the moist ocean air. I'd giggled and gurgled and squealed and watched her do her big-sis magic, building castles on the shore. I would need Dina, her and her magic.

In my earliest years, my family lived in New Jersey, but it wasn't long before Dina and I were making potions out of Long Island dirt instead of New Jersey's finest. Dad worked in New York City's Garment District selling little-girls' pajamas. Our dresser drawers overflowed with them. But Dad's commute was over two hours, and moving to Long Island would cut that time in half.

Our new house—Mom called it a town house—was located in Woodbury. It stood side by side with white, gray, brown, and brick homes, all shoved together like kids in a class photo. We went to see it one day when it was still under construction. I stood in the center of its bare skeleton and looked around. Instead of walls there were vertical slats of wood every two feet or so. There were no windows and yet I could see the sky. There were no doors and yet Mom pointed to rooms. My new house appeared to be made of life-size Tinkertoys and the thought made me curl my toes inside my sneakers.

"Dina, this is your room," Mom said, motioning to the left. "And, Cara, right next door is yours." Our two rooms looked like one giant one and I imagined our toys on the floor, our blankets on the beds, our clothes folded in piles on a dresser—I breathed a sigh of relief as I stared at the stage for what I believed would be one big, shared childhood.

Dina and I explored the house. We dared to walk through "walls" and jump over stacks of two-by-fours piled on the floor.

"Where are we now?" Dina shouted over to Mom, who, apparently, was in the master bedroom.

"You're in the bathroom," Mom answered.

"The bathroom!" Dina repeated and her eyes lit up.

"The bathroom!" I copied. We read each other's minds and simultaneously pretended to sit on potties. We made potty jokes. We were giddy. When Dina reached for imaginary toilet paper and turned around to "flush," I squealed.

We were on the top floor of a house that seemed to stand on stilts. There were no comforts of home, no sidewalks or bicycles, no friends, no memories. I could have been afraid. I could have been lonely. But I wasn't, because fear and loneliness were fleeting when I was with Dina. I loved to hear her say, "Cara, over here!" as she called me to her. I loved when she bossed me around. I knew that one day soon she'd push me down that new street on my Hot Wheels and shout, "Don't drag your feet, lift them up so you'll go faster!" I knew she'd pull me by my hand down the block, and carry our money to the ice cream truck. I knew she'd call for me, shout at me, push me and pull me, because I was hers and she was mine. I may not have been able to picture where the rooms in that house began and ended, but I could picture Dina with me. And in that would-be bathroom, I could hear the make-believe flushing sound from our pretend pair of toilets, and see the water swirl down the white porcelain drain. I looked up at her as she spoke.

"Don't forget to wash your hands," she said and motioned over to the future sink.

It didn't matter whether Dina fed me dirt or told me to wash it off my hands, I looked up to her. She took care of me, and I was happy to let her.

One night not long after we'd settled into the new place, a limousine pulled up in front of the house. I saw it from the kitchen window over the driveway. Dina came running downstairs and joined me. We both stared at the strange car. It was long and black and the size of our parents' two cars put together. Mom had told us earlier that we needed to get dressed up for dinner in the city with Dad's clients, but she never mentioned a limo. Dina and I wore matching black patent leather Mary Janes and the kind of kids' tights that slacked at the crotch and needed to be pulled up every five minutes.

We flew down the stairs to the curb. A driver came around the car to open the door for us, but I beat him to it. I slid in and tried out all the seats. They were plush and cranberry colored, more like opposing couches, and I half expected a coffee table to emerge between them. Dina and I took seats that faced the rear because it was more exciting—the seats in our cars faced forward. Dad sat across from me and stretched his legs out in front of him. His feet were a size thirteen—large feet are a noteworthy Mentzel trait—and I reached my miniature foot toward the sole of his shoe. Dad had curly hair like mine, but it was dark brown like Dina's. And he had a full beard. With his olive skin and blue eyes, my dad was good-looking, but with all that hair he learned to approach babies with caution, or he made them cry.

That night, like every night, Mom was put together perfectly. She was Farrah Fawcett with ash-blond hair feathered around her blushed cheeks. She wore a white silk halter top and full black slacks that swayed over her heels as she crossed her legs. She sat next to my dad, and placed her hand with its red fingernails on his thigh.

As excited as I was to be in a limo, I was annoyed that we were headed to dinner with Dad's clients. They would tell me that I was cute, maybe even pull gently on one of my curls. We'd go to a fancy restaurant—the kind with cloth napkins instead of the paper napkins I could blow my nose into. I'd wish I could eat dinner under the table with Dina, but instead I'd try to be polite and yawn through my nose so no one would notice.

I was happy but confused when we ended up at the Hard Rock Café and Dad's clients didn't show. I was even happier when, after dinner, our limo pulled over to another city curb. There was an awkward pause while Dina and I scooted over to see where we were. Out the window was a crowd and over their heads was a large marquee.

"Surprise!" Mom said. "We're going to see *Peter Pan.*"

"Are Dad's clients coming?" I asked.

"Nope," Dad said and laughed.

Dina and I were confused. We spent a few extended seconds puzzled as we pieced the evening together.

It wasn't until the limo driver came around and opened the door for us that I finally understood. We exited the car to the energy of an amusement park, to the brilliant colors and bright lights of Broadway. There were posters of a jubilant Sandy Duncan with her blond pixie cut, wearing green tights and shorts, her green vest and T-shirt, and her brown suede—let's be honest—fanny pack around her waist. The posters hung against the building, each one like a supersize invitation to a party, the *Peter Pan* party.

Soon there were tickets, and then ushers and playbills inside a palatial theater brimming with children who, on any other night at that time, would have been in the bathtub. Mom leaned in to us. She pointed. "That's the mezzanine," she said. "Over there is the orchestra. In the very beginning, they'll play the overture. There's the set. See the letters and numbers on the seats . . ." She liked to bring our attention to things, never wanting us to miss anything, and I appreciated that about her. I also liked that Dad was nearby. I once overheard someone ask him if it bothered him that he didn't have sons. "Never," he said, simply. I twisted around in my seat, the velvet kind with a flippy bottom that my butt would sink through if I let it.

The theater grew darker and my eyes grew wider. The overture began with a few notes from the song "Never Never Land." The music poured from the pit at the base of the stage and I wondered how all the musicians could fit down in that hole. The orchestra weaved through fragments of songs, but after a few minutes it became harder and harder for me to wait for the show to start. I looked at Dina, who stared expressionless at the stage, and wondered if she'd lost her patience with the overture as well.

It's a tall feat to keep a theater full of children seated for over two hours unless the show is at least as fun as recess. *Peter Pan* was better. Nothing could beat the excitement of Peter when he slipped through the Darlings' bedroom window and taught them how to fly. He sang, "I'm flying," and bounced into the air. "I'm flying," and hung above the stage, jumping and running and flapping his arms playfully. He didn't fly prone with a furrowed brow like Superman. He didn't fly for speed or with a sense of urgency. He flew for fun—no chores, no bedtime, and no school to weigh him down. Peter did what a theater packed with children dreamed of doing, what Wendy, Jon, and Michael Darling wished they could do, too. Then he grabbed a handful of fairy dust from his pouch and blew it onto the children. "Think lovely thoughts," he told them. *I can think lovely thoughts,* I told myself. *I want to fly.*

I felt so much a part of the play that I might as well have been on the stage in my favorite footsie pajamas because I'd forgotten where I was and the limitations of my seat. I stood up, my hands gripping the top of the seat in front of me, as the Darlings swung high above the stage, back and forth like pendulums. Then, unexpectedly, Peter flew straight out from the stage over the audience, and there was a collective gasp—a collective joy. My mouth dropped open. I watched as Peter swung over my head with his arms spread wide. When I caught my breath, I noticed Dina was up on her feet, too, beaming, her head following Peter back and forth through the air. The two of us, delighted. The two of us, dazzled.

On the limo ride home, Dina and I rambled on about the show. I wanted to be Tinker Bell, which was a little strange because Tinker Bell was a tiny light that darted around the stage. Dina wanted to be Wendy, which was much more understandable. Wendy was pretty and precocious and had a starring role.

We were in one of over a hundred cars filled with children who had just left the Lunt-Fontanne Theatre. Children telling their parents how they wanted to be Peter, or Wendy, or even Tinker Bell, how they too wanted to fly and star on Broadway. But that night was different for us than it was for other families. That night we were the exception; one of us *would* eventually star in another fairy tale production on the Great White Way. Like the flying boy in green named Peter, one day Dina would become the flying green witch named Elphaba in *Wicked*.

Sometimes I think Dina must have come out of the womb belting

"Everything's Coming Up Roses" like Ethel Merman, but my mom tells me that wasn't the case. "Actually, she cried like most babies." If you asked my mom when she realized Dina could sing, she'd say that her dad, my grandpa Nat, knew first. He was the one to introduce Dina to her earliest make-believe audiences. She used to hide behind our black velvet couch with a toy reconditioned to look like a microphone.

"Introducing the ONE, the ONLY, Idina Mentzel!" he'd announce in much the same way one would announce the heavyweight champion of the world. Dina would hop up from behind the couch, her microphone in hand, her hair in disarray from "backstage," and a big smile on her face.

But usually, when asked to pinpoint when they knew Dina could sing, and not just sing, but sing with a talent beyond that of her peers, Mom and Dad would tell you about the Brickman Hotel. The Brickman was a resort in the Catskill Mountains of Upstate New York, also known as the Jewish Alps or the Borscht Belt. The resort was part of a smattering of hotels in the area frequented by Jews in the 1970s, all of them so similar that they blur together in my memory. Typically, each had a golf course, swimming pool, tennis courts, often a pond with pedal boats, lawns dotted in goose shit, and, of course, a kids' camp for parents who wanted to take a day off from parenting.

At camp there was lots of glue and sparkles, lanyard bracelets, and string tricks played with partners, like Cat's Cradle. But one year there was a talent show for the older kids. They practiced all day, and their efforts culminated in an evening performance for their parents. They jumped rope, hula hooped, and sang and danced. And then it was Dina's turn. She walked to the rounded edge of a small stage—perfect for a comedian and his bottle of water. She took her time and waited for the room to quiet. Then, with a thick Long Island accent and a vibrato unexpected for a seven-year-old, she began to sing a capella, and her voice stilled the room.

"The sun'll come out, tomorrow . . ."

A few heads turned, as adults checked to see if anyone else was noticing what they were hearing. Dina continued, louder, forcing all eyes back toward her.

"You're always a day away . . ." she finished, and a stunned room clapped. A couple of people stood up, and according to Mom, one guy even shouted, "Encore!" When Dina sang she was captivating. Her voice was beautiful, but it was also big—several times bigger than what was expected from her gangly, forty-pound stature. And her voice had power. Even though she was only seven years old, about as mature as her newly forged front teeth, her voice had the emotional depth, tone, and timbre to really move people. That night, the first of countless audience-rousing performances, Mom and Dad understood their daughter in a way they hadn't before. Lots of little girls sang, but Dina didn't just sing, she was a *singer.*

Unlike my mom and dad, I don't have a singular experience to point to and say, "That's when I knew my sister was a singer," or, "That's when I knew she'd be famous." There was no beginning to singing. Dina always sang, *we* sang. We played and we sang and often at the same time. As long as I was with Dina, I didn't know there was a difference between the two.

The *Annie* album was a fixture in our childhood. The record jacket was bright red with large white bubble letters centered in the middle that read "Annie." Against the "i" stood a cute girl in a red-and-white dress, with curly blond hair and her arms folded across her chest. (Later I'd come to know her as the Little Orphan Annie with signature red locks.) We listened to that album over and over until we knew almost every word to "It's the Hard-knock Life." We sang full-throttle, loud enough to drown out the music.

Once we saw the show on Broadway, images from the performance added fervor to our at-home renditions. We crawled around and pretended to scrub the floor with clumsy sponges and metal buckets. I liked to play Molly, the youngest girl in the orphanage. I sang with a pout, "Santa Claus we never see," and Dina replied, "Santa Claus, what's that, who's he?" We sang and made up the words we couldn't quite make out. Instead of "It's a hard-knock row we hoe," we sang, "It's a hard-knock life you know." But the words didn't matter as much as the jumping around and singing. As much as the choreography and histrionics. As much as the pretending and the way we felt the story through the songs. Maybe Mom was talking on the phone in the kitchen and Dad was downstairs watching the football game, but that didn't mean Miss Hannigan wasn't in the house, too, ready to bust through the bedroom door and startle us. Singing was a way to make myself feel bigger, to imagine I was being seen. When I sang I felt significant. When I sang, I was with—and like—Dina.

I came to understand Dina's talent in the same way a portrait is drawn, one line, one curve at a time: one performance for family and friends in front of the couch, one repeated verse sung from the bathroom, until eventually her likeness stared at me from the stage.

Mr. Roper was the music teacher at Baylis Elementary School. He was a scrawny, graying man always equipped with a conductor's wand or a plastic recorder, and perpetually ready to lead classes in a clunky rendition of "Three Blind Mice" at the drop of a hat. Every year, with his piano and, I suspect, a bottle of ibuprofen for the inevitable headache, he directed the fourth-, fifth-, and sixth-graders in a musical. He cast Dina as the lead in each production: Mabel in *The Pirates of Penzance* in fourth grade, Dorothy in *The Wizard of Oz* in fifth grade, and Laurey Williams in *Oklahoma!* in sixth grade.

Dina was waiting back in the music room when we found our seats for the production of her first big performance, *The Pirates of Penzance*. Mom made sure we got there early to claim our seats in the front row. I sat on a metal folding chair among many others placed in straight lines across the gymnasium floor. In front of me was a stage of plywood bleachers, and on the wall behind them were long sheets of butcher paper painted to look like a pirate ship. Families began to file in and take their seats. Mothers draped coats over chairs to reserve them as fathers parked the car. Mr. Roper's productions were heavily attended, and before long the gymnasium was filled with nearly two hundred people.

Earlier, Mom had helped Dina get ready at the house. I stood in the bathroom and watched as Dina sat on the closed toilet and Mom combed her hair, dabbed eye shadow over each lid, applied a light layer of blush to her cheeks, and stroked lipstick onto her full lips. The makeup ritual was fun to watch, and I knew I could count on Mom to call me over and sweep a tiny bit of blush on my cheeks so I wouldn't feel left out. Dad had had one of the seamstresses from his office make Dina's Mabel costume. Intended to invoke the style of 1870s England, it hung to the floor in red and blue with puffy short sleeves and a bonnet. In that dress, with her rosy cheeks and the tissue paper ruffles of the bonnet framing her face, she looked like a collectible porcelain doll.

The lights went down over the audience and I waited. When the lights came back on, the stage filled with prepubescent pirates. They sang, and I waited. The stage filled with maidens, young girls lathered in makeup and melodramatics, and I waited. Finally, Dina snuck on stage, paused for her cue, and then pierced the silence with an operatic soprano-size " 'Tis Ma-bel." Then she sang the song that I had heard her practice in her room, in the shower, in the mirror, and in the car for weeks. She sang the song like she was pushing a feather through the air with each note. "Poor wand'ring one. Though thou hast surely strayed, Take heart of grace, Thy steps retrace . . ."

The show was fun. I was happy and I was proud. But every now and then I turned around and peeked at the dimly lit audience as they watched Dina. They saw *her,* but I saw *them.* I had an odd feeling. My body buzzed with excitement and yet there was a fixed, tight place in me, a pressed finger against my chest.

When the lights came back on, when the applause started and people stood up from their seats, I clapped so hard I bounced onto my toes a little. I found Dina center stage, holding hands in a long line with her cast members, a chain of cut paper dolls. They took a bow and there was a new wave of clapping.

This time I stood on my chair, alternately waving at Dina and smacking my hands together until they hurt. But the feeling I'd felt earlier, the tight feeling I'd ignored, lingered. It lingers even now, but now I understand it in a way I couldn't back then. Within my pride was a sense of loss. I was sharing my sister—not with a few friends from the neighborhood, but with too many people to count. Row after row of them. That night, even with my eyes still on Dina, I started to miss her as if she'd gone away, lost to the crowd the way a balloon is lost to the sky. She was no longer mine alone.

Dina had just moved on to junior high when I finally reached fourth grade at Baylis Elementary and had my first audition for Mr. Roper. He was casting the opening solo of "There's No Business Like Show Business" for the school concert. I practiced near the front door of my house in our hallway mirror, an art-deco square large enough to see myself from the waist up. I watched myself sing there after school for days prior to the audition. I sang loud and proud like my sister did. I was eager and innocent and had no clue that there were things I couldn't do. After all, I could ride a bike down the steep hill in front of my house, swim across the lake at camp, and run—I often won the field day 100-yard dash at school. Dina just opened her mouth and sang, and I assumed that's all there was to it. But one day after school, Dina heard me at the mirror.

"Why do you do that with your voice?" she asked.

"What?"

"That thing. That thing where you hit a note and then drop down to another note. You do that every time, like two notes in one." My stomach curled like a pill bug poked with a tiny stick. I didn't understand what she meant. I think I was hitting the wrong note and then adjusting afterward to fix it. I instantly felt small, vulnerable, and my enthusiasm evaporated. I watched her, not sure I wanted to hear what she would say next, but also wanting the help she offered.

"Try it like this," she said and proceeded to sing each note with precision. She wasn't showing off. She wasn't belting out with some crazy vibrato, trying to make me feel bad. She was problem-solving. But up until then, I didn't know I had a problem. I sang it again, and again my voice dipped down after each note. She repeated the line and it floated in the air for a few seconds after she finished, the way her voice always did. I tried to match her, but I couldn't stop doing *that thing*—whatever it was exactly. I felt like the notes wouldn't stay still long enough for me to catch them. By the third time, it was clear to me that Dina was frustrated, and her impatience made me anxious. She repeated a little louder, "Like *this*." My tears were on standby even as I willed them to stay put. It was no longer clear to me whether I was trying to sing or trying to please her, whether I was aiming for the right notes or for her to smile in approval. If hitting the notes was as effortless for her as it appeared, then how could she understand how difficult it was for me? She couldn't. When Dina turned around and headed up the stairs, I looked back at myself in the mirror. I took a deep breath and tried to sing one more time, but the air was full of failure.

On audition day, the soloists went up to the front of the room one by one. Mr. Roper sat at the piano and played the same sequence for each of us. He had written the lyrics in red marker on large sheets of butcher paper for the class to see, and they hung over the chalkboard. I was staring at them when he called my name. I pulled myself out of my chair and turned my back to the lyrics—I knew them by heart. I looked up and saw the faces of my fourth-grade peers and became acutely aware of my own heartbeat. When the piano began, I nearly startled. I heard my chord and sang, "The butcher, the baker, the grocer, the clerk, are secretly unhappy men because . . ." My windpipe narrowed to a straw. I squeezed the words out off-key and uneasy. The line repeated an octave higher, "The butcher, the baker, the grocer, the clerk . . ." I sang louder, fighting it, chasing the notes, but every time I reached for them they moved farther away. The entire fourth-grade class stared. I don't remember finishing. I do remember crying. The student teacher took me to the back of the room and offered me a Hershey's Kiss.

In those thirty seconds of singing it was clear to me that no one would ever mistake me for my sister. Not Mr. Roper. Not my friends. Not me. No one.

I loved singing but was suddenly, and I feared irrevocably, embarrassed to utter a note by myself, to let anyone really hear me. I retreated. I backed away from solos and took my place in the chorus. When it came to singing, when it came to Dina, life had changed. The stage was pulling her away from me, and thinking lovely thoughts was suddenly a lot harder than it had been when Sandy Duncan sang about them.

Lesson 2

HOW TO WORK THINGS OUT—OR NOT

Dina got a perm.

For a short period of time, a young hair stylist with tight jeans and pasty coral lipstick would come to our house to give us haircuts. Dina and I would shower right before the stylist arrived and Mom would set up a chair in the kitchen, where our hair clippings could be easily swept off the tile floor. The stylist showed up at our door with shears, a smock, and, on this particular day, a perm solution.

She twisted strands of Dina's wet hair around narrow pink rollers and then stretched a black rubber band from one end of the roller to the other to hold the hair in place. With a small-tipped squirt bottle she doused each roll in a solution that I'm guessing was chemically related to both ammonia and skunk spray until the fumes made my eyes burn. When the process was over, Dina's smooth brown waves were gone and in their place were fuzzy curls. Puberty struck soon after the perm, and thanks to a flood of hormones, that permanent solution was, quite literally, permanent. She never needed another treatment to keep her hair curly. Dina's perm marked the beginning of her teen years.

I wanted a perm, but my hair was naturally curly and this fact was a source of great frustration for me. Perms were trendy. The coolest girls had perms—Ilana Decker had a perm. With fake curls, girls could easily blow their bangs out and tease them into tall cliff-like structures over their foreheads. Natural curls, on the other hand, resisted straightening and therefore resisted the cliff trend. No amount of Sebastian Shaper hairspray could remedy the problem.

Then Dina got a crop top.

It was peach and off-the-shoulder and had a respectable brand name in Syosset's high-fashion scene. One day, Mom, Dina, and I sat in the driveway in our new slate-colored Audi 5000 S. It was a replacement for our aging Chrysler Cordoba. I remember the Audi well because it had a leather interior and it made me feel a little more like I belonged in Woodbury, and its neighboring town Syosset, among the mansions and the girls with nose jobs and $150 jeans. Dina was sitting in the backseat with her big hair, teal eyeliner, and frosted pink lip gloss—commonly referred to by the girls at camp as #44. She and Mom were talking about the shirt.

"I like it too, Mom," I chimed in.

"Oh really? I bet you don't even know how to say the name of it," Dina said.

"I do too." (I would have dressed as her twin every day if the mere suggestion wouldn't have made her eyes roll.)

"How?"

"E Spirit (ee-spear-it)."

She laughed at me.

"It's Esprit (eh-spree)." This, the pronunciation of brand names, was the kind of thing sisters bickered about on Long Island. Esprit signified Dina's budding teenage attitude, and the years she spent mastering the art of scoffing.

Even with her new perm and the occasional bickering, Dina and I remained close. My memory is filled with images of us snuggled up in bed with abundant blankets and pillows, our legs and arms tangled together. Sometimes we hopped out of bed and played Superman on the floor. Dina would lay on her back, press her bare feet against my belly and then lift me up into the air. With outstretched arms I'd balance on the soles of her feet.

Weekly, we'd climb into bed with Mom and Dad and watch black-and-white movies on the Turner Classic Movies channel. Love stories, musicals, or Westerns, with actors like Fred Astaire, Cary Grant, or John Wayne. Actresses like Elizabeth Taylor, Katharine Hepburn, or Lauren Bacall. My dad loved *A Place in the Sun* and my mom loved *An Affair to Remember.* Dina loved having her arm tickled as we watched. "Do mine first," she'd say and then flip her arm over and place it on the bed between us. I'd gently tiptoe my fingertips over its soft underbelly until she fell asleep—or feigned sleep to get out of returning the favor. I didn't feel slighted that I rarely got a turn. I never told Dina, but I didn't love arm tickling—it made me itchy. I loved *her.*

If the football game was on, then sometimes our family was divided between the TV upstairs in Mom and Dad's bedroom and the one in the basement. More often than not, I stayed with Mom upstairs, where the blinds were drawn and we could hibernate. Dina stayed with Dad downstairs, where the lights were bright and the television was loud.

Dina had always been a tomboy. When we were little her pajamas were mostly fashioned after athletic jerseys, while mine were fashioned after princesses. Dina was ambidextrous and had what people called a "wicked two-handed backhand" in tennis. I had blisters. And Dina understood football. She knew what the commentator meant when he said "first down" and why a coach would choose to go for a field goal over a touchdown. She understood why Dad would shout things like, "He's gonna go for it? What a moron!" and then sigh with his forehead in his hand. I didn't know much about football, but when I opted to hang out in the basement during a game, Dad and I sometimes tossed an orange Nerf football back and forth across the three yards between us. Occasionally I made the ball spiral and Dad would flash me one of his big smiles, the kind that stretched straight across his round face and made me feel adored.

I knew Mom didn't like it when Dad watched football. A couple of times I overheard her tell him that his football "habit" was the reason she believed we didn't do enough as a family. (Today she'd tell you that she alone planned our family trip to Disneyland and that marathon movie days at the Syosset Movie Theater were her idea.) But I remember only one fight between Mom and Dad. I walked into the kitchen one night and saw Mom crying. She and Dad were shouting at each other and she pitched the car keys at him, missed, and the keys hit the countertop.

Mostly, though, if there was noticeable arguing in our house, it wasn't between Mom and Dad, it was between Mom and Dina. Even before Dina became a teenager, she and Mom had screaming matches. It seemed they could fight about anything and that any disagreement, no matter how trivial—a forgotten textbook at school or missing shoes for one of Dina's costumes—could escalate.

One morning, in the rush to get some breakfast before the school bus came, Mom and Dina got into it. Dina was at the kitchen table and Mom was at the sink. I was eating my toast off a paper plate on the kitchen counter. We were spread out in the kitchen like the three points of a triangle.

"Can Linda come over for dinner?" Dina asked.

Mom sighed, which wasn't a good sign, and said, "I didn't defrost enough chicken cutlets."

I set my toast down and looked at Dina for her reply.

"Can't we just order pizza?"

"I'd rather not. Couldn't you have asked me yesterday? The house is a mess—you still haven't cleaned your room."

"Well, I didn't know yesterday," Dina replied. "Can't you just be spontaneous for once, like other moms?"

"I can be spontaneous—"

"No, you make a big deal out of everything," Dina said.

I took a deep breath and then forgot to let it out.

"I'm not making a big deal," Mom said.

"Fine. Whatever. She won't come over." Dina got up and started to walk away.

"Don't roll your eyes at me," Mom said. She couldn't see Dina's eyes, but given the tone of Dina's voice, the eye rolling was a safe bet.

"I don't know why I even ask for friends to come over. *I* don't want to be here, why would my friends want to be here?"

"Oh, right. I *never* let your friends come over, I *never* let you do anything?" Mom gave the sponge a quick squeeze and then dropped it into the sink.

"I didn't say that—"

"I'm such a *bad* mom."

"I didn't say that!"

"Why are you starting with me again, right before school?" Mom asked, but it was an accusation, not a question.

"Oh, *I'm* starting?"

"Don't talk back to me."

"How many days' notice do you need for a sleepover? Is a month enough, Mommie Dearest?"

Mommie Dearest was a 1981 movie starring Faye Dunaway as famed actress and abusive mother Joan Crawford. Mom, Dina, and I had watched it together. In one scene, Joan is furious because her daughter hung up some clothes on wire hangers instead of satin ones. Joan's hair is pulled off her tall forehead in a headband, her face is ghostly, covered in greasy, white cold cream, her eyes are bulging beneath her arched, penciled-in eyebrows, and with a handful of wire hangers she screams through the circle of red lipstick she'd yet to remove, "No. Wire. Hangers. EVAHHHHH!" After the movie, Mom, Dina, and I took turns reenacting the scene, unable to keep a straight face, always breaking into laughter on "Evahhhhh!"

I don't remember exactly when it happened, but at some point "wire hangers" weren't funny anymore. In heated moments Dina started to call Mom "Mommie Dearest." It was the surest way to hurt Mom's feelings.

I heard the engine of the school bus as it turned the corner. Dina grabbed her stuff and said, "You know what? Keep your fuckin' chicken cutlets. I'll go to Linda's house instead." Then she bolted out of the house and the screen door slammed behind her.

Mom followed after her, and as Dina raced to the corner for the bus, Mom reopened the screen door and shouted, "Selfish! You only think of yourself!" Dina must have been too embarrassed to shout anything back to Mom with the other kids standing around, but I'd seen their fights enough to know that as she took that first big step through the bus's folding doors, she called Mom a bitch.

As an adult I'd finally understand why a clean house and a good meal were so important to my mother. I'd learn that my maternal grandmother had been abusive, possibly an alcoholic, that my mom had taken care of her brothers since she was five years old, and that their house had been a pigsty. As a little girl Mom had been too ashamed to have her friends over. To Mom, a nourishing meal and a clean house meant she was a better mother than her mother had been to her. It meant she was doing things "right." But Mom wanting to get everything right was often the reason things went wrong with Dina. The ever-present threat of being like her mother made Mom defensive to any criticism. And Dina could be critical. She was sometimes more firecracker than candle. After too many blowups with Mom, Dina started to feel like something was wrong with her, like she was bad—even as a child I sensed this (but lengthy discussions as adults would confirm it). Fighting became a way to defend herself, to convince her own mother that she was good. And ironically, Mom fought for a similar reason, to convince her own daughter that *she* was good. And yet the louder they screamed, the worse they felt about themselves.

Sometimes I'd intervene, and I did this for myself as much as for them. I hated it when they fought. They were two of my three favorite people on the planet (Dad was the third one). And they took care of me. I was the little sister and the younger child. But when they argued, *I* wanted to take care of *them*. More as mediator than referee, I tried to inject objectivity into the scant lulls in their arguments, but my attempts to resolve their conflicts failed repeatedly. Instead, Dina would redirect her anger at me: "Why do you always take Mom's side?" she'd ask, and the question hurt my feelings. I was Dina's biggest fan. I didn't want there to be any sides.

Over time I learned that my efforts to make peace were futile and I was better off outside their conflicts than in the middle. But keeping my distance had its drawbacks, too. One day after one of their screaming matches I came out of my room and saw Dina in Mom's arms sitting at the top of the stairs. They were crying.

"I love you so much," Mom whispered into the air over Dina's shoulder.

"I love you too."

"You're a wonderful daughter," Mom said and let go of Dina for a second to pull a strand of hair off Dina's damp cheek. "Sometimes I just think we're so much alike . . . and that makes it hard."

"I'm sorry I get so angry," Dina said, looking down into her lap. "You *are* a good mom."

I felt the impulse to move toward them. But I hesitated. It wasn't *my* moment, it was *theirs*. They were in their own little world and I didn't want to trespass.

I think that seeing Mom and Dina fight so much is one of the reasons I have so few memories of Mom and Dad's fighting. With the exception of Mom's pleas for Dad to quit watching so much football, or the night she threw the keys at him, any clues that my parents were unhappy together were scarce. They played doubles tennis, spent afternoons laughing together on their friends' boat, tanned next to each other on lounge chairs while Dina and I jumped off the diving board, and coordinated their Halloween costumes—a ridiculous photo of Mom as a devil and Dad as a vampire comes to mind. So when they told us they were separating it knocked the wind out of Dina and me.

The news of my parents' breakup came on Thanksgiving Day, 1986. Dina was fifteen years old and I was twelve. Nothing had been planned that day. Unlike most Thanksgivings, we didn't have a turkey in the oven, and we weren't having company or mashing bananas into sweet potatoes to take over to my aunt's house.

Dina left Dad in the basement with the football game and came up to the kitchen, where Mom and I were taking a break from watching movies. We talked about who knows what for an hour maybe. Then, one of us mentioned Dad: "Ask Dad," or, "I wish Dad were here to weigh in," and there was an uncomfortable pause. Dina and I looked at Mom. Her eyes were fixed on a spot on the empty table and something about her seemed empty, too. She wasn't mad, there was no muscle to whatever she was feeling. Instead, she seemed limp, resigned. Dad showed up in the doorway and we all looked at him. He stood there like the inattentive kid in class whose teacher had unexpectedly called on him. He stood there like a kid without an answer. I was worried for him.

When Mom asked us to leave them alone for a little while I didn't know what to do. No one outright said that anything was wrong, yet I sensed that there was a threat in the room. I didn't want to be near the threat, but I also didn't feel safe turning away from it. Instead I turned to Dina, who said, "Come on," and we walked up the stairs.

A couple of years earlier, Dina and I had performed Kenny Rogers's "Through the Years" for one of Mom and Dad's anniversaries. (I had no idea Kenny was on his third marriage when he sang about those years, which has since left me wondering which years he was referring to exactly.) It was Their Song and it had played on cassette through our living-room speakers on countless occasions. Kenny sang, "I never had a doubt, We'd always work things out." Dina played the piano and sang while I accompanied her on the flute. We even made Mom and Dad tickets for the show and served Pillsbury cinnamon buns.

Dina and I took their marriage for granted. We had friends whose parents were divorced, and some whose parents *should* have been divorced, but we never worried about Mom and Dad. We knew their story well. It was a first love. A hometown love from the Bronx. It became a Dad-was-in-the-army-Mom-was-waiting-tables love. Mom and Dad became adults together. I'd recently asked Mom how I would know when I met the man I should marry and she'd said, "You'll know." That's how it had been with Dad, she'd just known.

I lay on my bed entranced by a brass finial and then the stitching on the underside of my comforter and then probably a strand of my hair. Every now and then the trance broke and I could hear enough of Mom's and Dad's voices to know they were still talking downstairs, but not enough to make out what they were saying. I waited for a reassuring knock on my door, someone to peek a head in and tell me what was going on. Mostly, I waited for someone to tell me how to feel. I knew how much I loved my parents as individuals. My father woke up early every Sunday morning to wait on line at the deli for bagels, then returned home and cooked us his signature salami and eggs. He walked in the front door after business trips armed with stuffed animals for Dina and me, and he always brought me water when he tucked me in at night, even though he knew it was just my ploy to delay my bedtime. And I idolized my mother. She was beautiful and athletic and I thought she knew the answers to nearly everything. But until that night, I didn't know how much I loved Mom and Dad as a couple and how much I needed them to be together. My family was the one place I knew I belonged, and I needed to belong somewhere. We were one interdependent system, and if the parts of that system started moving or breaking, I didn't know how my life would change. How *I* might change. I'd been safely tethered to my parents' togetherness my whole life, and suddenly I felt myself dangling over the unknown.

I was antsy and eventually found Dina eavesdropping at the top of the stairs. She looked at me and mouthed "shhh" with her finger over her lips. I hoped the floor wouldn't creak as I stepped closer to her and she took my hand. I don't know how long she'd been standing there or exactly what she had heard, but I could feel the weight of her thoughts in her tight grip. Soon, Mom called us downstairs to join her and Dad in the kitchen.

They both sat there at the table, but it was Mom who spoke, and I remember her words exactly; knowing Mom, she'd chosen them carefully. She said, "Your Dad and I are separating. We think we can be happier apart than we are together."

In those first milliseconds I felt nothing. Then my heart constricted as if a hand were squeezing it to keep it in one piece, and I wondered, *If I cry, will it make Mom and Dad feel worse?* Mom had often told me I was wise beyond my years and I remember that when she told me they were separating I wanted to be wise. I wanted to say the *right* thing. In fact, like Mom, I'd always wanted to say the right thing, do the right thing, even feel the right thing. I was consumed with getting everything right and trying to make everyone all right around me. *Is it okay to want them to stay together?* I continued to wonder. *If Mom and Dad think they could be happier apart, then shouldn't I want them to be apart? Is my happiness more important than theirs? But how can I be happy if they're not?* I heard Dina start to cry and her sadness put an end to my spiraling thoughts and gave me permission to cry, too. Then Mom and Dad stood up and the hugs started and with the hugs came more tears, even from them. Tears all around me and the fading echo of the word "happy" in my ears.

Mom, Dad, Dina, and I have different accounts of that Thanksgiving Day. What's important and consistent in Mom's and Dad's versions is that they'd been planning their separation. What was sudden for Dina and me was not sudden for them, they just hadn't planned to tell us on Thanksgiving. What's important from Dina's version is that I'm not even in it, which she told me as an adult while shaking her head, "That should tell you how self-centered I was."

Though nothing spoils an appetite quite like an imminent divorce, what's indisputable among the stories that we all tell is that we had Thanksgiving dinner at the Fox Hollow Inn. We hopped into the car like the intact family we'd been only a day earlier and drove over to the restaurant. Dinner was a blur. I'm sure there was a white tablecloth with some kind of centerpiece, and mashed potatoes and gravy, but I can't be certain. Dina and I spent most of the meal standing in the restroom crying together in front of a pair of sinks. I remember how broken Dina seemed, and how strange it felt to stand next to her and share tears, and how when she wrapped her arms around me, she wasn't only taking care of me, but I was taking care of her, too. And how, because she needed me, there was a flicker of satisfaction in my grief.

I knew then that marriages may end but sisterhood does not. If there was one thing she and I would always have in common, it was that we were sisters and when it mattered most, we'd be together.

Lesson 3

HOW TO PLAY A PART

On the East Coast it's customary for parents to spend a small fortune to send their kids to sleepaway camp for the summer. In the weeks before camp starts, parents buy their soon-to-be campers brand-new summer wardrobes—"ten pairs of socks, eight pairs of shorts, ten T-shirts, and one rain jacket." They pack everything into one huge duffel bag and one large trunk. Kids ages six to sixteen went to camp to spend their days playing kickball and soccer, to swim, canoe, and weave lanyard bracelets in arts and crafts, to spend their nights flirting at the canteen over Heath bars or chips, and to stay up late with friends in a flashlight-lit bunk, the smell of skunk a frequent reminder that rodents enjoyed skulking beneath the floorboards.

Dina went to sleepaway first. When I was six years old and Mom and Dad were still together, I was old enough to go with her.

"I wanna go too," I told Mom.

"But you'll be away from home, from Dad and me," she warned, and then added, "for a long time."

"I know," I said. "But I'll miss Dina more if I stay than I'll miss you guys if I go."

Dina meant home to me. In my mind, I belonged with her, to such an extent that I would leave my actual home to stay with her.

Mom and Dad let me go to camp that summer and I was miserable. While Dina loved camp, it wasn't for me, at least not yet. She had a close-knit group of girlfriends—they had beaded friendship bracelets and matching haircuts. I didn't connect with girls my age. I felt closest to the foreign counselors, especially the ones from Scandinavia who always had candy for me and taught me that real licorice tasted nothing like Twizzlers. It surprised me that even with Dina at camp, I was homesick. I missed Mom and Dad. I cried each night at bedtime. I subsisted on letters from them and crossing paths with Dina, who made sure she checked on me daily. I even got sick. I'd had high fevers as a child and I had a couple that summer. Dina worried about me and made frequent visits to see me in the infirmary. The highlight of that summer was when I received a package from home and opened it to find a Snoopy Sno-Cone Machine. The savvy beagle helped me bridge home and camp, and I spent one jubilant afternoon making "The World's Flavorite Icy Treats" for Dina's friends and my bunkmates. By the time I had enough ice shavings to fill the Dixie cups, my "snow cones" were hard-earned swigs of diluted juice.

The snow-cone machine had been retired for a couple of years when I decided to give sleepaway camp another try. Though I was older and didn't miss home as much, I still had trouble forming lasting friendships. For the first time, I considered that the best place for me might not be with Dina but on my own. In the summer before seventh grade—the summer before Mom and Dad's Thanksgiving separation—I sought a greater sense of belonging and a fresh start at a new camp.

The theater program at my new camp was putting on a performance of *Guys and Dolls*. I went to the audition hoping to be part of the show, to have a line or two much like I had in Baylis Elementary's performance of *Oliver,* in which I played a milk maiden and sang, "Any milk today, monsieur?" Or in *My Fair Lady,* in which I played the Queen of Transylvania at the Embassy Ball and said two words (three if repeats count): "Charming, quite charming."

At the audition I stood on the large, scuffed stage looking into a recreation hall where before me were rows of empty wooden benches, and in the darkness above, bats clung to the rafters. The hall was dank and had an old-building musty smell like worn wood and dirt. The director, a spunky African-American woman with busy hair of kinky curls, handed me what I assumed was the audition scene for all the girls. It featured Adelaide, who was a hopeless romantic and the lead dancer at a 1950s nightclub called the Hot Box. Having seen the movie multiple times on Sunday afternoons in bed with Mom, Dad, and Dina, I knew the part well. I reached for my best New York accent—in retrospect it wasn't as much of a stretch as I'd thought.

"Nathan, dawling. I can do without anything just so lawng as you don't stawt running that crap game again."

It felt good to be the lone voice in such a large room.

On the rec-hall stage that day my heart was pounding and I felt it through my whole body like the bass of a boom box. I read the scene with the director, occasionally peeking down at the lines and then at her on the floor near the edge of the stage. She looked pleased. A couple of times I glanced out over the invisible audience and imagined the seats filled with campers, the girls on one side, boys on the other, as they always sat there. I felt hopeful and excited. Unfortunately, those feelings were short-lived.

"Can you sing?" the director asked, and I froze for a second that felt like a minute.

Dammit. Those three words. My joy of acting was inextricably linked to my fear of singing, and I wished that it were not.

"No," I answered.

"Sing something," she said.

"No, I can't sing," I told her.

"How 'bout 'Happy Birthday'? Just sing 'Happy Birthday' for me."

"Really, I can't."

But the pianist, a graying, heavyset man, tapped on some keys, and that surprised me because up until then I didn't know he was sitting there. He was off to the side of the stage behind an old standard piano and I wished we could trade places. I'd taken piano lessons for four years and would have preferred to pick through a version of "Sing a Song"—"make it simple to last a whole life long"—than actually to sing one.

The pianist bounced on the same note a few times, my cue to begin singing. The note he played was higher than I wanted it to be and reminded me of singing for Mr. Roper, like I'd need to reach for each note again. I didn't know enough about music to ask for a different key. I could feel my lips pressed together, and with a deep breath I let them part. The notes sounded right in my head, but the moment I opened my mouth they were wrong. I started, "Happy birthday to you. Happy birthday . . ." When I strained to hit the high note toward the end, "Happy BIRTH-day dear so-and-so," I was embarrassed and wished I hadn't let the director make me sing.

"Thank you," she said with a smile—a smile I returned, though it was forced, a mere copy of hers, then I headed out of the dark rec hall and into the sun.

At dusk I stood on the wide wooden planks of the rec-hall steps where the assigned parts were posted on a sheet of paper. I waited a couple of feet away in a crowd of my peers amid an outbreak of disappointed sighs and the squeals of the soon-to-be Nathan Detroit, Sister Sarah Brown, and Sky Masterson. The chatter was garbled, as if it traveled to me through a strand of yarn and a paper cup. Then someone was shouting, "Cara!" I stepped toward the sheet of paper. I lifted my finger and ran it across from my name, Cara Mentzel, to the next name, Adelaide. My eyes crossed the page a second time to make sure I wasn't mistaken. *I'm Adelaide? I'm Adelaide!* I felt that boom box in my chest again. People were looking at me, at *me,* congratulating *me.* My smile looked like any other smile, but it felt different. I wondered if this was what it felt like to be Dina.

I'd never allowed myself to think I'd get the part. Then, I started to worry that some kind of stupendous mistake had been made and that ten seconds of "Happy Birthday" had misled the director. After all, I knew how to sing "Happy Birthday"—I'd obviously sung it before. Then the thought of birthdays led me to the old adage, "Watch what you wish for." I wanted to believe that I belonged on that stage, that the director had seen something in me that others had overlooked. I wanted her to be right. I wanted to surprise *myself* and be better than I had thought I was. I wanted to impress a rec hall filled with campers. I wanted to be good enough—whatever "enough" meant, I wasn't sure. But maybe it meant being more like Dina. Maybe it meant being as exceptional as she was.

In any case, what I wanted was a tall order.

I took a yellow highlighter to each of my lines; some pages were more yellow than white, and the neon visual reminded me that I was a lead. My xeroxed copy of the script looked like Dina's scripts always did when I sat on the floor in her bedroom and helped her run lines. Adelaide sang five songs, including a long-time favorite of mine, "Adelaide's Lament," where she tells her fiancé of fourteen years, Nathan, that her chronic cold is a psychosomatic symptom of being unmarried. I was proud to have ownership of the song. I'd often had fun singing it around the house when no one was home. I especially liked to say "poyson" instead of "person" in Adelaide's accent when she sings, ". . . a *poyson* can develop a cold."

That summer I ran lines on the grass with the cast, studied them in my bunk with a flashlight after "taps" played over the campus speakers, and rehearsed onstage. I could have used Dina's help; what was a new experience for me was routine for her. But she was too far away to help me. I was on my own. Besides, winning the part had been exciting, but it also made me feel vulnerable. I knew that if Dina ran lines with me or helped me with my solos I'd be even more self-conscious. No matter how kind she would try to be with her feedback, I'd worry about what she was *really* thinking, and that worry would be a distraction. So, maybe being on my own wasn't so bad. With

Dina elsewhere, I could focus on myself rather than on her perception of me—at least I could try.

The performance was scheduled for the night before Visiting Day, a day halfway through the summer all campers looked forward to when parents were invited to drive the three hours up from Long Island (where most of us were from) and spend the day with their kids at camp. Campers loved Visiting Day, not only because we missed our families but because of the large garbage bags filled with junk food that they schlepped all the way from home.

That year the best part of Visiting Day for me wasn't the food but that it fell on the day after the performance of *Guys and Dolls*. Parents weren't typically invited to camp theater productions, but given the timing of the show it seemed reasonable for my parents to drive up the night before and attend. I wanted them to see it. I worried that without them there my performance would eventually exist only in my memory, and I knew that memories faded. If they were with me, my Adelaide character wouldn't be easily forgotten. I also wanted them to be proud of me, to watch me the way they'd watched Dina so many times. Unlike Dina, who could rely on getting solos and leads, I knew I might never get the chance to star in a show again. And though I hadn't wanted Dina to be there during rehearsals, by then I wished she could be there for the performance. I always wanted to be the center of her attention and a stage could force the issue. I wanted to stand in front of her and have her feel as proud of me as I'd so often been of her. I wanted her to experience the rush that I experienced when *I* watched *her*.

A week before the show, I was on the dirt path on my way to dinner with a friend and I spotted the camp director.

"Barry," I called to him and walked over. "Can my mom and dad come see the show this week?"

"We don't invite parents to our shows," he replied. "They're just for campers."

"I know, but it's the night before Visiting Day and I'm one of the leads."

"Sorry," he said too quickly.

"What?" I asked, giving him another chance to say what I wanted to hear.

"It wouldn't be fair to the other campers, but don't worry. I'm gonna videotape it." It wasn't until he turned me down that I realized how much I'd wanted him to say yes.

The afternoon of the performance, I was walking through camp with a friend—picture matching Keds and leg-warmer socks—when I spotted Barry coming toward us with someone's parents. I was taken aback and instantly felt tears forming. Sometimes my sadness and anger sat so close together I couldn't tell them apart. But I also suspected that when I was upset, sadness was the default. Subconsciously I preferred sadness to anger; it was easier to manage and more socially acceptable—for a girl, anyway. Except, in that moment with Barry, something felt different. I wanted to shut the tears down. If I could resist those tears I could prevent myself from dissolving into the hurt little girl I was quickly becoming, and instead become the pissed-off teenager I wanted to be. Dina knew how to put her sadness on hold and identify with her anger, and I wanted to be like her. Bold and strong. I was trembling when I addressed the approaching adults with an unfamiliar bravery.

"What are *they* doing here?" I asked, gesturing toward the parents.

"Excuse me?" Barry said.

"Why are they here?" I repeated as if we were on equal footing, as if he weren't a foot taller than me, a man, and an authority figure.

"They're my friends."

"They're parents of campers," I reminded him. "Aren't all the other kids going to be upset if they see them here before Visiting Day?"

My snotty tone didn't appear to remind him of our conversation only a week earlier. He looked confused.

"You said *my* parents couldn't be here tonight. I really wanted my parents here." On the word "really" my tears came loose and with them he seemed to remember.

"This is different. They're friends."

I could feel myself shrinking under the downward stare of three apathetic adults, and I didn't want to shrink. I could feel my argument slipping away, my words vanishing. And then something shifted. I *made* it shift. I overpowered my impulse to disappear with my desire to be heard. Suddenly I didn't care about being good or liked. I wanted Barry to take responsibility for being hypocritical. I wanted to embarrass him and make him feel as awful as he'd made me feel. And so I banished the little victim in me and discovered my inner truck driver.

"Fuck you!" I shouted into his shocked face. "Fuck you!" I shouted again and then shot a string of insults at him like projectile vomit. He wasn't just an asshole, he became a fuckin' asshole and then fuckin' selfish and then he didn't give a fuck about kids. If my intention was to embody a pissed-off teenager, I may have overshot a bit. No matter how many times I said "fuckin'," or how loud I shouted it, my parents wouldn't be there that night. Right or wrong, I hated him for that.

I stormed off and, probably because he knew he couldn't stop me, he let me go.

A couple of hours later I headed over to the rec hall to get ready for the show. By the time my makeup was on as well as my first costume—heels and a tiny silver tube top with a matching tiny tube skirt—I'd mostly recovered from my emotional rant. My hair was huge, pulled back off my face, hanging long behind my bare shoulders and down my back. I looked hot, hotter than a thirteen-year-old late bloomer dressed as a thirtysomething dancer at a strip joint should look.

I could hear the kids filing into the hall. The louder their voices, the more nervous I became. I was terrified. *Why did I do this to myself?* I wondered, until the room quieted and the show began. Then it was my turn to step out onto the stage. My body was buzzing and I had to clench my teeth together to keep them from chattering. The words from each of those yellowed lines I'd rehearsed nonstop for days were pin-balling inside my skull. I managed to say, "Hello, Nathan dear," and then, "You go ahead, girls. Order me a tuna fish on rye," and with those first lines my time as Adelaide began.

The show had its high points and its low points. For one thing, Dina had once told me that her nerves subsided after the first few minutes onstage, but my nerves stuck around. Before long I started forgetting my lines. In one scene, I took a running start through the lines that were familiar, hoping the lines I'd forgotten would suddenly show up, only to realize that I was doing the wrong scene.

I also noticed that in front of an audience, I'd developed an awkward mannerism. I liked to wave my right arm about as I talked or sang, the kind of gesture that, had I been seated at a table, surely would have knocked a drink or two to the floor. I tried to act natural, but natural was as hard to find as my lines were.

Then there was a strange moment during "Take Back Your Mink" in Act II when I felt the undivided attention of the audience. The attention held an electric charge that made me feel powerful. But while I'd craved that power, the attention felt invasive, and I suddenly had the urge to resist it. I'd given over a hundred darkened figures access to something I held sacred, something private that I couldn't name. And they hadn't earned that access. They hadn't earned my trust. I stood there confused and exposed.

The show went on too long and we lost the attention of the audience, but it wasn't all bad. I enjoyed singing "Adelaide's Lament," and with the exception of some embarrassing high notes, my singing had been decent. When I remembered my lines, I was proud of my acting. I relished my final bow—partly because I was relieved it was all over and partly because I was grateful to share the experience with the cast. The audience offered up courtesy applause, glad it was finally finished. Over their heads, I noted the far wall where Mom, Dad, and Dina, would have been standing and clapping had they been invited. Then I moved on and took my racing energy to the canteen, where I celebrated with my cast mates and gnawed on a frozen Charleston Chew.

With my flubbed debut behind me and seventh grade in front of me, I began H.B. Thompson Junior High.

Dina was in the thick of her dramatic teenage years. She was usually studying, out with friends, or on her phone. She had her own line in her room—a

1980s social necessity the equivalent of today's smartphone—and more often than not, she kept her bedroom door shut for privacy. But if I ever needed advice about friends or boys all I had to do was tap on her door and she'd invite me in.

One day I came home from school crying because a boy lifted up his shirt on the cafeteria line and asked me if I was jealous.

"He did it in front of everyone," I cried. "I was so embarrassed. Am I ever gonna go through puberty?"

"First of all, yes you will," she assured me. "Second of all, you're gorgeous and one day he's gonna wish he'd been nicer because he'll want to ask you out and you won't give him the time of day. And lastly," she continued but then paused for a second, "he has bigger boobs than you?"

I laughed. "Yeah, kinda." And we left it at that.

Another time, the night before my boyfriend, Ryan, and I had arranged to have our first bit of alone time together, I went to Dina.

I think I'm gonna kiss Ryan tomorrow," I told her. "Like *really* kiss him," I clarified.

Ryan entered junior high from the cooler elementary school, the one with the reputation for being more "advanced" than mine—and I don't mean academically. Supposedly, Ryan knew what he was doing. It was rumored that at his school there wasn't a pretty girl he hadn't kissed.

Dina waved me into her room, where we sat down on her bed, and I explained how a couple of friends would join me over at his place after school, and that he'd take me up to his bedroom where we could be alone.

Like a true teacher, Dina didn't believe in stupid questions and offered thorough answers. She listened as I asked:

"What do I do if I'm chewing gum?"

"How do I know which way to tilt my head?"

"What do I do with my tongue?"

"How do I breathe? Swallow?"

The logistics were overwhelming and nothing about kissing seemed sexy to me. I was a long way from the hormonal infusion that would bring true passion to kissing, but that didn't stop me from being a romantic (or a perfectionist). My kiss with Ryan was a rite of passage that I was determined to get right. And Dina was my ticket to success, so I listened intently as she answered my questions one at a time.

"If you have a chance, you can go to the bathroom and spit your gum out first," she advised. "If not, just swallow it." I thought about the ten years I was once told that it took to fully digest chewed gum and was briefly concerned about the many pieces of Doublemint that could be lounging around in my belly by the time I went to college.

"Don't worry about tilting your head," Dina continued. "That usually comes naturally. You won't bump noses or anything."

"Are you sure?" I asked. "Nothing about this feels natural to me."

"You'll be fine. You wanna keep your lips soft, you know?" But I didn't know.

"That's easy for you to say, you have those full lips. The minute I pucker, my skinny lips get all tight."

"Well, they don't have to. You don't pucker them so much as push them against his." She lifted the back of her hand to her lips. "See, like this." And I watched her mushy lips meet the skin on the back of her hand. "You try."

I was a little embarrassed to kiss my own hand, but I gave it a try anyway, pressing my lips against its tender skin. She was right. My lips were still soft.

"When do I open my mouth?" I asked next and dropped my hand back onto my lap.

"Whenever you want," she answered. "He'll probably do it first so you can follow his lead. And you can breathe through your nose if it's hard to breathe through your mouth."

"What about my tongue? What am I supposed to do with my tongue?"

"Keep it soft, just like your lips. You're not sticking it out like some kid making faces out a car window."

"I know," I said, but again, I didn't know exactly. I couldn't be sure what tongues looked like in the darkness of two kissing mouths.

"Here," she said. She grabbed a handheld mirror off her dresser, the one Mom used when we were younger to show us what our braids looked like in the back.

She held the mirror a few inches from my face and said, "Stick your tongue out."

I stuck out my tongue.

"Too far," she corrected. "You barely have to stick it out at all. Pretend you're tasting something good."

"You mean something other than a guy's tongue?" I joked.

"Yeah. Think more . . . uh, ice cream or cotton candy."

"Like thith?" I asked with a lisp, my tongue resting slightly out of my mouth like a napping dog.

"Yeah, more like that."

"Tho thexy," I joked with my tongue still out and we giggled.

"You'll be fine," she assured me with an encouraging smile. "Let me know how it goes."

As it turned out, even with all of Ryan's experience, he didn't really know what he was doing. He only had one criteria for being a good kisser and that was the length of time we kept our mouths pressed against each other's. He'd clearly taken the term "lip-locked" literally. He actually had a watch and timed us! When we made it past seven minutes he told me that was the longest he'd ever gone and said I was a great kisser. I managed to feel flattered even though part of me knew I couldn't trust his judgment.

When I got home, Dina and I debriefed. She was appalled by Ryan's fixation on the time. I told her that between my tired jaw and his copious saliva, I could have been at the dentist, and in fact, I'd wished I had one of those suction straw thingies the hygienist used. At this, Dina looked stunned. She sat there speechless, just shaking her head. But I explained to her that the worst part wasn't Ryan—it was me! I was so nervous that I could feel little gas bubbles expanding and then popping in my stomach. The more my stomach gurgled with gas, the more nervous I became and the louder it got. I kept clenching my butt cheeks so as not to let even the tiniest one escape. When we finished our marathon kiss, possibly because he'd broken his record (but maybe because my stomach was so noisy) he noted my growling belly and said, "You must be starving. Let's go get you a snack."

"He thought I needed a snack!" I shouted as I recounted the moment to Dina.

She cocked her head to the side, stuck out her tongue, and said, "Tho thexy," and then we laughed until our stomachs hurt. I left her room wondering who had taught her how to kiss, wondering what girls without big sisters do. I left her room feeling lucky.

The summer before I started high school I returned home from camp with mono. If I had to guess, I caught it the night I went with Geordan Reisner to the empty soccer field and let him spend twenty minutes swinging his tongue around the inside of my mouth. A step up from Ryan, Geordan did *not* take the term lip-locked literally so I was able to take advantage of the ample oxygen the outdoors had to offer. Geordan was hot, but the trade-off for our make-out session hardly seemed fair. I missed the first month at Syosset High School.

Dina was a senior there when I was a freshman. When I recovered from mono she showed me around, made sure I knew where all my classes were, and introduced me to teachers and friends. When I met people at school, I wasn't just Cara, I was Dina's Little Sister. It was a title that existed before I took my first official step through the school's double doors. Dina even introduced me to David O'Brien, my first high school boyfriend and biggest heartbreak. People sang jingles about David and me, jingles spiked with sexual innuendo that pretty much summed up our relationship. His, to the tune of the o.b. tampon commercial, "O.B. set yourself free. Just try O.B. and you'll see." Mine, to the tune of the Sara Lee baked-goods commercials: "Nobody *doesn't* do it like Cara Lee." (A play on my middle name, Leigh).

And when David broke up with me—probably for not "doing it"—I was devastated. Dina crawled into bed with me, leaned her head against mine, and folded herself around me. She spooned me while I sobbed and until we woke up for school the next morning.

Besides helping me with my romantic troubles (and tending to her own), Dina spent much of her time in high school developing her voice. She studied everything from classical music to contemporary. She even started to write her own music and recorded her first demo, titled, "Too Late for Love," which she'd written during a brief breakup with her long-time boyfriend, Glen. I remember thinking that if high school was too late for love, then things weren't looking so good for me.

Perhaps the biggest contributor to Dina's growing vocal versatility was the weekends she spent singing at weddings and bat mitzvahs. In her junior year she lied about her age and took a job in a wedding band. Two to four times a weekend, she would slip into a black cocktail dress and then into her red Nissan coupe and drive all over the tri-state area singing songs from four generations, Motown to Madonna, and learning lyrics en route. I remember when Madonna's lyric-rich "Vogue" was released and that it took a lot of practice for Dina to memorize all the words, "Greta Garbo and Monroe, Dietrich and DiMaggio, Marlon Brando, Jimmy Dean, on the cover of a magazine . . ." I once got to see Dina sing a duet of "Tonight I Celebrate My Love for You" with the slimy wedding-band leader. He was Italian, wore white suits, and had a thick mustache. Every time they sang the line, "When I make love to you," and looked longingly into each other's eyes, I worried that he had bad breath and wondered if Dina wasn't only destined to win a Grammy one day, but an Oscar.

Mom supported Dina's job as a wedding singer, which reflected a change from her previous position on Dina's pursuing a career as a professional singer during Dina's childhood. When Dina was in elementary school, Mom was at the bus stop with her one morning and watched a mother pull her crying daughter off the bus for an audition in the city. "Mommy, I don't wanna go!" the little girl screamed and the mother insisted, tugging her daughter by the hand to a nearby car. Mom told herself she'd never be that kind of mother. And she never was. She encouraged Dina's singing, but not a career as a child star. When Dina saw an audition announcement in *Backstage* magazine for Broadway's *Annie,* Mom refused to take her, and she didn't hunt down acting agents for Dina either. She protected Dina and wanted her to have a real childhood and strong sense of self. There was enough time to open herself up to the criticism that waited for her in the world beyond school.

Dad wanted Dina to succeed, too, but he worried about her entering a competitive industry where so few people found success.

"Just make sure you have a plan B," he told her when she was applying to New York University's new musical-theater program. Mom was quick to disagree with him.

"You can't have a plan B, Dina. You can't let a fear of failure take your focus away from a dream like that." That may have been easy for Mom to say because she never doubted Dina's future success. Somewhere a stage waited for Dina and Mom knew time would take her to it.

I appreciated Dad's caution, but I admired Mom's insight. There was an inherent maternal wisdom in my mother that prevailed despite her own mother's failures. There was a light in Mom, like her unwavering faith in Dina, that reached us through what—given her upbringing—could have been an impenetrable cloud.

When Mom told Dina to pursue her dream wholeheartedly, I wondered what would happen to someone like me, someone who didn't even have a plan A. While I'd often told people I wanted to be a veterinarian—I loved animals and biology and the image of myself as a brainy doctor—I wasn't as certain about it as I let on. My wanting to become a veterinarian was partly an attempt to identify with something the way Dina identified with singing. When it came to having dreams, I only had one: to be a mother. But being a mother didn't feel like enough of a dream when set beside Dina's dream of stardom. As a mother, I would be one of many, not one of a few like Dina. To feel accomplished, motherhood might have to be paired with something else I hadn't identified yet.

Furthermore, my fantasy of performing in some way, singing or acting, being on a stage, persisted. I was embarrassed by it and tucked it away in my back pocket where I could keep it safe without having to fully acknowledge it. But sometimes, like one morning during choir, the fantasy was impossible to ignore.

"Stand up if you want to give it a try," my choir teacher said in ninth grade, as if trying out for a solo were as benign as recording an outgoing answering-machine message.

I sat in a metal folding chair in the top row of our auditorium-style classroom and watched as half a dozen girls rose to their feet. Some shot straight out of their seats, some stood up slowly, tentatively. I knew them and weighed their potential: *Nicole, I bet she'd be good. Natalie, I think she takes voice lessons,* and others. But me? I considered my chances. I wasn't certain that I would suck, but there was a good chance I would. My singing had proven unreliable. Plus, I was nervous, and when I was nervous my trachea tightened around the notes and warped them on their way out. But I also wondered if it was possible that time or estrogen (or a miracle) had tuned my vocal cords. Was it possible that my voice would glide through the room the way Dina's voice always did?

The girls on either side of me remained in their seats and I wondered if they were tempted to stand up, too. If, like me, they were too afraid to try. But wasn't the risk of failure greater for me than it was for them? If *I* sang, I wasn't going to be compared to Nicole or Natalie, I was going to be compared to the best—to Dina. It meant that if I failed, my failure was bigger than anyone else's. It meant that my mistakes would be louder. And this was a downside to being Dina's Little Sister. Teachers and classmates always asked, "Can you sing like your sister?" "No," I'd say, and then smile in the awkward pause that usually followed. *I'm fine with it, with the "no,"* I liked to tell myself. I was proud of Dina and of being her sister. But behind that smile and in that pause, beneath the "fine" and "proud," was the belief that something was missing in me. Because every "No, I can't sing" was a subtle reminder of who I wasn't and what I *couldn't* do, at a time when I'd yet to figure out who I was and what I *could* do. With Dina near, my identity was developing in relation to her; I wasn't figuring out who I was as much as I was coming to understand that I wasn't her.

I could feel my pulse tapping in my ears. I wanted to stand up and try to sing the solo, but my limbs felt numb, thick, and heavy, like drying cement. I was looking at my feet and wondering if they could even hold my weight when the sound of the piano drew me out of my thoughts and back into the classroom, where, through no fault but my own, the teacher called on a girl who wasn't me.

In Syosset High School, if you had acting aspirations but couldn't sing, your performing options were limited. Syosset didn't put on plays, only musicals. Plays were so scarce that apart from Shakespeare's Juliet and Blanche DuBois from *A Streetcar Named Desire,* I couldn't even name a play with a leading female role. In my high school, as in elementary and middle school, people starred in musicals or they didn't star at all. If you weren't one of the top singers in school, you were relegated to the chorus. If you wanted to act, the only option was the Forensics Club. In Forensics, students prepared eight-to-ten-minute extemporaneous pieces or dramatic interpretations for competitions. Forensics wasn't full-on theater—but it was better than nothing.

Dina had departed for NYU's musical theater program, when, in the beginning of my sophomore year of high school, I considered joining the Forensics Club. Dina had participated in Forensics, and the teacher, Ms. Eslinger, was an elegant blond woman who had been her champion. They'd been close and were still in touch. Even with Dina gone, the thought of trying out for Forensics felt like knocking on the door of their private party. I couldn't shake the feeling that I didn't belong there.

I imagined performing a monologue for Ms. Eslinger. How would she keep my performance separate from Dina's performances? I remembered listening to Dina rehearse a monologue from the play (and later a movie starring Barbra Streisand) *Nuts*. Would Ms. Eslinger watch me on a split screen, with Dina—her sloppy-haired Barbra Streisand in a psych ward, conjuring tears, declaring, "I won't be nuts for you!"—on the left, and me on the right—performing who knows what? Would it matter? Whomever I played, I'd be performing side by side with Dina, and I didn't want to risk looking ridiculous in comparison. I didn't want to be pitied. "Did you see Idina Mentzel's sister trying to act today? Yikes, must be rough," someone might say.

Even if I showed promise, all possible outcomes made me uncomfortable. At best Dina and I would be different, but at worst one of us would be found lacking. I didn't want to be the one lacking, but I didn't want Dina to be, either. I didn't want her to be less so that I could be more. I simply wanted to be extraordinary in my own way.

There were countless imperceptible ways that I backed away from interests that overlapped with Dina's. But because of Forensics, there was one notable moment when I consciously decided that singing and acting were pursuits that belonged to Dina alone. On the day that the Forensics Club would be starting after school, I closed my binder, waited for the bell to ring, and went home.

Dina wasn't the only reason I moved away from New York after high school, but she was one of them. My desire to be close to her remained, but I knew I needed to be someplace she hadn't already been.

In my thirties, I found the old VHS tape of the *Guys and Dolls* camp performance in the bottom of a rubber storage bin. I watched myself sing "Take Back Your Mink." There I stood in a white dress at the edge of the stage.

"Take back your mink," I sang, and removed the first shoulder strap of the dress.

"Take back your pearls," and removed the other strap.

"What made you think, that I was one of those girls," and I shimmied the dress down to the floor until I stood more than half naked in that silver tube top and miniskirt.

When I shimmied and lost the dress, a hundred boys whistled and screamed like young men at a bachelor party. I winced as I watched the striptease of my thirteen-year-old self with the eyes of a thirty-year-old teacher and mother of two. I remembered that moment of contradiction, how it felt good to be liked, but it didn't feel right. How I loved that everyone's eyes were on me, but still wished I could find a sleeping bag to slide into. Then, staring at a freeze-frame on the television screen of myself with the dress at my feet, it occurred to me that starring as Adelaide may have had less to do with any talent I possessed and more to do with my olive skin and long legs. I felt sorry for the girl on the screen, sorry as if she were my daughter. I wished I hadn't watched the video. I wanted that young girl to think that she'd scored the leading role *because* of her talent, not *in spite* of a lack of it. A few minutes earlier, I thought I'd found a sweet memory in the bottom of that bin. But really, I'd lost one.

PART II
MOVING ON

Lesson 4

HOW TO MEASURE A YEAR

I found my place.

At first glance, the University of Colorado at Boulder looked like it was plucked out of Tuscany. The vast majority of its buildings were constructed of pink sandstone from Colorado quarries and Tuscan-red barrel-tile roofs, features that gave continuity to architecture that ranged from college Gothic to modern, and reflected the changing styles of the university's 135-year history. The university stood in a valley against the Flatirons, monstrous red rocks that jutted out of the foothills of the Rocky Mountains and slanted away from the university like giant hands gesturing toward a work of art. "Voilà. Here's Boulder," they said.

On a self-guided tour of the campus with my parents, I noticed three fraternity-type upper classmen across the street. While looking at the college incarnation of "the cool kids," I walked straight into a parking meter. If there were a way for a halo of twittering birds to circle my head, they would have. There was no question that the laughter across the way was at my expense. But more jarring than the impact or the embarrassment were the realizations that although the landscape had changed, I could still make an ass out of myself, and still had no idea where I was going.

I originally applied to CU because just north of Boulder was Colorado State University. CSU has a prestigious veterinary graduate program, and completing my undergraduate in Colorado would bring me that much closer to a study of veterinary medicine. But during my senior year of high school I interned at Syosset Animal Hospital and realized that veterinary medicine wasn't for me. Not because the enema blow-out of a chocolate Lab was the most vile experience I'd had to date, but rather because being a vet seemed like a lot of guesswork, trial and error, and I didn't like that the treatment for most questionable diagnoses was a pill or a surgical procedure. I changed my mind and applied to CU as an "Undecided" major.

CU was a fresh start. I didn't know of one student from my high school attending with me and there were approximately twenty-five thousand students there at the time. For once I looked forward to getting a little lost in the crowd. My first order of business was to get rid of "Long Island." I traded in my four-hundred-dollar jappy Justin cowboy boots for a pair of wool socks and Birkenstocks—and yes, I wore them together. I wore no makeup, had no hairspray, and listened carefully to my Colorado roommate, who, to me, sounded like she had an accent, but really what she had was a lack of accent. I wanted that, too. I wanted an absent accent.

"Where ya from?" people would ask.

"Long Island," I'd say.

"Oh, Lawng Oyland, hah?" They'd repeat like it was an original reaction, like I'd never seen Mike Myers do "Coffee Talk" on *Saturday Night Live*.

In Boulder I wasn't Dina's Little Sister, I was just another freshman student with a new Target comforter and Brother word processor. But I didn't entirely fit the incoming freshman profile for CU. In 1992, CU was one of the top-ten party schools in the country and I didn't party. I chose the substance-free dorm (an odd concept since all dorms were theoretically substance-free). I had a copy of that "Footprints in the Sand" motivational passage, the one that ends with "When you saw only one set of footprints, it was then that I carried you," in a Lucite frame next to my bed. I wasn't religious. Judaism was my heritage, but to me it was about brisket and chopped liver, bat mitzvahs, and the calming depth of our cantor's tenor. I was spiritual. I liked to meditate and talk to God. To me, God wasn't a gray-haired bearded man in a robe—not Jesus or Allah—God wasn't so much a person as a symbol of Love and a guiding force in the universe. I believed in platitudes like "God never gives you more than you can handle" and "Whatever is meant to be is meant to be." At college I had hoped to surround myself with like-minded peers, but in that first month at school I learned that the substance-free dorm had less to do with booze and more to do with Bibles. Incessant invitations to Bible study nearly drove me to drink.

In Boulder the only person comparing me to Dina was me, and I didn't compare us often. But occasionally, in the white solitude of a rounded library study carrel, I would remember that Dina had graduated from Syosset High School with a 94 grade-point average and I had graduated with a 92. I don't know how or when I stored our high school GPAs in my memory, but I could retrieve them as quickly as my own birthdate. Remembering them was irrefutable evidence that I compared myself to my big sister more than I liked to admit. The shame of having remembered those numbers was far worse than the inadequacy I felt because of the difference between them. And what *was* the difference between them? Two points. Were two points even statistically significant? Probably not, but part of me believed Dina's 94 meant that even when the variable of our ages was controlled for, she was better than me, smarter than me. This was another tricky part of being Dina's sister, of being anyone's sibling, probably. Comparison is built into your very existence. Someone is always the Smart One. The Talented One. The Funny One. You can't both be fast, one of you has to be faster—the Fast One. Even if someone else isn't passing judgment, you're making the comparisons on your own.

School was hard. Friendships were fleeting and I was lonely, but I also felt accomplished, if for no other reason than that I hadn't walked into any more parking meters. I'd hauled myself more than halfway across the country and I was okay. I did my work and found my bearings around campus and town. It helped that I lived against the dignity of the Rocky Mountains. They were the spine of Colorado's landscape and I felt stronger and more stable in their company.

Dina came to visit me during my second semester. She was fighting a cold and her voice was hoarse.

"I get the whole Boulder hippie thing," she said and looked at my shoes, then up at my frizzy ponytail, "but who says you can't take a shower?"

"I showered on Wednesday," I assured her.

On Long Island I'd worried that someone might notice if I wore the same pair of jeans twice in one week. In Boulder, a city listed as one of *GQ*'s worst dressed in the country on more than one occasion (though as a fitness mecca, it has earned recognition for having the best-looking naked people), nobody seemed to care about my clothes or my appearance, so I didn't either. For what felt like the first time, I was comfortable.

I was excited to show Dina around Boulder. I took her to Norlin Quad, off of the library. We grabbed a snack and sat on the steps around the University Memorial Center fountain. We walked along the red brick of the outdoor mall on Pearl Street. It felt good to be the one who knew whatever there was to know—the school, the town, anything. And then for some reason I can't remember, Dina and I decided to roller blade.

I'd bought a pair of Rollerblades before I left for college. I'd planned to cruise around corners and weave through pedestrian areas agilely, like an athlete. I'd made my Rollerblade purchase using the same criteria I'd used to make most purchases throughout high school—the most expensive item must be the best. This was a standard takeaway from an adolescence on Long Island. Despite my vision of swift Rollerblade grandeur through campus, I'd barely put mine on. At the time, Dina was even less skilled—she'd later cruise down NYC streets like the expert I aimed to be, but back then, we borrowed a pair from a friend of mine, and Dina and I were off.

By the time we were ready to Rollerblade, Dina had full-blown laryngitis. She could barely whisper so I gave her one of my campus whistles to hang around her neck in the event she needed to get my attention while we were out and about. Slowly, side by side, we found our footing. We bladed over sidewalks, slick new asphalt, and bumpy bike paths patched with tar and cement. We laughed at each other's wooden awkwardness as we passed through the student parking lots, behind the campus's Fiske Planetarium, and down into a tunnel underpass beneath Boulder's Twenty-eighth Street.

In my minimal Rollerblading experience, I'd learned to stop via local lawns. I'd get going and when my speed exceeded my comfort zone, I'd hop off the sidewalk or street onto an adjacent lawn. Lawns provided the right amount of deceleration, and in the event I needed to fall, a lawn was a soft place to land.

We arrived at a frontage road that ran the length of a steep hill and ended on the outer side of a main intersection. Dina experimented with her heel brake. I attempted to do the same, but I had picked up too much speed and couldn't bring myself to lean on the brake out of fear I'd falter. Dina disappeared from my peripheral vision. I peeked down at the rough asphalt as it whipped by beneath me. The friction between my wheels and the street sent a vibration up through the soles of my feet that tickled in the worst way. I checked to my right for a handy lawn, but there were only parking lots. Petrified, I raced toward the bottom of the hill where a Stop sign stood like a moot point at the edge of Colorado Avenue, a four-lane cross street. The hill leveled out and I held my breath as I cruised through the Stop sign, took a wide turn, narrowly avoiding a median, and then crossed back over two lanes of traffic toward the curb on my right. I cut off a city RTD bus in the process. I took a quick step up to the curb, hopped my wheels over a strip of grass along the sidewalk, and then slammed into the concrete on my hands and knees. The bus whizzed by, pounding its angry horn.

I was sitting on my ass in the middle of the sidewalk, squinting, and pulling a small glass shard out of a scrape in my palm when I heard the whistle.

"Toot tooooooot. Toot tooooooot." Dina came rolling down the sidewalk. "Toot tooooot." She smiled and the whistle dropped out of her mouth. She was animated and excited when she tried to speak, but her voice wouldn't cooperate. It only worked intermittently. "Oh—gosh, you're awe—! You're like—pro!"

I was confused. Didn't she know my collision course through traffic was a mistake? I looked up at her and the whistle that hung from a string around her neck. Before I could set Dina straight I exploded into a soggy mess of snot and tears.

"I almost died," I managed to say.

She sat down next to me and whispered, "Well, at least you looked great," and we burst into laughter. "Let me get th—stupid—ings off—you." She unclasped one of the buckles and then croaked, "Whose idea was—anyway?" We walked back to my place in our socks, carrying our Rollerblades in protest.

Maybe I remember that day because I almost died, that's certainly good enough reason, but I think—at least in part—I remember that day because it was symbolic for me. My sister, whose voice had defined so much of my life, had come to visit me and shown up without, of all things, her voice! Then, she watched me successfully (successful perhaps, only because I lived to tell the story) tackle a huge hill and, despite my fear and flailing, she was impressed. I'd moved a thousand miles away from home to a place where her voice was quiet enough for me to begin to hear my own, and it seemed like Dina knew that was what I needed to do. It seemed like she was proud of me.

I fell in love with an aerospace engineering student, Ken. He was tall and skinny—too skinny, he'd say. He had warm brown eyes and an even warmer smile. We moved in together. He wanted to be an astronaut. An astronaut! I didn't know people still wanted to be astronauts. Wasn't it a cliché straight out of a career-day presentation in elementary school? I had a boyfriend who wanted to venture into the stars and a sister who wanted to be one. Dina was willing to face repeated rejection, something that would be unbearable for me. And Ken was willing to suffer through differential equations, something that would be impossible for me. I envied their clarity. I envied their drive. And I worried that without an extraordinary goal, I might never be an extraordinary person. *Am I destined to be ordinary?* I wondered. *Am I okay with that?*

It was about the time Ken taught me how to drive a stick that I unearthed my hair dryer, reintroduced black boots and tights to my wardrobe, and started to feel a bit like a badass. I declared a major in psychology and planned to attend graduate school to become a clinical psychologist. My interest in psychology was simple and honorable: I wanted to help people. Then someone told me that psychology was the largest major at CU. Because it had the fewest science requirements, many students deemed it the easiest route to a degree. I couldn't confirm the accuracy of their claim, but true or not, "easy" bothered me. I hadn't come across the country to join a throng of people with a reputation for being mediocre. Suddenly, I didn't feel as much like helping others as I felt like outperforming them. Honorable? Definitely not. On the upside, I'd found some drive.

I loved my neuroscience classes most of all and excelled at them. One day, I was in the elevator of the Muenzinger Psychology Building with a few classmates and one of my neuroscience professors. We were talking about our future studies.

"I'm pretty sure physics and I are incompatible," I said. "I mean, I still struggle to borrow and carry when double-checking the bill." I giggled. My professor looked me square in the eyes and said, "Don't do that. Don't act less intelligent just because you're a pretty girl." His use of the imperative was jarring. I'd never heard the words "intelligent" and "pretty" spoken in such a severe tone, and I didn't know how to react. Had I been insulted, reprimanded, complimented? All of the above?

"Okay," I said, "I won't."

"I'm serious," he pressed. "You're too smart for that."

I swallowed hard to clear the lump in my throat. "Okay," I repeated.

I walked to the bus stop replaying the brief interaction in my mind. I hadn't intentionally acted less intelligent. Sure I was exaggerating—I mean, I *can* borrow and carry—but my earlier statement wasn't an outright lie. The quantitative sciences had never been my strong suit, and I'm embarrassed by how long it would take me to calculate a 15 percent tip. But maybe my professor was on to something. Maybe I put myself down a lot. Maybe giggling was a sign of insecurity. It felt like a reflex, a way of sweetening my delivery. A little giggle or nervous laugh was my way of ensuring that whatever I'd said would be well received. Though I didn't quite understand what that had to do with being "a pretty girl." The truth was I didn't always feel smart and I certainly didn't always feel pretty. But intellectually, at least, I had no doubt a woman could be both. If not because my mother and my sister were great examples, then because *Working Girl* was one of my favorite movies. Every now and then I called upon the image of Melanie Griffith on the Staten Island Ferry and Carly Simon singing, "Let the river run, let all the dreamers wake the nation," for inspiration.

The following semester, when, as a junior, the same professor asked if I'd like to teach recitations for the lower-division Biological Psychology class, I wanted to bat my eyelashes and say, "I'm not sure my pretty little brain can handle that." But I was too excited about the opportunity to teach my favorite subject to make a joke.

Dina came to visit the semester I taught Biological Psychology. She'd been working as a reservationist at a popular restaurant in Chelsea, auditioning in her off-hours, gigging with some of her own music, and trying to find an alternative to singing at weddings and bat mitzvahs on the weekends. She came to class to watch me teach. She sat toward the back of a sunny classroom behind a U-shaped configuration of tables where a class of approximately thirty students sat facing a large green chalkboard. I stood in front of the class and reviewed the week's content from the professor's lectures on synaptic transmission. Dina listened as I answered questions, drew diagrams, and offered detailed explanations of, but not limited to, the propagation of action potentials, the depolarization of cell membranes, calcium channels, and the difference between excitatory post-synaptic potentials and inhibitory post-synaptic potentials. I was knowledgeable in front of the class, poised and confident. And Dina saw me. In the back of a room full of college students begrudgingly fulfilling their science requirement, Dina sat beaming. On our way out of the classroom, she locked her arm in mine and said, "Holy shit, I'm so impressed. How do you know all that stuff?" I didn't have an answer. I was too busy soaking up her praise.

That night, Dina, Ken, and I went out for dinner at Sushi Zanmai. Back then it was the only place to get sushi in Boulder. Sushi Zanmai is a relatively small restaurant with one of those tiny bathrooms situated inappropriately close to the kitchen. There was a sushi bar on one side and tables scattered around the bar's perimeter. On Friday and Saturday nights patrons might wait an hour for a table. We were seated around 8 P.M. To our surprise, around 9:30 the staff started rearranging the chairs and tables to clear a corner for karaoke. Apparently, Saturday night was karaoke night. Truly, I hadn't known.

Some people would have reached for their sake or Kirin and begun a mental search for the song they'd sing. Not me. Not Ken. Not even Dina. Dina rarely sang in public unless there was an official performance. When we were younger and family or friends asked her to sing—just 'cause—like at a family friend's house on a Saturday night—Dina resisted. She wasn't a show-off and making herself the center of attention in an unofficial capacity made her uncomfortable. But making her the center of attention in an unofficial capacity didn't make *me* uncomfortable, and there in the corner of the restaurant a microphone on a flimsy stand waited for a singer, my favorite singer.

"Come on, Dina. Sing something," I said.

"Why don't *you* get up there?" she asked.

"Oh *right*. That's not happening."

"I get to sing all the time," Dina said. "Seriously, I have my own mic. Let someone else sing, someone who doesn't get to do it otherwise."

"Fine," I conceded.

Then, with comedic arrogance, Dina added, "Besides, I doubt it would be in my key," and dramatically flung her hair off to the side.

Boulder didn't know Idina Mentzel like Syosset did, and while I appreciated the anonymity and the chance to be Cara—whoever she was—I still wanted the world to know that my sister was special. Of course, at the time *the world* may have been an ambitious goal, so the patrons of Sushi Zanmai had to suffice. But Dina was adamant.

The lights dimmed until the room was almost dark, and we stayed and watched drunken college students slur the words to "Livin' on a Prayer" and "California Girls." Occasionally, there were brave souls with the microphone who were very serious about their performance, but struggled to stay on pitch. These were the people I watched while in search of an appropriate facial expression, something authentic that acknowledged their courage and concealed my discomfort. But the harder they tried and the worse they sang, the worse I felt; I was convinced that I couldn't have felt more embarrassed if I were up there myself. And yet there was nothing empathetic or noble about my feelings. Me, the girl who was afraid to get up there herself because she might suck, was embarrassed for those who had the gumption enough to try—or better yet—would enjoy trying; I didn't need to be a psychology major to know that my discomfort was all about me and not about them. It was a projection of my self-consciousness onto innocents who would soon be too busy selecting their next song to care about my uneasiness. Painful as it sometimes was for me to watch, I envied them.

Then there were the karaoke die-hards who wanted to be singers and, unlike Dina, used karaoke as an opportunity to take center stage. They may not have been able to make a career of singing, but they were eager to get up there for three minutes of local stardom and two minutes of post-performance accolades. Some people wanted their fifteen minutes of fame, but would settle for five minutes of karaoke. I remember one such person from that night who fit this description.

I returned to our table from a quick trip to the restroom and the restaurant was cheering as a woman, close to my age, was taking the "stage."

Ken leaned over to me and explained, "Apparently, this woman won the regional karaoke contest last month."

"There's a regional karaoke contest?" I asked. He shrugged his shoulders as the first notes of Gloria Gaynor's feminist anthem "I Will Survive" began.

"At first I was afraid, I was petrified."

She wasn't fabulous, but she was good, and unlike her predecessors, she could hold a tune. She had pitch and hints of vibrato. More than talent, though, she had stage presence. I think she'd grown accustomed to having an audience. She was probably used to solos in high school. I caught myself thinking *Dina's so much better,* and immediately coached myself to be a better person. *Be kind, Cara. Root for wanna-be Gloria Gaynor. Wish her the best.* Still, all I could think was that I wanted my sister to get up there and put that girl in her place, show her how it's *really* done. *Oh my god, I'm an affront to feminism. I'm a terrible person.* At the same time, I was shamelessly proud of my sister, and wasn't that a good thing?

I leaned over and tapped Dina's arm.

"Please," I said.

Dirty look.

"All I'm askin' . . . is for a little 'Respect'?" I was begging, but I was careful. I didn't want her to get annoyed with me.

She smiled and I felt relieved.

"Just a little bit," I added and smiled back. I knew I'd won. If there was a surefire way to make me happy, Dina would do it.

Before long, Dina stood in front of the mic, dotted with the colored lights of a cheap disco ball. I scanned the crowd, then looked back at her. I was the only one in the room who knew what was about to happen. Not even Ken, who had heard her on cassette tape, knew the power that the unassuming girl at the mic with the poufy hair was seconds from unleashing. Horns played the first couple of measures of "Respect" and then Dina began.

"What you want! Baby I got it."

All table chat ended. There it was, the best feeling. The reason I wanted to put Dina on display that night. The satisfaction of a stunned audience. The meteoric force and unique texture of her voice and the way it charged the crowd. She drew her head back, instinctively measuring her volume and her distance from the mic, and continued. When Dina sang I was fully immersed in her performance. She made it impossible for my focus to wander beyond that moment and I loved the feeling of being 100 percent present.

Finally, "R-E-S-P-E-C-T! Take care. TCB."

When Dina finished, the audience whistled and applauded. I'd done nothing but sit there, shout a few *whoo*s, and dance in my seat, and yet I felt triumphant. When Dina performed, she both inspired me to be my best and reminded me that I didn't need to be *the* best to be happy. In fact, with Dina onstage, I could feel better than ever as one of the many faces in a dimly lit crowd.

A little while later we grabbed our coats. On our way out, a woman stood up from the sushi bar and stopped us.

"You could be a singer," she said to Dina, as if recognizing talent in Dina were rocket science. I tried not to laugh.

"Here, I'm a voice coach," she added and handed Dina her card. Had this woman made a practice of scoping out potential clients at karaoke night? Smart.

"Thank you," Dina said and took the card. Then, as we walked on, Dina turned back and added, "I do a little singing back in New York."

On a long weekend in the fall of my senior year at CU, I arrived at the Newark airport and stepped on the Down escalator, heading toward the baggage claim. I could see Dina and Dad waiting at the bottom and imagined the hugs in the seconds before they happened. Dina was good with a hug, but she was more of a kisser. I loved that even as we grew up, she still kissed me, usually on the lips. There's an old photo of us—a favorite that I opted to feature on this book cover. I'm four—our ages are carefully noted in my mom's script on the back side—and Dina is seven. I'm in my little red-and-white sundress with the strawberries on it and there's a matching red yarn ribbon in my hair. Dina's in a bedazzled short denim skirt, a future favorite hand-me-down. She's squatting down with her arms wrapped around my waist, her head level with mine as we smooch. Kissing Dina is a special kind of kiss. It's a split second that manages to say, "I love you. I'll take care of you. I see you," all at once. At the bottom of the escalator a kiss waited for me.

Dad had been living in the city since he and Mom divorced, so visiting meant I could spend time with both him and Dina and we might all be able to grab a movie together. Mom was no longer living in New York. During my sophomore year at CU, she left the Long Island town house behind for a fresh start near me, in Colorado.

I enjoyed New York City in bite-size pieces—maybe five days at a time. After five days, the pace was too swift for me, and I typically found I was ready to return to Boulder. But Dina loved the city and knew how to maneuver in its chaos. She knew how much tip to give the take-out delivery guy. She knew the subway, and when to get annoyed because a cab driver was taking the wrong route in rush hour. She even knew how to fall asleep in the clamor of sirens, horns, and drunks down on the street. It was different from Boulder. When I was with her in the city I didn't bother to look at street signs; I just tried to keep up.

I stayed with Dina that weekend. She shared a three-bedroom apartment with her best friends, Debbie and Suzy. Five-inch-tall glossy white colonial moldings traced the perimeter of the worn parquet floor. The narrow strip of kitchen was mostly the receptacle for take-out remnants, and the window at the far end made it the perfect place to smoke a few rare Parliaments.

The apartment was the launching pad from which each of them dug into life after college. They often met on the fly or talked on the phone. Their schedules had them bumping into each other on the way in or the way out, but there was a warmth to their friendship that bridged the skinny, short moments. It was a warmth that thrived in every dried-flower arrangement—Suzy had taken up the art—missing hand towel, and Indigo Girls DVD. They knew each other well—Dina's auditions, their job interviews, dating troubles, sexual encounters—the walls were thin. They knew how to navigate each other's flaws, they'd argue and make up, and had free reign in each other's closets. I was jealous of their connection. It was a connection I didn't have with anyone, not even Dina. Their closeness wasn't just about the trust and understanding expected of good friends, but also about knowing the details that took them from Sunday to Sunday. I didn't have Sunday to Sunday with Dina.

I imagine Dina and I were like a lot of sisters. When we were younger we shared a laundry basket and chores. We couldn't veer farther from each other than a closed bedroom door. But we were getting older. We no longer shared a home, and no longer saw each other every day. Yet our bond was indisputable. There was a tacit quality to our closeness, an abiding undercurrent of security, unaffected by physical distance or the frequency of our phone calls. I often consider all the possibilities, the ways the bond between sisters is developed. For Dina and me, perhaps it can be traced to the length of time we'd known each other? The familiarity of each other's face, skin, smell, or voice? Our shared gene pool or shared past experiences? Or maybe, as the younger sister, I was (and continue to be) bound to Dina because I know no world without her in it.

Still, I wanted to feel like a friend to Dina, not a perpetual little sister. I'd hoped the difference between our ages would feel more narrow the further we traveled into our futures. But even in our midtwenties, I didn't feel like it had. Moreover, I felt more self-conscious with her than with anyone else. I tried not to be, but *trying* not to be self-conscious is like trying not to yawn. I was even anxious talking to Dina on the phone. If I knew she was going to call I'd construct a mental list of discussion topics, news I could share with her and questions I could ask her. If I was prepared, I could avoid awkward silences, or worse, I could avoid her ending the conversation before I did, something I dreaded because I'd feel personally rejected. I couldn't justify feeling rejected, but I also couldn't help it. I didn't have enough time with Dina as an adult to find the ease and confidence I wanted to feel when I was with her, an ease and confidence that in college I was beginning to feel more often.

I was sitting cross-legged on Dina's couch when she approached me and dropped a few pages on my lap.

"Can you read this for me?" she asked.

"Sure."

"I have a callback for this off-Broadway thing called *Rent,* but the sides—the pages of the script—are of this weird monologue and I don't get it."

Dina had read a lot of scripts. When we talked she always seemed to be going on an audition, but nothing had panned out. I imagined she tried not to get too excited about auditions anymore, but I didn't know for sure. If she was discouraged, she seemed too busy to feel it for very long.

I sat with the script on my lap feeling hopeful. Dina was looking to me for an answer—maybe because I knew about postsynaptic potentials she thought I might also be able to explicate the poetic elements of her script? Suddenly, I wasn't too young anymore, too inexperienced, or too annoying. I was a young woman, just like her, and nearly a college graduate. I took the script carefully into my hands like I was holding the beginning of our grown-up relationship. The one we would build on a level playing field.

I looked at the first page and tried to focus on the print, but I couldn't. I was preoccupied by my desire to impress her. I stared at that page, willing away the pressure to please. I noticed the title, "Over the Moon," and read on.

"Last night, I had a dream. I found myself in a desert called Cyberland." At first, I was able to follow the script, though I wondered about the connection between deserts and Cyberland. Was it some kind of "wasteland" metaphor?

"Out of the abyss, walked a cow, Elsie. I asked if she had anything to drink."

Weird, I thought.

"She said, 'I'm forbidden to produce milk. In Cyberland, we only drink Diet Coke.'" *Definitely weird.* I backed up and reread a little. *A desert, Cyberland, a cow, Diet Coke. Shit.* I read on, understanding the script like I understood *Beowulf.*

"It's like I'm being tied to the hood of a yellow rental truck, being packed in with fertilizer and fuel oil, pushed over a cliff by a suicidal Mickey Mouse!"

Come on!

I read the lines, tried to read between the lines, and eventually stared at the white space on the page and waited for an epiphany. After half an hour, the meaning of the short piece still eluded me.

I pictured Dina and me on that couch in the ethers of an alternate universe where she hung on my every word as I postulated the piece's themes and used multisyllabic words like "antiestablishment." But that's not how it happened.

Instead, when Dina walked by I handed her the script.

"That's crazy, Dina," I said to her, too afraid of sounding stupid to even guess at its meaning.

"I know, right? Thanks for trying."

I was flattened.

Dina continued to go about her business. She took care of mundane tasks like picking up in her room and chatting briefly with Suzy about what movie to rent from Blockbuster. I sat there on the cusp of Dina's stardom feeling as inconsequential as a throw pillow.

The following day, while I flew back to Colorado, Dina auditioned for *Rent.* She performed "Over the Moon." She sang "When a Man Loves a Woman" and Bonnie Raitt's "Something to Talk About" for *Rent*'s director, Michael Greif, and its creator-composer, Jonathan Larson. She scored the part of the raunchy lesbian performance artist, Maureen Johnson.

Dina rehearsed for the show at the New York Theatre Workshop while, back in Boulder, I spent most of my time in the basement lab of the psychology building. I'd decided I wanted to graduate with honors, a recognition that required a minimum 3.5 grade-point average and the successful completion of an honors thesis. I was determined to put an exclamation point at the end of my undergraduate story.

My Perception professor agreed to be my thesis adviser, and soon I was spending more time in that windowless psychology lab than in my apartment. I was particularly interested in unconscious perception. Unfortunately, as my research progressed, the fascination with which I began it was lost to the details of computer programming and statistics, and the fact that at the time, there was little consensus in the scientific community regarding the definition of *unconscious*. Which led to a thesis far more tedious than compelling as evidenced by its mouthful of a title, *Perception Without Awareness and Signal Detection Theory*.

My visit to see the earliest off-Broadway *Rent* performances, including opening night, was supposed to be a welcome reprieve from school. But the visit was bittersweet—way more bitter than sweet. Mom, Dad, and I had planned to see the first preview together when Dina called to let us know that Jonathan Larson had been found dead in his apartment that morning. Jonathan had suffered an aortic aneurism that went undetected at two different emergency rooms earlier that week. He was thirty-five years old.

I knew Dina and the cast and Jonathan were close. He wasn't only breaking new ground in theater with his rock opera about young artists in New York City's East Village living in the shadow of HIV, but in the process he had created a family, and my sister was a part of it.

Rent was the fruition of months—years, for many—of devotion and work by Dina's *Rent* family. By Dina's account, the dress rehearsal the night before had been exhilarating and sent the cast home eager and buoyant. But in the short distance between dusk and dawn the *Rent* world changed. Jonathan, a visionary, was dead. His vision was in limbo. And somehow, in a cloud of grief, a decision had to be made about how to proceed.

A modified version of the show was performed that night. The cast honored Jonathan by singing his score to a theater filled with his family and friends. The cast sat in chairs that lined a series of long tables set end-to-end across the stage. No special lighting or costumes, props, or staging. The first half of the performance went as planned, but by the end of Act I when the cast sang the riotous ensemble piece "La Vie Bohème," the cast was out of their seats, dancing on the tables, performing the piece as staged. A performance that began somberly grew into a cathartic celebration of Jonathan and his work. In the end, an audience of mourners were on their feet cheering and crying, all at once energized and exhausted. But afterward, the grateful noise quieted and the full theater shared a sustained silence.

I don't know if I was there that night or at the following night's preview. I've heard the story so many times that I can't be certain if the memory is from the story I've been told or from my actual experience. What I *do* remember is that I watched *Rent* for the first time while intermittently holding back sobs so big I worried they'd burst from me and disrupt the show. And I remember one of Dina's lines, a line Jonathan wrote for her to say to Angel, but that from then on she'd always say to Jonathan: "You always said you were so lucky that we were all friends. But it was us, Baby, who were the lucky ones."

Rent became a huge success and was moving to Broadway. Dina was in newspapers and magazines and even on television; *48 Hours* aired a piece on *Rent* that featured her. The highlight of most weeks in Boulder was my visit to the Eads News and Smoke Shop. In the pre-Internet era, Eads carried nearly every newspaper and publication in the United States, and it was where I found Dina's press—each photo, article, and review that mentioned her name or included her picture. I spent months cutting them out and passing them around with bragging rights. Her success energized me and I needed to be energized. I was overwhelmed with school. My thesis had put my self-esteem through the wringer and I was bored with my daily tussles with self-doubt. By the time I flew to New York for the Broadway opening of *Rent,* my mini-vacation had been well earned.

I sat in the Nederlander Theatre on West Forty-first Street in New York City, between my mother and father, and my grandmother to his right. It was April 29, 1996. And I was over the moon.

The Nederlander was a regal theater housing twelve hundred red velvet seats, and like most Broadway theater seats, they were made for asses that find airplane accommodations roomy. The theater's interior was a glossy wood laminate with ornate gold-leaf accents and layers of elaborate moldings. There were three sets of box seats on either side of the broad stage and front and rear mezzanines that helped fill the space between the floor and towering ceilings. The theater underwent significant transformation to achieve the East Village grunge atmosphere where *Rent* was set, and even the theater's marquee and external facade were altered.

In front of me, the stage depicted a sparse apartment in the Lower East Side's Alphabet City. The back wall was painted faux brick, and a fire escape hung just in front of it with stairs that led to the floor. Off to the right was scaffolding and above it hung a massive sculpture, a pile of urban clutter including bicycle parts, a sidewalk grate, rebar, and a steering wheel. As a finishing touch, colored string lights were haphazardly twisted around it. Later in the show, when the lights were turned on, the sculpture would look like a Christmas tree, or like an amusement park ride had collapsed in the night. Several silver-and-red metal folding chairs were scattered on the stage and a few were set around a rectangular table.

That night the Nederlander was filled. Theatergoers moved through aisle thoroughfares and ushers handed out playbills. I thumbed through mine. I flipped past advertisements and tried to find a table of contents or Dina's picture and description in the "Who's Who in the Cast" section. Finally, I found "Maureen Johnson, Idina Menzel," with a tiny version of her headshot and a short bio noting *Rent* as her "Broadway debut." Dina had recently taken the "t" out of our last name to help with pronunciation. People had often said "MEN-sul," like pencil, and she wanted her name to be pronounced "Menzell," like gazelle or mademoiselle. It occurred to me that Dina removed the better letter. That if ever I wanted to change my name slightly, I'd have to remove the "z" and be Cara . . . Mentel. *Oy.*

The lights dimmed and brightened a few times. A voice through the speakers said, "Please take your seats." The last few people squeezed past those of us already seated. I was sweaty and shaky, but not because I was nervous. I wasn't worried that Dina would forget her lines or that her voice would crack on a high note; I'd never seen Dina screw up a performance. I knew she got nervous and was nervous backstage somewhere, but Dina was the kind of performer who knew how to harness adrenaline to strengthen her performance.

It was anticipation that made me shaky. My dad turned to me wearing a stiffer smile than his usual one, probably because he was so happy, that his mouth had been locked in that position for an hour. My mom had her hand in mine the way we'd done just months earlier for the off-Broadway show, and the way we always did at Dina's performances. In those last few seconds before the show began, it occurred to me that Mom, Dad, and I loved Dina so deeply that we held her dreams as if they were our own, maybe even tighter.

Roger, played by Adam Pascal, walked out onstage and sat down. He began fiddling with his amp and guitar and the theater grew quiet.

Casually the rest of the company, including Dina, joined Adam. The audience stood and cheered. When they took their seats again, Anthony Rapp, *Rent's* Mark, said, "We dedicate this opening night and every performance to our friend Jonathan Larson," and the audience stood again and cheered. I wasn't sure how long the cheering would last, but no one was in a hurry. Soon enough, the show officially began. Within the first minute Mark was interrupted by the phone ringing, and he and Roger let it go to voice mail. It was Mark's mother. They listened as she left a lengthy message that ended with, "We're sorry to hear that Maureen dumped you, I say c'est la vie. So let her be a lesbian, there are other fishies in the sea."

It was hard to imagine I could be any more excited than I had been moments earlier, but the mention of Maureen sent a shiver through my body and

Mom must have felt the same way because she squeezed my hand. I knew it would be nearly fifty minutes before Dina made her official entrance. I watched each of them, knowing that each brought me closer to her debut.

When that fifty-minute mark neared, tension in the Nederlander started to build. Not just on the stage where plot lines came together, but in my stomach. If the seat hadn't been so small, I would have been on the edge of it. I returned Mom's squeeze from earlier.

"Christmas bells are ringing . . . ," the ensemble sang. "Got any C Man. Got any D Man," junkies asked as they followed their dealer around the stage. Angel and Collins haggled for a coat with a street vendor: "Fifteen. Sold!" "I should tell you, I should tell you," Roger and Mimi sang from their earlier duet. The key characters were all making their way to Maureen's performance and I knew somewhere behind it all my sister was taking a deep breath. "And it's beginning to, and it's beginning to, and it's beginning to . . ."

Pitch black.

The sound of a revving motorcycle.

A headlight.

And then Dina.

She stood alone, center stage. She pulled off her helmet, let the teeming locks of early nineties curly hair fall around her face, and with the melodramatic fervor characteristic of Maureen, she said, "Joanne, which way to the stage?"

"Snow!" the ensemble sang their final beat.

The stage was Dina's.

Brace yourselves, I wanted to say to the strangers in front of me who had never experienced an Idina Menzel performance. Instead of sitting next to Dina, watching a Broadway show like we had when we were young, or talking about starring on Broadway or wishing, hoping, working for it, Dina was there. Dina had arrived.

"Last night, I had a dream," she said into the black silence.

I knew those words well from the previews and because I'd wrestled with them in her apartment the night before her audition. But hearing them in the Nederlander wasn't like reading them had been less than a year earlier.

"I found myself in a desert called Cyberland."

I wasn't harboring the emotional burden of improving our relationship and providing an indispensable contribution to her professional life. There was only the sound of her voice. And love. And pride. And a quiet celebration in my heart.

"Out of the abyss walked a cow—Elsie. I asked if she had anything to drink. She said . . ." Dina's speaking voice shifted into a melody as she sang a capella:

"I'm forbidden to produce milk. In Cyberland, we only drink—[cowbell clink]—Diet Coke."

She only sang a couple of lines, but each note filled the theater. Her voice had precision, a warm, brassy timbre, and even though she was singing about milk, her voice had an emotional thrust unlike any other I'd ever heard. When they weren't laughing, the audience sat motionless.

Dina continued on Elsie's behalf, "She said, 'Only thing to do is jump over the moon.' "

Then she grabbed her throat and started swinging her head back and forth like a heavy-metal guitarist. She screamed:

"It's like I'm being tied to the hood of a yellow rental truck being packed in with fertilizer—and fuel oil. Pushed over a cliff by a suicidal Mickey Mouse. I gotta, gotta, gotta, gotta, gotta—gotta"—always pausing there and then adding one final gotta that made the audience laugh—". . . find a way!"

Dina was a force of nature, and when she stopped screaming and shifted to a jazzier melody—"That's bull, he said. Ever since the cat took up the fiddle, that cow's been—jumpy. . . . Maybe it's a female thing"—years of classical vocal training and wedding-band singing were evident in her versatility. By the time Maureen Johnson entices the audience to moo with her, "Moo with me," she says, there was no doubt they'd moo. She'd corralled them with her vocal range, her sense of humor, her unbridled talent. They mooed louder and louder, growing into a crescendo, until, like an orchestra conductor, she flung her arms through the air and cut them off with a pithy, "Thank you."

As Dina finished, a surge of energy shot through my arms and legs and propelled me onto my feet. The audience stood with me, not as individuals but as one synchronistic entity. I clapped so hard my palms tingled. I wished I could whistle—the cool whistle using my thumb and forefinger. *That's my sister,* I thought. *I have a sister who makes me wish I could whistle.*

By the end of the show Dina hadn't only made the audience moo—during the performance of "La Vie Bohème," she also mooned them. Then, after delivering one of my favorite lines, "There will always be women in rubber flirting with me," she sang a duet, "Take Me or Leave Me," with her lover, while climbing up and down metal folding chairs and tables in leather pants and heels. Dina was unforgettable. The show was unforgettable.

Hundreds of people gathered at Chelsea Piers to celebrate the opening night of *Rent* on Broadway. To accommodate guests, an entire ice rink was covered in AstroTurf and wooden dance-floor tiles. Tables were clustered near designated dance floors. The open space was lit with string lights that dangled like fireflies from cavernous ceilings. Were it not for the ice hidden beneath my feet I could have been at an evening reception of an outdoor June wedding.

I made my way to a small nest of tables where Dina's friends from NYU, my family and family's friends, and my sister's agent and manager were convening. Everyone in my sister's world except my sister, who was with the *Rent* cast for press and pictures in a striking kelly-green gown. I wore a fitted knee-length pewter dress that I'd bought the day before. A Broadway opening required a hot dress I definitely didn't have in my closet in Boulder.

At Chelsea Piers it was getting late for my grandmother, who tended to be short on smiles, but she wasn't that night. She was talkative and lively, wearing her joy like the red lipstick she saved for special occasions. When she started to peter out, my dad took her home. Mom and her friends were engaged in conversation and I sat with Dina's inner circle, Debbie and Suzy and a few others.

People were discreetly sharing a joint at our table. I'd never smoked pot—though once I got in trouble with a couple of friends for burning a sage smudge stick from the local health food store in my dorm room. (It smelled just like pot and caused other members of the substance-free community to call the police. I think it's safe to say that those girls and I are the only people in the history of college residence halls to get in trouble with the police over burning something as innocent as potpourri.)

I imagined that one day I'd smoke a joint in a cozy living room somewhere with a boyfriend and a bag of Doritos. But I definitely never imagined an ice rink or hundreds of people, cameras, or Leonardo DiCaprio on a nearby dance floor.

"Hold it in for as long as you can," Arie said. "You may need more. The first time you need more." I obliged, not sure if he was fucking with me or telling the truth.

Soon after, I spotted my sister and she and I had a chance to connect.

"Hey, Sis," she said and kissed me on the lips. "You look hot."

"Thanks. You too. Love the color."

"Is that a new dress?" she asked me.

"Got it with Daddy yesterday. You haven't seen the best part." I turned to the side and lifted my arm slightly, exposing an armpit mark the size of a fried egg.

"Classy," she said. "Watch this." She leaned in toward me and adjusted her boobs while looking off in another direction.

"Classy," I said and we giggled. "By the way, I'm stoned."

"What? Ca-ra!"

"Yeah, under Arie's proud tutelage."

"You feeling okay?"

"I think so. I don't feel much of anything."

"All right. Be careful. I have to do more press. We'll hang at home later. I love you." She kissed me again.

I watched as Dina returned to the press and the cast, including Taye Diggs,

Rent's Benjamin Coffin III. He had chocolate skin and a big smile that showcased teeth so white they belonged in a toothpaste commercial. I must have stared too long in Taye's direction because years later he'd tell me that he felt flattered because he thought I was flirting with him! Of course, the chances of *me* flirting with him were unlikely. I wasn't in a flirting mood. Since the joint, I'd been staring too long at everyone and everything. The more probable explanation was that I was lost in thought staring at the string of lights that hung a couple of inches over his right shoulder.

I headed back to my family and friends. Some of them were on the dance floor, and I merged with the swarm of swinging arms, bobbing heads, and twisting bodies. The music pounded in my head as if the speaker itself were in there. I looked down at the floor and stared at a sea of busy feet—bare feet and dress shoes and heels—and near misses between bare feet and stilettos.

When I looked back up into the crowd I noticed that my vision was impaired. Every time I turned my head it was as if I were scanning photo negatives. I couldn't paste the scenes in front of me together. Along with visual continuity, I also lost depth perception. Far, near—heck if I knew the difference. I saw a conga line. I saw Debbie's back. The conga line. Her back. I grabbed her waist and shouted, "Conga!" to which she turned to me dead serious and said, "Don't be touchin' me, girl." *Shit.*

I realized that the conga line was on another dance floor in the distance and Debbie had no idea why I had suddenly grabbed her. Mortified, I decided to go to the restroom and wait for the high to wear off before I embarrassed myself further.

Getting to the restroom was easier said than done. It was a long diagonal stretch across the rink and my heels were problematic. I'd bought them the day before with my dad, having fallen in love with them on a virtual catwalk through a narrow store on Eighth Street. They were black peau de soie sandals with four-inch stiletto heels and a paltry centimeter-wide strap that crossed the base of my toes. They'd been hard to dance in, even hard to walk in, and as I began my stoned trek to a toilet sanctuary far, far away, I worried that I walked like one of them was shoved up my ass. I took them off and held them in one hand by their straps. Shortly after that, I noticed that my feet were numb—I'd forgotten there was ice beneath the AstroTurf. I jogged the remainder of the way to a bathroom stall, where I covered the seat in toilet paper and sat down in my skin-tight dress.

I can't say how long I was camped out in there, but I think I could have read my entire thesis and the full Harry Potter series. Me. The stall. Minutes ticked by like hours, but my mind stayed very active.

I thought back to earlier in the evening and remembered Dina in her green dress standing among press and cameras. She pressed her lips together to ensure her lipstick was still on. She tipped her head in toward Daphne Ruben-Vega, *Rent*'s Mimi, and whispered something. Daphne nodded and then they laughed.

I heard laughing in the bathroom. *Is someone waiting for my toilet and wondering what's taking me so long? How long have I been in here?* I peeked through the crack in the stall door and saw a couple of girls, like me, in front of the sinks. *Are they laughing at me? Do they know what I'm doing in here—or rather, what I'm not doing in here? Do they know I'm stoned?* My eyes drifted from the crack in the door to the door itself where someone had scratched "Jocelyn sucks cock." Beneath the writing was a date noted with slashes, as if it were important to note the year Jocelyn sucked cock. *Hmph. Way to go, Jocelyn!*

One of the girls washed her hands and I heard the other tug on the paper-towel dispenser. When one dropped a brown wad of paper into the trash I stood up and used my foot to flush the toilet. At the time, I thought this was genius trickery on my part. In the event that the girls knew I was stoned and were in fact laughing at me, the sound of my flushing toilet might convince them otherwise. I stared at the swirling water and watched it rush down into the tunnel at the bottom of the bowl as they left. Then I resumed my seated position.

Jesus, Cara. Of all the places—all the times—to get stoned, what the hell were you thinking doing it at this party? What a shit sister I was, paralyzed by paranoia and stuck in the bathroom instead of in the party celebrating Dina. Of course, it wasn't like Dina and I were going to have quality time together. If I hadn't been in the bathroom, I would have been back out in the hullabaloo, smiling until my face felt frozen in place, conscious of my every word, trying to be eloquent and articulate, cool and relaxed. I'd scan the crowd for famous faces—maybe Keanu Reeves or Michelle Pfeiffer would be there. All the while knowing I'd be star-struck and never approach anyone, not even to say something polite like, "I really appreciate your work. I'm a big fan," which I'd rehearsed saying the night before in hopes I'd find the opportunity and the nerve. And maybe a ride on Keanu's motorcycle or your basic celebrity one-night stand.

I felt my hair swelling in the cold dampness of the East Coast and I looked down at my wrist for a hair tie, but there wasn't one. I heard another woman enter the bathroom and then the stall next to mine. I saw her patent-leather heels under the stall wall and the royal-blue cuffs of what I guessed was a wide-legged pantsuit. *Can she see my feet like I can see hers? My bare feet? She probably thinks that's weird, bare feet on the gross public-bathroom floor.* I heard her fuss with the defiant toilet-paper roller.

I set my elbows on my knees, set my head in my hands, and closed my eyes. *What time is my flight home tomorrow?* Back in Boulder I'd defended my thesis and passed. I remembered pushing the two flat bins of drafts and articles under my bed, first with my hands and then with my feet, sitting on the floor and shoving each one clear out of sight. "Take a few months off," my thesis adviser had said. "We'll get the paper ready for publishing later." "Later" wasn't far enough away. I wanted to publish my paper, but I'd exhausted myself and had nothing left to put on a page. I hadn't applied to graduate school; I couldn't—at least not yet. Underlying the excitement of a strong finish at school was an eerie sense of finality. If something was over, something else had to begin, and I hadn't a clue what that would be. Focusing on Dina for a few days had served as a recess from the stress of "what next?" But suddenly, stoned and in the stall, my focus on Dina was no longer a recess but a reminder. With *Rent* came the promise of a rich career for my sister. I was unmistakably elated for her. But *Rent* was Dina's beginning and reminded me that I didn't have one.

Someone opened the restroom door and a wave of music entered, carrying with it another memory of Dina from earlier in the evening. This time she was in a line along the edge of the stage with the cast singing "Seasons of Love" together. They were a family. I wished I could be with Dina as often as they were. *Is she closer with them than she is with me?* I wondered, and the question bothered me. It felt wrong. I couldn't name what I was feeling, but I was glad that despite my paranoia, I knew no one could hear my thoughts. More than anything, I missed Dina. Our lives were becoming more different and distant than they'd ever been. *But,* I reassured myself, *our roots run deep. They'll hold us together.* And it was from those roots that I loved Dina, from them and—as it were—from a toilet seat at Chelsea Piers.

Later that night, I went back to Dina's apartment and sat sober—finally—on the couch with Debbie and Suzy.

"Oh my god!" Dina screeched from her room. "Come listen to this." She popped out from around the corner and with a silly grin she waved us over. "Taye's drunk and he left a message on my machine."

We huddled around her answering machine as Taye slurred and rambled on about how beautiful Dina looked that night and how much he liked her. She listened like a giddy high schooler who had just been asked to prom. I felt lucky to be there with her. I'd look back on that night countless times and feel grateful that I'd been there for the beginning of her professional career, and the beginning of her relationship with Taye—Taye, who called her Dee. And Dee she would be from then on.

I knew that being Maureen meant being onstage eight times a week, and I knew it would be nearly impossible for Dee to make it to Colorado for my graduation. I knew and I understood and I didn't want her to feel bad about it and I tried not to care. But I did. When I walked across the stage and the dean placed a medal around my neck, magna cum laude, Mom and Dad were there, but Dee wasn't.

Lesson 5

HOW TO SING A SOLO

At twenty-three, I was no longer the little girl who sang lullabies to her Cabbage Patch dolls and strapped newborn diapers onto apathetic teddy bears. I had grown up and I dreamed of snap-crotch onesies, a BabyBjörn, and the drool that pools around a baby's brand-new bottom teeth. Having my own family was and always had been an ambition far more compelling to me than any career. Unlike the path to a fulfilling job, the path to a family was no mystery: Find a man. Make a baby. Set up house. The first order of business I'd already taken care of.

I met Jon at CU in the ashes of my relationship with Ken—you might say that Astronaut Ken and Long Island Jew Barbie "failed to launch." I was the kind of girl who didn't like to be alone, and Jon had dimples. He also had a smile more round than wide, and with curly brown hair that sat tall on the top of his head he made a good *Seinfeld*'s Kramer on Halloween. He knew how to throw big parties and I liked having a social boyfriend. He was also a business major and had the drive and ambition I'd always found attractive.

Jon won me over one night when he delivered a Subway sandwich and a latte to the psychology lab.

It wasn't a perfect relationship: he left me waiting one too many times and I started to wonder if he wasn't as sensitive as I'd originally thought. We spent six months apart, during which time he moved to San Diego. Eventually we chose to give things another shot and I moved there to be with him.

We rented the walkout basement of a large home in the village of La Jolla. The house was built of coral stucco, its edges were covered in climbing bougainvillea, and it was wedged into the side of a hill on a well-manicured lawn. Unlike the house above it, our studio was tiny and unremarkable—visitors needed help finding our door—but we didn't need much and it was only a short walk to the shore.

It was there, in that gray-carpeted hole-in-the-wall-of-a-real-home, that on a lazy afternoon Jon and I lay in bed in a postcoital fog. I was forming constellations out of the bumps in the popcorn ceiling when he shifted in the bed and reached into his end table, then sat up and faced me. There was a brief anticipatory silence and I sat up instinctively so our eyes were level. Jon opened his hand and in his palm sat two silver Tibetan spinning rings.

"Cara Mentzel," he said, so close to me that I could see the speckles in his green eyes. "Marry me? Please."

"They're just promise rings," he added—nervous, I think. "But I'll make it official . . . soon."

I wrapped as much of myself around him as I could, my arms, my legs, even craning my neck around, setting my chin on his back.

"Of course," I told him softly. Then I kissed him. "Of course," I said again, this time in tears.

I stayed in bed alone when he went into the shower. We weren't planning on a baby, and yet I lay on my back with my legs up in the air, my feet facing the ceiling. I pictured my microscopic eggs reeling Jon's frenzied chromosome-toting suckers in. After a couple of minutes, I pulled my knees into my chest and rolled on my side. With my cheek against the pillow, I imagined brushing my lips gently over the beating fontanel of a newborn, like a whisper.

I thought that my ambitions of young motherhood were culturally unpopular. I was part of a generation that wanted me to make my mark in a man's world *before* having a child. My generation wanted me to be Murphy Brown or Clair Huxtable. But I wanted to be a mother first and foremost. The sooner the better.

As if feminism's Rosie the Riveter fist weren't discouraging enough, I assumed Mom, Dad, and Dee would disapprove of a pregnancy then, too. For one thing, when Dad and I talked on the phone he still said things like, "Tell me again, why aren't you applying to med school?" and, "You sure you don't want to be a doctor?" I tried to convince myself to postpone motherhood five years, even two years, and it helped that I didn't have a choice; though we'd taken a risk that day, Jon wanted to wait to have children. *Had my hope to conceive betrayed him?*

Daily, I thought about having a baby and each time I had to persuade myself that the time wasn't right. The conversation with myself grew tiresome.

You don't have money.

We have enough. People have had less.

Focus on your career.

I'm not ready to. Why does my career have to come first?

Don't you want to BE something?

Yes, I want to be a mother.

You're too young and naïve.

Maybe. But there will always be something I don't know.

You don't understand how much work it is to have a baby.

It doesn't matter. I'll do whatever it takes.

You're not ready.

Is anyone? Ever?

Be patient.

Then patience would win, because I wasn't good at being patient but I wanted to be. My children would need a patient mother.

Two weeks later, I took a trip back to Colorado to visit Mom. I locked myself in her bathroom and unfolded instructions to a pregnancy test. I carefully examined the diagrams: two lines, positive, one line, negative. I flattened out the small sheet of paper on the vanity, unwrapped the stick, and peed on the "absorbent tip." When I finished, I stared at those tiny windows for a clue to my future like I'd just peed on a crystal ball.

It had been challenging to wait two weeks to take the test and just then it was tough to wait one more minute for the results. The moisture crossed the first window, leaving a blue line in its path like invisible ink in lemon juice. One. As the moisture entered the second window, I took a deep breath, suddenly scared and unsure what I wanted. I quickly found comfort in the possibility that conceiving a child from that slim opportunity with Jon might mean the child was meant to be, that the Forces of the Universe had intervened and helped make a difficult decision *for* me. Furthermore, acknowledging that something spiritual may have played a role in my pregnancy offered me shelter from the judgment of others. In the face of criticism, I could deflect some of the responsibility by suggesting there were other forces at play.

Then there it was. . . . Two. My lids dropped shut and sent tears down my cheeks. Until then, the happiest I'd ever been was when I watched Dee sing. But the news of a baby brought with it a new kind of happiness, not the adrenaline rush I often felt when Dee performed, but a stillness. Peace. I set my hand over my abdomen and pictured the embryo. My child was a tiny light in the darkness of my womb and my heart hung high above it, bright as the moon.

I called Jon and told him first. Pregnancy was *not* what he thought we'd talk about on the phone that day. He'd planned to tell me that he'd just bought a car, a fact that gave him pause after hearing my baby news. But of the many things he was probably feeling upon hearing we were pregnant, there was no question, one of them was joy. I told Mom next. She had the warmest reaction in my family. She hugged me. She cried. She said, "I know how much you've wanted this." But I knew she was worried. Her love for me, though unconditional and endless, was a veil too transparent to mask her concern.

I told Dad over the phone, and then Dee, and I shared the news with excessive enthusiasm. Perhaps I thought I could rouse their enthusiasm with my own, and that positive posturing might help me avoid a negative response on their part. But I knew they'd be shocked. After all, I was a good girl. I was Miss Substance-Free-Dorm, Miss Magna Cum Laude. When I heard Dad's initial shock, I assured him, "I want this baby, there's nothing I want more." Minutes later, I told Dee the same: "I want this baby, there's nothing I want more." So they tried to be happy for me, despite their concerns. But I was young, unmarried, and unemployed, and while I chose to minimize those realities, part of me knew that expecting my family to ignore them was unfair. And though I couldn't articulate why, part of me knew my sister was pissed; I'd learn more about why, later.

In the more than a year that Dee spent as Maureen in *Rent,* she recorded the original soundtrack, received a Tony nomination for best featured actress in a musical, and mooned tens of thousands of theatergoers, including the Clintons, Tom Cruise, Nicole Kidman, and Matt Dillon. Then she signed a recording contract with Hollywood Records and moved on from *Rent* to pursue her career as a recording artist.

Dee's voice had been her most apparent talent, but she wasn't just a vocalist, she was an artist. She had journals stuffed with lyrics and seeds for songs. The piano of our childhood—on which we rarely practiced for our piano lessons with Herb Strizek—resided in her apartment, and she often found inspiration for her own music in a new series of chords. But even with her gigs at The Bitter End and other venues around the city, Dee had spent the vast majority of her time over the years singing other people's songs. Her album was a chance to create her own sound and her own music.

I still lived in San Diego, and Dee lived between New York and Los Angeles while she worked on her album. Simultaneously and separately, she and

I nurtured our creative energies. She was in New York when I flew out there for a visit and joined her at the historic Bearsville Studios in Woodstock. Since its opening in 1970, musicians, including The Rolling Stones, Bob Dylan, Patti Smith, R.E.M., and Natalie Merchant, recorded at Bearsville, and Dee was thrilled to record in a space that carried the memories and spirit of the artists that were there before her.

I sat on a threadbare loveseat in a large loftlike room with tall ceilings and scuffed hardwood floors. A foot in front of me was a coffee table and just beyond it stood a wall with two windows. One window was long and narrow like an aquarium. Through it I could see Dee standing with bulky headphones next to a microphone that hung like a cattail. The other window was smaller, and invoked the image of an interrogation room. Through it was a mixing board, the sound engineer, and producer Milton Davis. Milton had produced Dionne Farris's "I Know." It was a catchy song I knew well and enjoyed, and I was excited about his collaboration with Dee.

That afternoon Dee was working on an original song called "Still I Can't Be Still." My first instinct was to call it a ballad, but there was a lot of movement in the music. It was hypnotic. The drums had a tribal quality that compelled me to move my head back and forth like it was tracing the shape of an infinity symbol in the air. I listened as Dee took the same few measures over and over. Her vocals were emotionally wrought and yet somehow still soothing. It occurred to me that I could probably recognize her voice on the radio, at a wedding, or in a bathroom at Macy's, even if all she sang was a note or two. I was attuned to the distinctiveness of her voice and knowing her that well made me feel special. She moved on, taking a chunk of the next verse, and I continued to listen. Sometimes she sang carefree, exploring the possibilities in each part, and sometimes carefully, chasing a particular sound. She and Milton collaborated throughout the process. Occasionally she asked me what I thought, which was kind, but futile, because I loved everything. In this way and over the course of the day, she worked her way through the whole song with the endurance of an athlete and the elegance of an artist.

When she sang the lyric, "I don't believe I'm beautiful, at least I have my sister's smile," I had mixed feelings. For all the ways I admired her, I liked hearing that she was happy to be like me in some way. I liked hearing that she thought we had something in common, and I was honored to be mentioned. Though if the lyric was to be believed, it was heartbreaking that she didn't think she was beautiful. And I knew there was some truth to it.

Later, when Dee's agent stopped by for a listen, Milton blasted the track through the studio. The song moved through me in waves where I was certain even my unborn child could feel it. "Meet your aunt Dee Dee," I whispered. "Your beautiful aunt Dee Dee."

I was over six months' pregnant when Dee and Mom came to town for my wedding. We were grabbing breakfast at the greasy spoon diner next door to the dress shop where we had an appointment for my final fitting. We reviewed the wedding plans. Jon and I weren't having a reception. We chose to have a morning ceremony that focused on our vows, followed by a small brunch buffet of fruit, croissants, and bagels. We didn't have a lot of money. Jon had been helping his dad build the family business and my pregnancy made it difficult for me to find a job; no one wanted to hire someone who could commit to only nine months of employment, and I wasn't comfortable lying in my interview. Mom gave us a lump sum that she had saved for me over the years and Jon and I wanted to save it for the baby and a down payment on a house.

At the diner I explained to Dee and Mom that to stick within our wedding budget Jon and I chose to keep flowers to a minimum. There would be a sunflower on each table, my bouquet, and boutonnieres, but that was all. No adorned arch, elaborate centerpieces, or flowers along the aisle. The ceremony would take place on a cliff in La Jolla and we hardly needed to make the venue more beautiful.

"That's all you're doing?" Dee asked.

"That's what we can afford."

"Let me take care of the flowers," she offered.

"You don't need to do that, Dee. I'm happy to keep things simple." I needed her to know I wasn't settling. Any evidence of disappointment on my part could prompt—or, worse yet, validate—her concerns that I was making the wrong choices for my life.

"No. I want to do it," she insisted. "Let's do something special."

I indulged her—or was I indulging myself?

"I always wanted a flower tiara, like made of teacup roses or something."

Mom joined the conversation. "Beautiful, like a ballerina."

"That'd be gorgeous," Dee added. "I bet they can do that. Call over there. Tell them we're swinging by later." Her words were swift. She was in rescue mode, which was generous, but I didn't feel that I needed saving.

"What about hair and makeup?" she asked next. "Do you have that set up for tomorrow morning?"

"No," I told her, knowing it was the wrong answer.

"Ca-ra," she said like she sometimes did, her voice taking a dip at the end, suggesting I'd been remiss. I always knew when Dee was annoyed with me. There was a tone and inflection in her voice that could make the most innocuous word bitter, in this instance, my name. Maybe Dee's tone felt harsh because I was so sensitive to her opinion, or maybe because it actually was harsh. I suspect both explanations are true. Regardless, my reaction to her was always the same: I retreated or gave in.

"It's really not necessary, Dee. I planned to do my own."

"But it's your wedding. It's part of the fun. Let me do it as a gift," she said, nodding her head.

"Do you think we can still find someone?" Mom asked.

"I don't know. Probably," I told them. "I'll ask around."

I thanked Dee, but I was disappointed in myself. I shouldn't have accepted her offers. I'd been desperate to convince her I could be self-reliant, but I didn't know how to push back and say no to her. And, if I'm honest, I was too easily led astray by my fondness for tiaras and professional updos.

After breakfast we hopped over to the dress shop. It was a modest establishment, dull, with a few dresses on muslin-covered mannequin busts, blouses hanging from four-armed clothing racks, and a small selection of wedding shoes on a round glass table in the corner. There was little question that the space was more for alterations and dressmaking than for shopping. At the time, maternity gowns were hard to find and this store was the only place in La Jolla that would build a custom wedding gown. Mom had been to the shop with me months earlier and we'd designed the dress together. We chose a cream chiffon gown that ruched tight across my bust and flowed to the floor. The empire waist would accommodate my growing midsection. We planned to adjust the hem last-minute depending on the size of my heels and the size of my belly. The dress was our idea of a safe bet.

I set a shopping bag down on a bench and pulled a shoe box out of it.

"Oooh. Are those your shoes? Let me see," Dee said. I opened the box and exposed a pair of cream sateen pumps. She paused, her face blank, and then said, "Are you sure you want to wear those?" Again, like I should have known better. "They're grandma shoes. They're frumpy."

"Dee—" Mom tried to interrupt, probably hoping to soften the blow, but I spoke instead.

"I'm pregnant," I defended myself. "Have you seen the stairs I need to walk down?"

"No, but—"

"I have sciatica," I stopped her, "and a whole new center of gravity. Besides, they won't even show. The dress covers them."

But she was right about the shoes. And she was kind to call them frumpy instead of downright ugly—which they were. The toe was square, the heel a thick stump. They looked like my grandma should wear them and stick a shiny gold buckle across the toe box.

"Still," she insisted, "you can't wear those. You can suck it up for a couple of hours. A nice pair of heels will make you feel pretty and feminine. Even if you can't see them."

I realized that much had changed since we'd lived together. Dee used to be the tomboy and I was the girly girl. I was the sister who once lost a whole set of Lee Press-On Nails while washing my hair in the shower. I was the sister who put on too much makeup and orchestrated amateur modeling shoots during sleepovers with my friends. Times had changed.

I tried not to feel insulted; after all, I knew Dee's intention was to help me, not hurt me. But despite her best efforts to be an enthusiastic and dutiful maid of honor, it was clear to me that she was frustrated. She was focused on ensuring that I had the wedding she thought I deserved, and given my constraints, I was making that difficult for her. But what I wanted more than flowers or hair and makeup or pretty heels was her genuine excitement and approval, and I sensed those were harder for her to give me.

Dee grabbed another pair of shoes from the table in the corner and asked the seamstress for my size. They were sandals with two-and-a-half-inch heels, and thin, elegant straps that trailed around my foot and up my ankle, where they finished in a tiny gold buckle. I slid my foot into one. Dee squatted down on the floor and fumbled with a buckle so small we needed Stuart Little to fit the prong into the pinhole. Of course, she was right. Instant elegance. Those sandals changed the expression on my face. I looked in the mirror and noticed that when I wore them, even in shorts and a zip-up sweatshirt, I naturally pulled my shoulders back and sucked my cheeks in ever so slightly.

I went into the dressing room and pushed my shorts down over my heels. I put on my strapless bra while the seamstress gently laid the dress in a ring on the floor. I carefully stepped inside it. She pulled the dress up and then drew the straps over my shoulders. She zipped the back. I adjusted my boobs and stood up straight, set the curtain aside, and stepped on the pedestal in front of the three-way mirror. In an instant, it was clear that Mom and I had made a mistake. While my toes were perfectly peeking out beneath the hem, my nipples were not-so-perfectly peeking out the top. We had bet on my belly growing, which was still more of a mound than a full-on baby bump. We should have bet on my boobs.

"Oh shit," I said and snorted. I flashed on an image of my grandmother's face as I walked down the aisle and her eyes dropped from my tiara to my nipples, a pair of rising suns on a chiffon horizon. She'd surely have a heart attack. She was a good sport about the whole my-granddaughter-is-knocked-up thing, but if I walked down the aisle with nipples shouting "Mornin'!" to all our guests, she'd walk her frumpy pumps with the gold buckles over the toe box right back to the hotel.

Dee, Mom, and I stood facing the three-way mirror. Dee held her hand over her forehead like she was shading her face from the sun. "I'm thinking that's not the look you were going for," she joked, and I squealed with my hand over my mouth, "Oh my god!" I turned to Dee and said, "Who knew the day would come when my boobs would be bigger than yours!"

Mom bent over into peeing pose. She crossed her legs and trapped her hand between her thighs. Her laughter was silent and she held her breath, her face turning pink. It's worth noting that this was our go-to don't-pee-your-pants strategy. None of us had ever explicitly articulated the theory behind the strategy, but we intuited it. If you hold in your breath, you can hold in your laugh, thereby holding in the contents of your bladder. Dee and I watched Mom successfully implement the strategy. When Mom regained her composure, her eyes widened and she approached me. She gave an upward tug on the bust of my gown and started to MacGyver me into that dress.

"We need another piece of fabric," she said to the seamstress. "Can you add it right here?" and pointed her finger just above the existing ruche. "Maybe even at an angle, like this," and she folded the chiffon over a little, to make it narrow at my cleavage. "Actually, it's even prettier this way. We need a different bra, one with less padding. Cara, do you still have that other one we bought? Can we let it out at the zipper a tiny bit, too?" The seamstress glared at Mom with a straight pin ready in one hand and another sticking out of her mouth like a toothpick. "We need it ready tonight," Mom finished.

While Mom and the seamstress pinned me up, I stared at myself in the mirror. I'd always been lean and lanky with a smallish chest, and arms so long they made me feel graceful in ballet class, but awkward when I danced at bat mitzvahs. I was a new woman in that mirror. I was a buxom brunette ready to salsa her way down the aisle in my augmented maternity gown, slinky sandals, new breasts, and shapely hips. *Va-va-voom,* I thought and smiled at myself.

Dee took Mom and me across the street and treated us to mani-pedis in massage chairs. We reminisced about bra shopping together back on Long Island, in a small custom-bra shop in Huntington. All the while, unbeknownst to us, a tow truck lugged my car with a trunk full of tuxes, dresses, and even the wedding rings, from the parking lot behind the diner to a lot forty minutes south of town. Three manicures and one rude awakening later, I prayed, *Please, God, don't let anything else go wrong in front of my sister.*

After a late-night drive to the tow yard, and a couple of early-morning hours of hair and makeup, I arrived at the wedding venue, a grassy area like a golfing green set atop a La Jolla cliff. There was an eager wind. The ocean below beat on the shore and could be heard beneath the harp and cello's Pachelbel's Canon. I stood above the green at the top of a steep stone staircase so narrow I had to descend the stairs alone. Each step had its own character: some were cement, some had pebbles, others had moss-covered rocks that were kind enough to fix themselves off to the side. Some were so thin they barely fit the length of my foot, others too bumpy to fully set down my heels. I looked out over sixty-some guests seated in white folding chairs, including my grandmother, aunts, uncles, cousins, closest friends, and Taye. In a line at the far end stood the ceremony officiator, my sister, and Jon with his family. At the bottom of the stairs my mother and father waited to link arms with me, or catch me—whichever the moment called for.

I grazed the railing with one hand for reassurance, and held my bouquet in the other. I confirmed the placement of each foot on each step. I trembled and tried to steady my nerves with a strong smile. I glanced down at the steps, up at the guests, down at the steps, up at the guests, until I reached the bottom and joined Mom and Dad.

I looked straight ahead. Waiting at the altar were both my groom and my sister, the unfortunate victim of a sea-foam dress and a curling iron. I walked toward them, toward his faith in us and her doubt in our future. I wanted what came next for me, to be a mother, to be a wife. I wanted Dee to believe I was up to the task and to be happy for me. I wanted her approval the way I always had. But I was pregnant. I was a big girl making big choices. I convinced myself that her approval wasn't important to me any longer.

At 3 A.M., two weeks past my due date, a series of modest contractions drew me out of a deep sleep and I started to regret the Kraft Mac & Cheese I'd eaten for dinner. It had been a nostalgic craving, a hankering for the nurturing quality of my childhood, but when the contractions became more frequent it occurred to me that a nutritious dinner would have been more sensible; I'd need sustenance. I tapped Jon on the shoulder a couple of times.

"Hey . . . hey. Call Molly."

"Really? You sure?" he asked.

"I think so. The contractions are little, but they're coming fast."

Molly was our midwife. I was having a home birth.

Having a home birth was important to me. I didn't feel safe in a hospital. To me, hospitals were places people went to when they were sick or hurt, and I was neither. I didn't like the stories I'd heard about nurses who encouraged epidurals, unnecessary C-sections, the overuse of Pitocin to progress labor, forceps, or vacuum extraction. I was committed to natural childbirth. Birth was the first official experience my child and I would share and I was insistent we do it as a team. If he (or she—I didn't know the gender) couldn't be numb, then I wouldn't be numb either. The birth was my first chance to do right by my child and keep him safe. Forceps would never touch his defenseless skull.

Dee didn't like the home birth idea. She was all about the what-ifs. "What if something goes wrong?" "What if you *need* a C-section?" "What if the baby's not breathing?" I tried to reassure her that those things were unlikely and that if there was any indication of a problem, either during the pregnancy or during the birth, I would reassess the situation. But my assurances didn't sway her. When we talked on the phone there was tension between us, the kind that would knot in my belly when the line sat quiet a few seconds too long. Dee seemed angry, but never said it outright, and maybe that's because hidden beneath her anger was what she really wanted to say: "Please let me keep you safe." And what she kept hearing me say was, "No."

Since my graduation, my fascination with the brain and my spiritual beliefs led me to a study in an alternative health modality called craniosacral therapy. This therapy incorporated a study of central nervous system anatomy and physiology, as well as more esoteric energy-healing techniques. My interest in a holistic approach to health could be measured in the length of my hugs—hippie hugs. Each time I pulled someone close I took a cleansing sigh that said, *I am fully present with you,* and then held them a few uncomfortable seconds longer than necessary.

When I became pregnant, my interest in craniosacral therapy grew because I often wondered about the inherent intelligence directing the development of my child. Every one of his cells knew where to go and what it was destined to become: part of the brain, heart, digestive system or lungs, part of an eyelash or a fingernail. I had a stethoscope with extra-long tubing and loved to fall asleep to the swish-swish-swish of my baby's bitty heart. During those times, I felt the presence of something sacred working beyond my understanding, and often beyond my consciousness. I trusted that presence. If it could safely build a baby, it could safely birth one.

On the phone with Jon, Molly asked how far apart my contractions were and suddenly Jon and I felt like idiots—we couldn't remember how to count contractions. From the end of one to the beginning of the next? The beginning of one to the beginning of the next? Molly clarified, from the peak of one to the peak of the next. But my contractions seemed never to end. There were slight periods of time when they were less prominent, but they never completely stopped.

I labored in my bedroom. Jon and I had moved to a new apartment and were living in a small one-bedroom a little bit farther inland. Our bedroom was just big enough to fit a queen-size futon that we kept open and used for our bed. Our sliding closet doors were mirrored and there was a window on the wall opposite them. When I went into labor, Jon turned the lights on and prepped the bed as Molly had instructed at our home visit a couple of weeks earlier. He layered the bed in Chux absorbent pads. (Chux compete with laxatives for the least-sexy item at the drugstore. They're mini-blankets, usually two feet by three feet in size, made of sanitary-napkin material, and used primarily for nighttime incontinence.) Jon covered the Chux with old flannel sheets we'd cleaned well and packed in an extra-large Ziploc bag, where they had been waiting for the labor. Then he set the pillows and blankets back up for me and turned off the lights.

Molly wasn't the only one coming to the birth. She had a sister, Judy, who would be joining her. Judy was a nurse-midwife and worked in a nearby hospital. My friend Anne, a doula, was also coming. And Mom would be there, too. She had flown to San Diego a few days before my due date and we were starting to worry that she'd have to return home before I went into labor. Dee was in Los Angeles and had planned to make the two-and-a-half-hour drive down to San Diego when the time came.

At first, the contractions were like menstrual cramps, but soon my lower back was so tight I felt as if I'd been arched in a backbend for hours. I had a sharp, short-lived pain that spiked from my cervix up through my center and took my breath away. At one point, I felt a sudden widening of my pelvis, not so much painful as startling, and I had the strange urge to move out of the way, out of *my baby's* way. But of course, I couldn't; I *was* his way. The feeling scared me and when it was over only mild contractions returned. After a while, I worried that my fear had caused my labor to slow and I was mad at myself for being afraid. I wanted to be brave and strong. I remembered a clip from a video Jon and I had watched in our birthing class. An aboriginal woman went into labor while gathering some kind of grain in a field. She kept working and then, without a fuss, simply squatted down and popped her baby out.

She caught her own baby! She held him like a football and set him in a sling. Within minutes she was gathering grain again. I don't see how this could have been true, but that's how I remembered it at the time, and I wanted to be Cara, the Incredible Squatting Tribal Woman.

After the scary contraction, the hardest part of the labor wasn't pain but exhaustion. I was desperate for a fifteen-minute respite, enough to sink my head into a pillow, refuel, and then awaken ready to rally again. But that was a gift rarely bestowed to a mother during natural childbirth and I knew it. I also knew that labor, especially with a first child, could take a while and I didn't want to wake Mom and Dee so early in the A.M. I waited a little and then had Anne call Mom, who then called Dee. Mom had spent the night at a nearby hotel and I remember the relief I felt when I heard her gentle knock on my bedroom door and then saw her face.

By eleven o'clock I was fully dilated. Molly gave me permission to push and my dampened spirit was revived. Being able to push meant that I could take control over the labor and no longer had to wait for some magical contraction—which might or might not come. There was light at the end of my baby's tunnel and I was more than ready to take him to it.

Jon sat in the bed against the wall with his knees apart and I lay within the curve of his body, baring down, pushing, his steady slow breathing like a metronome, setting the pace, keeping me calm. *Push.*

"You're doing great," Judy said and held a hand up in the air, pressing the tip of her thumb and forefinger together, forming a diamondlike shape between them.

"We can see this much of the baby's head," she added, which was a whole lot less than I thought it was and I wanted to slap the smile off her face.

An hour passed.

Dee was still on the highway when my baby's crowning head sent a burning sensation across my bottom. The Ring of Fire, it was called. A term I'd learned from a book I'd read so often during my pregnancy that more pages were earmarked than were not. Prior to pregnancy I understood the Ring of

Fire as a reference to tectonic plates and a series of volcanoes in the Pacific Ocean. But, spread-eagle in the final stage of labor, it struck me as an appropriate term for crowning, as my entire perineal region was burning with the heat of a hundred active volcanoes. Anne took a wet, warm washcloth out of a Crock-Pot and firmly pressed it against my perineum. The pain disappeared. Another push, another washcloth. Until I pushed one final time and the baby's head was out. One more push and, slick and quick, out came the rest of him. All at once the birth was over.

Jon slowly scooched out from behind me to cut the cord, and Mom, her face flush and wet with tears, rearranged the pillows for me. She kissed me on the forehead and with another round of tears told me she was proud of me.

"You did such a good job," she said. "You're already a great mom."

Then Anne set my child in my arms. A boy, Avery. His bare body lay against mine. In my body I had held him closer than I ever would again, and yet I had been desperate to have him in my arms. And then I did. I took in every detail of him. His face was rosy, hot pink like the bottoms of his wrinkly feet, and the rest of him was a milky white. He had a silver widow's peak and tiny fingers with tissue-paper fingernails. He was warm and fragile and lanky and all I could think was that he was the bravest and tiniest person I'd ever met. I was proud of him. He'd ventured from the secure confines of my womb to the open air of his new world and that journey took guts. He started to cry, a tight rattle of a cry, and I leaned my face close to his. I could feel the moist warmth of his breath on my lips, his heartbeat against my chest, his sticky fingers fumbling against my breast. Love was tangible. Love could be held and I held it then.

But something was wrong.

"Cara, I need you to push again," Molly said.

"What? Why?" I could see Molly between my parted knees. She had bulgy eyes on a good day; just then they scared me.

"The afterbirth isn't coming. You may be bleeding internally." I felt Molly's hand reach inside me and I noticed a circle of blood spreading out from under me. I ignored the blood. I wanted to stay in my peaceful love bubble with Avery. Then I felt a rough tug in my abdomen. *Is she pulling on the umbilical cord inside me?* Anne drew the pad out from under me and set two more in its place. More blood. A new circle growing quickly at its borders became impossible to ignore. I saw Mom off in the corner. Frozen.

"Cara, push. Push hard." Molly was nearly shouting. I wanted to be done pushing. I wanted nothing more than to hold Avery. Hadn't I worked hard enough?

I whispered into Avery's ear, "Daddy's gonna hold you. I'll be right back," and I kissed him on the point of his widow's peak. Then I pushed, but I was light-headed and each time I pushed I felt more light-headed.

"Call 911," Molly ordered, then Judy interrupted.

"No need. Pass me my bag, I have Pitocin in my bag."

After that, the voices in the room grew distant, like conch shells were pressed against my ears. My eyes were fixed on Avery in Jon's arms when the room started to disappear, first around the edges, then the remaining hole in the middle, until everything went dark.

The room was bright when I came to. Someone had drawn the blinds. Molly was shoving a pile of bloody Chux into a trash bag when Dee walked into the room. She'd arrived at the apartment during the hemorrhaging and had been told to wait in the living room. Dee looked at the blood, then at me.

"Hi, Mommy," she said with a smile, referring to me.

"Hi," I replied, so happy to see her. She walked over to Jon and took a look at my swaddled bundle of baby. "Oh my god, Cara," she said softly. "He's perfect. He's so perfect," and I couldn't have agreed with her more.

Anne held a straw to my lips and I sipped some juice. Mom sat next to me, unwrapping a protein bar for me. When I finished the juice, Judy fussed with the tube of an IV and then inserted the catheter into my arm and taped it in place. She held it steady as Jon came up next to her and placed Avery back in my arms. Avery was crying and his rosy cheeks were redder than before. I held him tightly, tilted my head down into the heat of his cries. I blew gently onto his forehead and then slowly whispered, "Welcome, my love." I took a deep breath. I wanted to inhale the very essence of him and at the same time draw any fear out of his little body. "I'm here," I told him, "and everything's okay."

When Avery settled, I offered him to Dee. Ever so gently she pulled him toward her heart. Dee had written a song that year to her unconceived, future child; "Reach," she'd titled it. I'd listened to the song repeatedly on an early release of her album, and when I saw Avery in her arms it was her alliteration that I heard: "Bathing beauty ballad of bliss you were born." Dee looked in Avery's slate eyes and in an instant became a doting aunt. Maybe her love for him left no room in her mind to think she'd been right and I'd been wrong, that having a baby at home wasn't safe (an opinion I continued to disagree with). Maybe his innocence against her chest made it impossible for her to feel angry, or worried. *Maybe.* But I was euphoric. I didn't think about what she felt or didn't feel. I thought only of my child. I was a mother. I had what I wanted: my baby, my beginning.

Lesson 6

HOW TO SING A DUET

Avery was a cherub, complete with apple cheeks and porcelain skin. His dark eyes had turned blue and he had a tuft of blond hair growing down his forehead. When he giggled, little spit bubbles formed in the corners of his mouth. When he nursed, he liked to stop mid-suckle to flash me a gummy grin.

Avery was still under a year old when Dee came to visit us again. She'd been dropped by Hollywood Records while working on her second album, and before her first album, *Still I Can't Be Still,* had even been released. Sales for *Still I Can't Be Still* were low and Dee was devastated. We all were.

Jon, Avery, and I were living in yet another rental apartment in San Diego. It was larger than the previous ones, a two-bedroom with a substantial living room, but the place was old, the tradeoff for larger square footage. Avery had his own room, but it was more of a storage closet where we kept his crib and clothing because he mostly slept in bed with Jon and me. The apartment was a perpetual rental that had seen many families and roommates. The walls and cabinetry had endured too many coats of paint and the cheap carpet was probably steam-cleaned after each tenant instead of replaced. Still, the residence had large east- and west-facing windows so it was filled with light and was home for us.

It was naptime. Dee had just finished reading *Moo, Baa, La La La,* one of my favorite baby books, to Avery. He was sucking and drooling on the board book's chunky corner when I lifted him up from her lap and carried him into my bedroom.

I set him down on the bed and his pudgy legs floated into the air where the soles of his feet met the palms of my hands. The noon light shone through the mini-blinds and landed on his face in stripes. I unsnapped his onesie and kissed his belly as he giggled. Then I started to sing to him as I always did at naptime—leaning over him, face-to-face, where we looked at each other like there wasn't another being in the world as perfect as the one our eyes were fixed on.

"Bum, ba, dee, duh, bum, ba, dee, duh, why are there so many, songs about rainbows," I sang to him like my breath was as easy as a breeze, each note sending him toward his dreams. My throat was open, nothing more than a channel for my love.

Sometimes when I sang to Avery, a voice emerged I didn't know I had. A pretty voice. That day, partway through the lullaby, I realized Dee might be within earshot. I wondered if she could hear me and what she'd think. Immediately, my throat began to constrict. I tried to pretend she wasn't near so that my voice wouldn't change, and Avery's gaze was helpful. He was still looking at me and listening. I continued our song with an awareness of Dee trailing behind each note. Avery's lids closed and opened again, ". . . the lovers, the dreamers and me." I sang through the next verse until his eyes remained shut, then kissed the delicious dimple on his chin before I pulled on the door, leaving it the slightest bit ajar.

When I stepped out of the room, Dee was standing there.

"You can sing," she said with the same gentleness I'd just used to close the door. They were three simple words that, until that moment, I didn't know

I'd longed to hear from Dee. I knew right then I'd hoped she would hear me. My need for her acknowledgment was inescapable. I was over an inch taller than Dee and yet I felt like I was looking up at her, as if I were a little girl again. My thoughts took me back to the hallway mirror where I'd rehearsed for my elementary school audition and she tried to help, the mirror where part of me had been waiting a decade for her to turn back around instead of heading up the stairs.

"Why didn't you take voice lessons?" Dee asked, and I returned to the present moment.

"I don't know," I answered, not far from a whisper.

"Was it my fault?" she asked.

Was it? I wondered.

"*You* were the singer—singing was yours," I said.

"It could have been yours, too."

"No. I couldn't sing like you."

"But you sing like you, Cara. Delicately, and it's beautiful."

"It's usually not, at least not when anyone is listening . . . except Avery, maybe."

We stood two feet apart and the tears came slowly for both of us. I could see the freckles over the bridge of her nose and the muscles along her clenched jaw roll beneath her skin. Her question, "Was it my fault?" was suspended in the air between us. I flashed on an image of myself as a little girl in my purple bedroom singing with arms outstretched in front of my daybed for an audience of stuffed animals, the way I often did back then. If I'd been an only child, I wondered, or if Dee hadn't been a singer, would I have loved singing as much as I did? And if I did, would I have taken more risks, taken voice lessons? Was there any way to distill my true nature and desires from a childhood obscured by Dee's influence? And was there any point?

"Did I steal singing from you?" Dee asked.

"What do you mean?"

"Like, did I overshadow you, hog all the attention?"

"No. Of course not."

"But I was 'the singer,' " she said with air quotes.

"Dee, we were little girls. No one stopped me from taking voice lessons and I don't know why I didn't." She was searching my eyes for an answer so I ventured a guess. "Maybe I thought talent was given, you either had it or you didn't. You definitely had it. I didn't." My explanation didn't feel entirely accurate, but it was my best guess at the time.

"But that's what I mean," she said. "Just because I could sing didn't mean you couldn't. If you didn't have to compare yourself to me, maybe you would have tried more."

"Maybe. But I didn't. I don't know, Dee, you didn't overshadow me. There was nothing dark about your singing or our relationship. There wasn't," I assured her, but by then she was looking through me.

"I'm sorry," she said and filled a short silence. The shame in her apology bothered me. What could she have done differently? Was she supposed to play down her own talents to make room for mine? Besides, if she'd done that, we might have been standing there in tears discussing how I'd held *her* back.

"I love you so much," Dee said with a big sigh.

"I love you, too," I replied, relieved the conversation was over.

But later that day, I recalled a conversation Dee and I had had years earlier in her New York City apartment. I can't remember its context, but I can remember it word for word.

"Why do you talk in a little-girl voice?" she asked me. "Speak from your diaphragm," and she placed her hand under her ribs. "From *here*."

"What do you mean?" I asked, hurt.

"All high up and airy. You don't sound confident. You should be confident when you talk. Confidence comes from down here," and with the fingertips of one hand she pointed at the central spot directly under her sternum.

"Oh. I didn't realize I wasn't doing that." Her lesson on proper voice projection made me feel less confident, not more.

"I mean, don't worry about it or anything," Dee added. "I just wanted to mention it."

But I *was* worrying. No longer was I concerned only about *what* I said to Dee, now I was also concerned about *how* I said it. I didn't even know how to continue the conversation for fear I'd do it all wrong.

"I'll pay attention," I told her—it would be hard *not* to.

It's true I was insecure, and I was aware of my social anxiety, but I thought I hid it well. I wasn't some wallflower. I was outgoing. I was even vice president of Syosset High School one year. And I think Dee knew all that. But I also knew confidence was something that at best I portrayed but rarely—if ever—embodied, which made me think that maybe Dee, like that professor in college, had a point. To me, being confident was a risk. It made me feel exposed and easy to judge. Insecurity, though ugly and vexing, in some odd way made me feel safe. If I'd already judged myself poorly, no one else had to do it for me. A first-strike assumption of failure on my part provided a buffer from rejection that I sometimes relied on, the very buffer that was probably responsible for my not taking voice lessons. The truth was that I had a love-hate relationship with insecurity and that if Dee's talent had cast a shadow in my direction, I stood in it willingly.

When I sang "Rainbow Connection" to Avery and Dee listened, she didn't judge me as insecure, and she didn't try to correct me. She called my voice delicate and it was a compliment. I felt she understood me in a way she hadn't before and that she understood us. Whether we were singing or talking to each other, she and I had different voices. Mine tended to be soft, sometimes tentative. Hers tended to be powerful, sometimes heavy-handed. We were different people.

But I was changing. I was emboldened by motherhood. I'd always wished my children and their cousins would be close in age, but something about having motherhood "all to myself" was satisfying. I never patronized Dee aloud, but I wasn't above thinking, *You're not a mother, when you're a mother you'll understand.*

Motherhood gave me the upper hand in disagreements with Dee, and the freedom to be self-righteous. Over time, Dee became frustrated with my all-organic, all-natural, all-knowing maternal disposition, but when she questioned my choices I didn't retreat from her like I'd often done in the past. Instead, I consciously marched through my anxiety into our conversations armed with facts and an uncharacteristic show of confidence.

Once, when Avery was still a baby, Dee was in town and asked if she could feed him.

"Yeah, let me get you some food," I answered and then sashayed into the kitchen with my babe snug against my chest in a sling. Dee followed me and watched as I took a bite of banana, chewed it thoroughly, and spit the slop into a little dish. I handed the dish to her with a baby spoon and a straight face.

"Seriously, Cara?" she said and raised an eyebrow, an expression that made it difficult for me to tell if she was being critical or curious.

"What? It's called kiss feeding," though in this instance I had to admit it looked more like "spit feeding." Then Dee looked at me like she was plotting an escape route whereby she would flee with Avery and treat him to his first Snickers bar just to spite me. I tried to fend off any judgment with a comprehensive explanation of the benefits of kiss feeding.

"There's an enzyme called ptyalin in your saliva that begins carbohydrate digestion. Young babies don't have it when they're first introduced to food, so I usually feed Avery straight from my mouth like a mama bird to her fledglings." Then I added, "Moms do it in Africa."

Another time, Dee asked about vaccinations.

"Don't you think you should vaccinate Avery?"

"No, I don't—at least not yet. Vaccines are all about greedy pharmaceutical companies. Did you know that the incidence of infectious disease was dropping before vaccines? Yeah, because of improved hygiene practices? Or that half the people who contract pertussis are actually vaccinated?"

And yet another time, she asked about nursing.

"You're going to nurse for *two years*? Don't you think that's a long time?"

"No. Why? Because I'm part of a culture that doesn't support it. What do I care? Nursing secures the bond between mother and baby. It helps stimulate the growth of his cranial and facial bones. Breast milk is filled with nutrients and protects the baby from all sorts of bacteria and viruses in his early years."

There were a number of other points of contention between Dee and me regarding my parenting, including behavior management. I spent the first three years of Avery's life employing a philosophy that encouraged parents to avoid the word "no." To most outsiders, and to Dee, it appeared I had set no boundaries and he was running amok—and sometimes he was. What neither Dee nor I understood at the time was that at the core of my convictions was my need to feel in control of my life and my need to prove to her that I had control of my life. But it wasn't easy facing Dee's criticism, and the tension growing between us was thick like Floridian humidity.

Of course, I didn't always feel bold, either. Postpartum depression found me six months after Avery was born. It was like some parasite sucking the life out of me. I often felt like I was watching life through a windowpane; I could see the world and the people in it, but I was separate, disconnected. The depression was exacerbated by two miscarriages and the destruction of the Twin Towers. I wanted to be near my family again, and Jon and I opted to settle back in Colorado, where my mother still lived.

We bought our first house in the urban sprawl of Erie, Colorado, a giant step up from our previous rentals. We were proud of our front porch, burgundy front door, and expansive western view of the Rocky Mountains. We built garden boxes in the backyard and I took up gardening. I was pregnant again. I'd made it through my first trimester and I finally felt confident enough about taking the pregnancy to term to start planning for the baby.

I sat in a winged, claw-foot chair, with my feet on the ottoman, and talked to Dee on the phone. I was anxious because I needed to tell her that I planned to have another home birth. After hemorrhaging with Avery's birth, I suspected she wouldn't take the news well.

With the phone pressed to my ear and my heart pounding, I took a deep breath and told Dee my plans.

"I'm having this baby at home."

"What?" she said. It was only one word, but sufficient to convey her disapproval.

"Yeah. I'm gonna have another home birth."

"But what if something goes wrong?" she asked.

"Nothing's gonna go wrong. I'm young, I'm healthy, I have a much better midwife than I did the first time, and I trust her."

"But why take the risk? It's not safe."

"It is. I actually feel safer at home. At home no one's going to force me to have a C-section—they're thirty-three percent more likely in hospitals, you know. At home, I don't have to be on guard. I'm relaxed."

"But you never know. Something could happen."

"Something could always happen, anywhere."

She didn't like my response. "Why do you always have to do things differently?" she asked. "It's like you try to be extreme just to stand out."

"What? What does that even mean? Do you really think that?"

"What I think is that you're being irresponsible."

"Well, I disagree. I'm not irresponsible."

"Really?" she said. "'Cause you're *so* responsible. That's how you ended up pregnant at twenty-three?" And there it was, her truth, the allegation she'd withheld for years, but that I had sensed nonetheless.

"I bet I was more careful than you were back then," I argued. "I just happened to get pregnant."

"But you didn't just *happen* to get pregnant. That's my point," she said. "Nothing happened *to* you. You wanted to get pregnant. You wanted to get pregnant even though you didn't have the means to take care of a baby."

After all this time, after being an aunt, was she still suggesting that my pregnancy was irresponsible? I knew how much she loved Avery and she knew how much I loved him. I couldn't understand how she could have the impression that my life had somehow taken a wrong turn because I'd become a mother. Did Dee really think she knew better than me what *my* life was supposed to look like?

"You realize you're talking about your nephew, right?" I reminded her.

"I love my nephew! This isn't about him. It's about you. That's so unfair."

"Well, you're the judge," I told her. "You'd know what's fair." I knew that calling her "the judge" was hurtful when I said it. She knew she was critical and hated it about herself. I knew I was hypersensitive and hated it about myself. But regardless of my sensitivity, the reality was that when Dee was upset, she was good at making words sting, and she didn't even have to raise her voice to do it. I wanted words that could sting, too. For the first time, I wanted to hurt her.

"Who are you to talk to me about motherhood?" I yelled. "Who are you to question my decisions?" I hadn't realized that I was shouting. Until then, I'd never shouted at Dee. But yelling at her felt like a way to protect myself. Like if I screamed loud enough maybe I could stop her words midair and they'd never reach me, never hurt me.

"Come on, Cara. Don't you think you got pregnant because you needed attention, because I had *Rent* and you needed your own thing?"

Her words hit me hard and the fight in me quickly faded. I thought about that year when *Rent* began and how proud I was of her. I pictured the deep plastic bin I still had in my basement filled with magazines and newspapers and clippings of her as Maureen in that black catsuit. I thought about how hard it had been, but how gratifying it was, to leave Colorado when I was buried in my thesis and fly to New York for a couple of days to watch her onstage, to share that success with her.

I couldn't bear to listen to Dee anymore and I'd lost the ability to shout her away. I said nothing, but she continued.

"You're impulsive," she snapped. "You had to have everything right away.

Have a wedding, have a baby. You needed to make sure people were looking at you, too."

I didn't understand. Was she accusing me of jealousy? Didn't she know how good it felt every time I saw her take the stage, or how good it felt to hear her belt out the last note of a show-stopping song, or jump to my feet for her standing ovation? But I quickly realized that she didn't know. She'd never seen me like I'd seen her. She'd never felt that proud of me.

Dee's anger hurt, and once I understood what I'd done to make her feel that way it hurt even more than the anger that had masked it—I'd disappointed her.

I started to cry gasping, audible tears and she heard them and stopped talking. As much as I could, I spoke through my tears.

"You don't get to decide what I do or tell me why I do it. You don't get to tell me what mistakes I've made. What do you know about being me, Dee? I've spent my whole life rooting for you, being proud of you, watching *you*. Have you any idea what it feels like to hear how disappointed you are in me? And for the very thing I'm most proud of, my family."

"I'm sorry," she said. "I didn't mean it like that. I *am* proud of you."

"And to tell me you think I did it all because of *you*? Because you had fame and I didn't." I felt betrayed. I'd been loyal to her and she'd turned on me. I hadn't just been her sister, I'd been Idina Menzel's sister, and I believed I'd been really good at it. And the truth was that if I was desperate for attention, it was mostly from her.

"I don't think you did it all because of me," she backpedaled.

But I wasn't finished.

"Can't having my baby just be about me? Does it have to be about you, too? I've never competed with you for attention."

There was another pause, like we'd just parked a car and pulled the keys from the ignition.

"My baby is *my* success," I insisted, feeling as if I was reaching through the phone, begging for her to agree, begging for her to accept my choices, to accept *me.*

"I know. I'm sorry, babe. You're a great mom. I just . . . imagined so much more for you."

Another jab, this time unintended. I couldn't speak. In Dee's mind, my adult life was shaped around my need for attention, and that made me feel like my desire to have a family had been impure. In her mind, I was supposed to be *more,* and that made me feel like I wasn't enough.

"I love you," she said.

"I know."

We hung up. Dee was gone, but the conversation stayed with me. *Was she right?* Did I have a baby because I needed attention, because she had *Rent* and recognition? I didn't want to be the person who would have a baby to get attention, even unconsciously. The possibility haunted me. I desperately wanted the answer to be no. The answer *had* to be no, because if it wasn't, then in some obscure way, Dee was the impetus for the best thing I'd ever done—have Avery. And I wanted Avery to be all mine. All *my* doing.

After eight years of dating, Dee and Taye were getting married. Their destination wedding in Montego Bay was about six months away, and Dee and I were on the phone again. Several months had passed since The Argument. We'd talked, but we hadn't revisited the subject. Maybe we'd said all there was to say, or maybe the matter was too sensitive to touch again. For my part, the hurt lingered, but it also didn't hold any answers, so I kept moving forward, hoping to leave the interaction with Dee further and further behind until it was less a part of me and more a part of history.

I was slouched in a loveseat in my bedroom with my hand over my pregnant belly, my baby big enough to kick at my palm. I watched as Avery pushed Thomas the Tank Engine's Percy around fragments of train tracks and listened to Dee talk about her dress, which villa everyone would stay in, and how she was flying in her favorite wedding band—one she'd sang in years ago—and the karaoke party she had planned after the rehearsal dinner. Then she surprised me.

"Sing with me, Cara," she asked. "At karaoke, sing something with me."

Oh shit.

Dee had tossed her request for a sister duet at me like it was as light and harmless as a playing card. I had a vision of us belting into microphones like Joan Jett and Debbie Harry, then realized I was neither Joan nor Debbie—not even close.

"It would mean a lot to me," she added. Dee had to know that she was asking a lot, but it felt like she was asking as a kindness, an attempt to put all the heavy crap behind us and sing like we had when we were little. Before I was self-conscious or afraid to sing. Before I was afraid to fail her. Way back when singing was playing, and playing was fun.

But I knew that singing with Dee after her rehearsal dinner wouldn't be like singing a lullaby to Avery in our private corner of the universe. It meant standing up in front of a hundred familiar and unfamiliar faces and offering up the perfect opportunity to compare me piece by piece—note by note—to my sister, something I'd worked hard for a long time to avoid. In my mind, if I agreed to sing with Dee I needed either the ability to sing well or the confidence not to care. And I was fairly certain I didn't possess either of the two.

Whenever someone learned I was Idina Menzel's sister they still always asked, "Can you sing?" They asked it before anything else—usually right before, "Who's older?"—and they asked with the nonchalance of a barista wanting to know if I preferred whole milk or nonfat.

"Can you sing?"

"No, thank you."

The safe answer was always no. Though sometimes I made light of it and said, "In the shower and in the car."

To get onstage and provide evidence that I couldn't sing was another matter altogether. With an audience I'd very likely suck. I'd suck in front of Jon and my parents, my aunt and uncle, my cousins, Mom's friends, Dee's business manager and two agents, the groom, his family and hot friends—the latter, a gross understatement. If I got up onstage and sang karaoke with Dee, it wouldn't be, "No, Dee's sister can't sing," but would very likely be, "Whoa. She *really can't* sing."

I can't do it.

I wanted to say yes to Dee, which made me wish I could sing more than ever. My singing ability remained fleeting, and unreliable. Like my blueberry pie, my voice came out differently every time. Would it have been so difficult to spread the wealth a little bit, to more fairly distribute the Mentzel-Goldberg gene pool? I didn't need to sing like Dee, but the basics would have been nice—to hold a microphone and a tune at the same time. I wanted a voice I could count on, pretty or raspy, loud or soft. But even as an adult, I was embarrassed to want it. When no one was around, I tried to sing. In the car driving, I tried to match pitch with a random song, or harmonize with Radiohead's "Creep." I practiced singing in the shower, where the acoustics were in my favor, and in the vacant house, where the emptiness was in my favor. Often I sang with my sister's songs because those were the ones I knew best, the ones I'd sung over and over and over, "Take Me or Leave Me" or "Still I Can't Be Still," her version blasting in the background. Once I even recorded myself for objectivity—*What do I sound like?*—and listened quickly before anyone caught me or I was sidetracked and forgot to delete the recording. But I had a vocal range the width of a nickel. I started a song in one key, only to switch midway through the song to hit the higher notes or reach the low ones. I struggled to match pitch. I could hear a tune in my head, but then couldn't find the notes once I opened my mouth. I could hardly imagine singing in front of people and guessed it would be like smiling while being strangled; I'd be hard-pressed to sing when I could barely breathe.

Avery had connected the tracks, formed a large oval across the carpet, and was sitting in the middle of it. The phone was still in my hand, Dee on the other end, the "Sing with me?" question still patiently waiting, and the singing shit back for a visit. I hated that I couldn't sing. I hated that Dee felt guilty about it and I felt inadequate. If I had a magic wand, my favorite spell would be "Singing shit begone!" I'd wave that fuckin' wand and stop wishing I could sing, stop caring what everyone thought of me, and stop wondering what could have been if . . . I'd wave that wand and grant myself the wish I wanted more than anything, to be the bold, unapologetic woman who would welcome the chance to sing karaoke with her sister, and who would love it. I was tired of waiting to become that woman, and so I answered Dee, "Yes."

Yes.

I gave birth to Jacob safely at home in my bed. His hair was as dark as Avery's had been light. His eyes were black, his skin the color of a gingersnap. At five pounds twelve ounces, Jacob was the smallest baby I'd ever held, but he was strong, a tight bundle of muscles. Avery crawled into bed next to me and I watched as he lovingly ran the tip of his forefinger over Jacob's brow. *Brothers,* I thought to myself. *Ha!*

"Aunt Dee Dee" came to visit that week. She'd recently had a small part in the film *Kissing Jessica Stein* and a series of theater projects: Kate in an off-Broadway production of *The Wild Party* that never moved on, Amneris in *Aida* (but as a replacement, rather than originating the role), and as one of myriad rotating performers in the Westside Theatre's production of *The Vagina Monologues*. While these roles were some of my favorite Dee performances—as Kate she got to fake pee onstage—the momentum of Dee's career seemed to have abated and she was discouraged. Discouraged, but driven. Dee was always driven.

I was in my bedroom and Dee was giving Avery a bath when I heard her call to me from across the hall.

"Cara, Avery and I want to show you something. Grab the video camera!" (A baby-shower gift from her.) I crossed the hall with Jacob cocooned in a sling hanging over my left shoulder, and found Avery standing butt naked in the tub with a faux-hawk molded from shampoo suds. Dee was sitting on the closed toilet lid.

"Avery and I need you to film our commercial," she said. At the mention of their commercial Avery pressed his lips together into an infectious smile, and then added with high-pitched enthusiasm, "For soap!"

"I can't wait," I said from the doorway, then opened the flip-out screen of the camera. "Ready when you are."

"Do you remember your lines, Avery?" Dee asked.

"Yep," he answered and reached over to lift the yellow bottle of Johnson & Johnson baby soap from the ledge of the tub. When he leaned over I noticed his wet eyelashes were clumped into a few distinct points and a wave of adoration swept through me.

Dee said, "Take one: Johnson and Johnson Baby Soap Commercial, starring a brand-new big brother, Avery." She clapped her hands together to simulate a clapperboard and said, "Action!" and Avery raised the soap bottle up over his right shoulder.

"This Junsun Junsun soap is sooo great," he started. "It doesn't hurt if it gets in your eyes." He looked over at Dee for his next line and she rubbed her hands together. He picked up the cue and continued. "You wash your hands with it if they get dirty," then he paused, "or if you pick your nose . . . so you can touch the baby." He pushed the bottle toward the camera and smiled again as if his grin were the punctuation at the end of his sentence.

"Cut," Dee said. "Nice work, Avery! You're a natural at this." He was, and she was too—a natural auntie.

The calendar glared at me from the day I agreed to sing with Dee until the day we left for Jamaica. I routinely imagined the details of our karaoke set. I imagined the songs we might sing, felt the adrenaline and buzzing of my hyperactive nerves, and then practiced deep breathing until my anxiety dissipated. And still the date shouted at me from every calendar, "Look at me! Look at me! Over here!"

When I arrived in Montego Bay, everywhere I turned I saw symbols of relaxation. Placid water and white curtains blowing in the breeze. Stunning villas and infinity pools. Lounge chairs, hammocks, and frothy beverages; a crowd favorite called the Dirty Banana, which still makes me laugh, was made with bananas, Kahlua, and cream. Beauty surrounded me—lush greens, blue skies, my sister in an off-the-shoulder midriff-revealing cotton top, and her groom, the gorgeous, dark Taye Diggs, in a fedora. The resort was the same place he'd given Angela Bassett her "groove back" in the film *How Stella Got Her Groove Back* in 1998. There were sea urchins to entertain Avery and fluffy white towels under beach umbrellas to shade four-month-old Jacob during naps. And of course, there was karaoke.

Before the rehearsal dinner, Dee was kind enough to find me a sitter and, like typical sisters, we played dress-up. She loaned me a pink satin sundress. It was fitted over my chest, which I liked because it allowed me to place nursing pads over my breasts without having to wear an unflattering, nursing bra. Braless and pink, I slicked my hair back into a tight ponytail and was ready for an evening to remember.

The tiki-lit buffet was outstanding and lined the shore. Guests held kitschy piña coladas in pineapples with little umbrellas. When a storm rolled in, the staff deftly transferred all the necessities to a covered porch nearby. Then it was time.

Let me be very clear, there was none of that fifteen minutes of fame, karaoke wanna-be-a-superstar crap at this rehearsal dinner—these were *actual* superstars. Many of the attendees were talented singers—so many, in fact, that Dee could have sold tickets. I knew Dee and Taye's Broadway friends could sing, but apparently every other actor and actress could sing, too. Whether they'd been on Broadway as dancers in the ensemble or were Broadway stars. Whether they were actors who did a guest spot on a sitcom or starred in a soap opera, they had Broadway-worthy voices. Even one of her agents killed it with a rockin' rendition of "Ain't No Mountain High Enough." I gawked at five beautiful men who stood in a line and sang, "Papa Was a Rollin' Stone," and the groom, signed up against his will, who sang "Day-O" from his early career days performing at Tokyo Disney.

The show was well under way when Dee approached me, the black binder with the list of song options in her hand. "You up for this?" she asked.

"Yep," I answered, but my throat tightened like I was seconds from a tongue depressor and strep swab. I found a phony smile and stuck it on my face.

"'Enough Is Enough'?" Dee asked, remembering we'd listened to the song growing up, on a cassette tape of Donna Summer's *On the Radio: Greatest Hits* right after "Sunset People." The song was actually titled "No More Tears," but the chorus repeated the words "enough is enough" so many times that that's how people usually remembered it. Donna Summer sang the song as a duet with Barbra Streisand, one of the few duets between two women. I used to know the song well, but that evening I could only be sure I knew the first two lines, lines that in total added up to four appropriate words given the weather, "It's raining," and "It's pouring." Dee and I never discussed what song we'd sing. We probably should have; it might have helped my nerves, but despite the significance of our singing together, I'd been trying to play the whole thing down. *Breathe. Relax. It's only a big deal if you make it one.*

I agreed to the song, and Dee walked our request up to the karaoke deejay. I didn't know how many people were ahead of us or how long I had before our turn. If I hadn't been nursing, it would have been prime time for a drink. But quickly I heard the deejay announce, "Dina and Cara singing 'Enough Is Enough,'" and hearing the pairing of our names, "Dina and Cara," reinforced that we were sisters, first and foremost. Dina and Cara signed together on the bottom right corner of a Mother's Day card. "Dina and Cara, 1980," written on the back of a photo. Or, "Dina! Cara!" shouted up the stairs from the kitchen, "din-ner!" Dee found my hand and clasped it in hers. I watched my feet as we walked through a mess of white folding chairs to the patio stage. We fumbled with the microphones and took our places in front of the crowd. I looked up and faced sixty or so disheveled partiers, including my mom and dad and at least a dozen of my sister's closest friends, all their eyes fixed on us, fixed on me. I faced the music.

I traded the chance to sing the only words I knew for the opportunity to delay the embarrassment, and let Dee start. She began, "It's raining. It's pouring.

My love life is boring me to tears." *Ah, that was the next line.* Her voice drifted through the air and lingered in the space after her last note ended. I picked up the next verse. The mic made it impossible for me to hear myself. I had no idea how my breath translated into sound. I couldn't feel the notes as I sang them. I couldn't hear the notes as I sang them. My throat felt numb, and still I tried to cram air through it as the hot-pink words jumped around the blue karaoke screen. I abandoned all hope of singing well.

Adrenaline kept me afloat, and when the tempo picked up, Dee and I huddled together, bouncing up and down, shouting "Enough is enough" at the tops of our lungs. When we briefly bounced apart I watched Dee. She was beaming in her white cotton and lace skirt, her matching blouse, her bronze skin and prominent cheekbones. She was giddy and silly and childlike—my favorite kind of Dee. Our bouncing grew into impassioned jumping, my heels hitting the floor repeatedly. The movement coupled with my vision of Dee managed to knock something loose, and a weight fell from my shoulders. Just like that, I let go. My throat not so much numb as irrelevant. I wasn't paying attention to my singing anymore. I didn't care about being able to sing. I only cared about being a sister and being with Dee. I only wanted her to be happy.

I'd finally resumed breathing and was—dare I say it, having fun—when thanks to all the jumping, something else came loose—one of my nursing pads. It snuck beneath the seam under my bust and took a detour out the bottom of my dress, landing *plop!* like a silver-dollar pancake into a puddle on the patio floor. I looked up at the pool of confused eyes that strained to make sense of it. *Seriously?* I'd worried for months about embarrassing myself during karaoke, but it never occurred to me that my undergarments—or lack thereof—would be the source of that embarrassment, rather than my vocals. Not once had I imagined having to explain to the attendees of Dee's wedding exactly what a nursing pad was and why one of mine was on the floor. I did the only thing I could think to do. I dug my hand into the top of my dress and pulled out the remaining troublemaker. I flung it like a miniature Frisbee into the crowd, a gesture that was well received with raucous cheers and whistles. I retrieved the other pad from the puddle and flung that one as well. Dee and I were hysterical. It was clear, I wasn't a singer. I was a mother. But I'd gotten what I wanted. I'd become the person who loved singing karaoke with her sister—a sister I was about to need more than ever.

PART III
FLYING HIGH

Lesson 7

HOW TO FAIL

Despite motherhood being all I'd ever wanted, I wasn't a perfect mother and I wasn't a perfect wife. At my worst I was depressed, sleep deprived, and had a temper I'd never had before. I worried that I was changing in ways I didn't want to change, often feeling impatient yet meek and insecure.

My relationship with Jon was also changing. My love for him had become elusive. I looked for it everywhere: at the passenger side of the car when he opened my door first, in the beautiful bed frame that he built for us, in his green eyes and the dimple I'd once adored, in his social charm and willingness to help family and friends. It seemed my feelings for him were the direct result of where I focused my attention. I could convince myself that everything was all right simply by deciding to look one way and not another. By choosing to love that he'd do the dinner dishes while I bathed the boys, instead of worrying why he'd choose to do dishes rather than spend time with them. By appreciating how much time he invested fine-tuning business plans instead of complaining about how little attention he paid to me. By calling him at work just to say I love you, because maybe the more I said it, the more

I acted like it, the more my love would be true. And I wanted to love him. I wanted my marriage to work.

But Jon had a temper, too, and when I was able to be objective, I knew I'd slipped into the familiar role of mediator in our family. Among other things, I didn't like how he raised his voice with Avery, twisted his doughy arm because he was laughing too loud in a movie theater, or yanked him by the ankle if he wouldn't sit still to put his shoes on. Over time I realized I was mediating and managing and exhausting myself making sure everyone was okay all the time, making sure no one felt too sad or too angry and no one ever got hurt.

While I didn't always like Jon's behavior with the boys, nothing about it ever seemed black-and-white to me, not easy to judge as bad, wrong, or sufficient reason to leave him. Furthermore, I was so fixated on my own shortcomings, I had a hard time holding him accountable for his. (Even now, there's a shakiness in my heart where the internal conflict continues, where I weigh my mistakes against Jon's and question my right to pass judgment, and worry that I'm being too hard on myself—or not hard enough.) I was often confused. Where was the line between a poor-parenting moment—the kind most of us have had on a bad day—yelling at an inconsolable toddler, for instance, instead of holding him tight and kissing his sweaty forehead? Where was the line between acceptable and unacceptable?

I didn't know until the night I decided Jon had crossed it.

The table was set. Three place settings and one high chair on the end of a rectangular mahogany table. I lifted the pan with the salmon off the burner and scooped the steamed veggies into a large ceramic bowl. Jacob was already in the high chair, sliding soft carrots shaped liked pennies around with his palms, and Avery was playing at his train table in the den off the kitchen.

"Aves, go wash your hands," I called across the room, my voice traveling into the vaulted ceilings as Jon walked in from work. He set his computer bag against the wall and I finished zigzagging through the kitchen from countertop to fridge to stovetop to table to countertop again. It was a hot summer evening and an orange sun peaked over the distant mountain horizon like a watchful eye. Jon kissed me on the cheek.

"Perfect timing," I said to him.

"How's it goin'?" he asked me as he kissed Jacob on top of his head, then sat down at the table.

"Pretty good. It was a long day, but a good one." I set the veggies on the table, then continued. "The boys had no interest in naps so our field trip to the grocery store was a little ambitious, but we had fun at the park."

I noticed Avery still hadn't made it to the table and called to him again, "Avery, dinner's ready," this time a little louder than before. I didn't want to yell at him. Avery was distractible, but rarely defiant, and in this instance he was probably deep in imaginary play on Sodor Island with Sir Topham Hatt and his steam engines.

I set a full plate on the table in front of Jon and walked around to the other side to set down Avery's plate. Avery's chair was still empty. "Avery! Dinner. Is. Ready!" I yelled.

The rest happened in an instant—and yet it seemed in slow-motion. In a volume that exceeded my own, Jon shouted, "I just want to get home, sit down, and relax!" Then he set both his hands flat on the table in front of him, pushed all six feet two inches of himself straight out of his chair, and added, "For once!"

When I saw Jon turn toward Avery I was still standing on the opposite side of the table, too far away to intercept him. I felt a dark hole open in my stomach as he shot toward Avery in two big steps, grabbed him just beneath his shoulders as if his arms were the lifeless rails of a chair and not the soft limbs of a child. He quickly carried him partially up the stairs and then slammed Avery's tiny bum down on one. Gravity would have been more gentle than Jon had been. Avery froze, his eyes wide, vacant at first, like his spirit had been ejected on impact.

"Jon!" I shouted and slipped in between them with my back to him like a fortress. I knelt in front of Avery and placed my hands on his knees. Life returned to his eyes in the form of fear, and he tried to breathe, but he couldn't. And briefly, neither could I. I was certain his back was broken and that he couldn't feel my hands.

"Look at Mommy, baby. Mommy's here. Breathe." Avery tried, but it seemed as if fear itself were lodged in his airway. A necessary calm fell over me. I realized he'd had the wind knocked out of him. I placed a few fingertips under his chin and leaned toward him until he could see nothing but my eyes and the world was just us. Avery watched as I took a deep breath and coached him to do the same. Then he took a short series of staccato breaths that finally led to one big inhalation and on his exhale he started to cry.

"Can you stand up, Avery?" I asked, and I held his hand as he came to his feet on a step. *He can stand,* I thought and breathed a sigh of relief. *Kids blame themselves,* I thought, something I'd heard about children who knows when, maybe from Oprah, that was suddenly relevant in a way I'd never imagined it would be.

"Avery," I said, still looking at him. "That wasn't your fault. Daddy made a mistake." I turned around and looked at Jon, whose temper was already a thing of the past. "Jon. Tell him. Apologize."

"You okay, bud?" he asked.

"Yeah," Avery answered in a whimper.

"Daddy lost his temper, buddy. I'm sorry." Jon choked up midsentence and started to cry.

"It's okay, Daddy," Avery told him.

"No," I interrupted. "It's not. It's Daddy's job to protect you, not hurt you."

I turned to Jon. "I'm gonna go run him a hot bath," I said, then carried Avery up the stairs, away from his dad. From dinner. From a stove that might or might not still have been on. From a fridge that might or might not still have been open. From a baby who might or might not have been scared. And from a man suddenly more stranger than lover.

The bathwater rushed into the tub. It was loud, but I wished it were louder. I wanted to drown out the voices of my guilt. *I* was the one yelling at Avery.

I'd triggered Jon. It's *my* fault Avery got hurt. I was smart enough to know those were the thoughts of a victim, but they felt true nonetheless, and no amount of psychobabble would assuage my sense of failure. It was my job to protect my son and I hadn't. For a minute I was obsessed with assigning blame—to myself, to Jon; so long as I was ruminating, I could avoid replaying the events in my head. But in front of me waited a wounded five-year-old, so I forced my attention back to the little boy who needed it.

Avery stood on the navy bathmat and set a hand on my shoulder. He lifted one foot and then the other as I pulled his socks over his heels and off his feet, then slid his nylon shorts and Blues Clues underwear down to his ankles. He took one foot out, then the other.

We knew the bath routine well. It was a routine Avery usually loved. But that night, the mood was subdued, not silly. I tested the water with my hand, then gave Avery a gentle smooch on his tush. It was blotchy in places. As I raised him into the tub, his skin slid slightly over his ribs.

"It's gonna be hot," I warned in a singsongy voice ill fitted to the circumstances, then set his feet down into the water. "Let your feet get used to it before you sit down," I added. A wave of nausea fell over me when I heard myself say "get used to it." *Was Avery getting used to being pushed around by his dad, used to his dad's unpredictability?* I remembered a time a little over a year earlier when Avery had accidentally hit Jon on the bridge of his nose during a Sunday-morning pillow fight. Jon reacted by biting him on the shoulder. I remembered how quickly it happened. How stunned I'd been, the way Avery's joy disappeared from his face in an instant. The shock and hurt I watched fill his eyes. And the walnut-shaped mark that formed on his once-flawless skin.

Avery sat in the tub, dunking his plastic red boat in the water.

"Look at me, boo," I said. "What happened downstairs wasn't your fault. Daddy's a grown-up. Daddy needs to control his temper." Avery quickly changed the subject and showed me how he could make his boat jump out of the water.

When the bathwater began to cool I held out an oversize blue towel. Avery stood up and swung his leg over onto the bathmat. I wrapped the towel around his body a couple of times and then sat on the toilet seat with him bundled on my lap, his pruney feet dangling out the bottom. I ran my hands quickly up and down his sides to warm him up the way my mom used to do for me when I got out of the swimming pool. Then I gave him a big squeeze and kissed him on top of his head.

"I love you, Avery."

"I love you, Mommy," he said, and with his back damp against me, I rested my head over his and let a few secret tears fall.

Later that night my tears were no longer a secret—at least not from Jon. Speechless, he spooned me in bed as I sobbed into the down comforter so the boys wouldn't hear me. Maybe it was strange that Jon could comfort me, strange that he was still comforting after what he'd done, but for six years Jon had been the man to hold me, and I needed to be held. I considered pushing him away, but I was too emotional to be decisive, and too tired to act. I lay there in an unsettling duality. In Jon's arms I felt both loved and trapped.

Hours had passed when I felt Jon pull his arm out from under me and turn over in bed. I folded the blanket back and sat up, then headed toward the light that shone through the crack in our door. I entered Jacob's room, leaned over his crib, and listened to him breathe for a few minutes. Then I entered Avery's room through the Jack and Jill bathroom they shared. Avery was asleep in his undies, sprawled out in bed with his head where his feet should have been. I liked to joke that he slept like the hands of a clock, making circles in his bed all night. I knelt down and smelled his breath like I was breathing life itself.

When I slipped back into my bed, Jon woke up a little and asked if I was okay.

"I will be," I told him.

I drifted through the next few days in a dissociated fog. I pulled into the driveway with no memory of the turns I'd made or the exit I'd taken to get home. I took the kids to the park and pushed the swings out of habit, and emptied the dishwasher as if nothing had changed. Shock, I imagine. And perhaps I was distancing myself from reality as a stall tactic; I didn't know my next move so I didn't make one at all.

I wanted to call Dee and I didn't want to call Dee. She offered me a sense of safety. I knew I'd never fall too far without her catching me. When it came to me, she carried an air of *I won't let anyone fuck with you.* And she'd fly across the country to put Jon in his place if I asked her to. But she was also judgmental. No misstep of mine went unnoticed. Whether she chose to acknowledge my mistakes aloud or to let her criticism percolate beneath the surface, I could detect her irritation in a sigh, an awkward pause, a change of subject, or a question: "Why didn't you just . . . ?"

Before that night, I'd rarely called Dee with marriage complaints and concerns the way I imagine a lot of close sisters would have. If I disclosed that anything was wrong in my marriage, Dee would worry, and I didn't want her to worry. I had the sense that with her, I was either happy or I was a burden. And when it came to the marriage she doubted, I was either happy or I was wrong. Part of me wanted to stay with Jon so that I wouldn't have to be wrong. Another part of me—admittedly a disgusting part—was relieved that he'd fucked up. It gave me an excuse to leave him. It meant our failed marriage could be more his fault than mine, and that people—my sister especially—could be angry with him instead of disappointed in me. Finally, there was the part of me, the part that yearned to be closer to Dee, that wanted to confess every little thing I'd ever withheld from her. I wanted her to know it all. But there were too many parts of me. I was in pieces.

As it turned out, I didn't have to decide whether to call Dee or not. Mom had filled her in and she called me.

"How's Avery?" Dee asked over the phone.

"He's doing okay." I was picking up toys in the living room and looked over at the stairs where Avery had sat for those few scary minutes a few days earlier.

"I'm worried about his back and neck, but at least for now he appears to be fine." I took a seat on the couch.

"Do you want me to come out and talk to Jon, see what his deal is, see if there's anything I can do?"

"I love that you'd do that, Dee, but it's not necessary. And besides, I know how hard it would be for you to leave New York right now." Dee was in rehearsals for a new show called *Wicked* and she'd piss off a lot of people if she took a few days off. "I don't want you to worry. I'll figure this mess out."

"Like I'm not gonna worry."

"I know, sorry." I paused and then asked, "Do I leave Jon?" I wanted her permission. I didn't want to make the decision alone and then have to justify it to her.

"I don't know, Cara. You haven't been happy for a while, right?" I guess I hadn't withheld as much from her as I'd thought.

"It's all a matter of perspective, I suppose. Sometimes he's great—he taught Avery how to remove the stamen from a honeysuckle, for Christ's sake. But then sometimes he's not and we know what that looks like. But I'm not perfect either. I lose my temper, too."

"Stop it. Who doesn't? We're not talking about perfect here. You'd never put Avery in danger. You always put your kids first."

"I think that's what bothers Jon. I put them first and *not* him. It's awful, but sometimes I wish Jon was more stereotypical, straight out of an after-school special or something. I mean if he were the kind of guy that came home drunk, said 'where's my dinner, woman,' and then gave me a black eye when I didn't bring him his beer fast enough, I wouldn't question myself. I'd leave him. But he's not, and it's all his shades of gray that screw with me."

The line was quiet for a moment and I wished I knew what she was thinking. "I don't want to overreact," I finally added. "I know you think I'm impulsive sometimes." Then I started to cry, which was nothing new. For days my tears had been on their own schedule, showing up unannounced on line at the grocery store or on the phone with a rude customer-service representative.

"That's not *this,*" Dee said. "And who cares what I think?"

"I do."

"I know."

"What about Mommy and Daddy?" I said. "Did they try hard enough?"

"Maybe not, but who the hell knows? And your situation is different, Cara."

"There's no way to do right by my boys now," I explained. "If I stay with their dad, I run the risk of them thinking their dad's behavior is okay—not to mention, I think I'll lose my mind. But if I leave him, then they'll be alone with him more often *and* have divorced parents. I'll never be able to give them the kind of family they deserve . . . I just don't trust myself to make the right decision anymore—" Then she cut me off.

"*I* trust you," she said. *I trust you* meant she saw me as a competent grown-up and I had her respect. *I trust you* meant there was no *wrong* move for me to make, just a next move. It meant that she wasn't going to fly out and solve my problems for me (though she was tempted), because she knew I was capable of solving them myself.

"And there's no rush," Dee added. "If you're not ready to make a decision, don't make one yet." She waited for my crying to subside and then said, "But please don't stay with Jon because you're worried about money. If that time comes, Taye and I will help you. Mom and Dad will help you. You'll be fine."

"I know you guys would help, and that's a huge relief, but I don't think I could stand to be a charity case."

"You're gonna have to get over that. If the time comes, let me help you. It makes me feel good to help you."

"I know. Thank you. Really, that's peace of mind."

Before she could say goodbye I realized we hadn't talked about her at all.

"Shit," I said. "I'm so self-involved I haven't even asked how the show is going."

She sighed. "That's a whole other story. They're still throwing new pages at me. I'm an emotional wreck. But I don't want to talk about it right now. I'll fill you in later."

"You sure?"

"Yeah."

"I miss you."

"Miss you too. I'll be up late. Call me if you need anything."

" 'K. You too."

Mom took the boys to dinner a few nights later. Jon was out back, meticulously working on the new patio. His focus on the project struck me as odd given the tenuous circumstances of the week. The patio was a diversion, and each Home Depot paver symbolized Jon's denial. I could almost hear him saying, "I'm going to put this thing together even though everything else is falling apart," or maybe *because* everything else is falling apart. But to me, building that patio was like whitening a rotting tooth, or watering a dead plant.

It was dusk when I popped my head out the sliding back doors where Jon was still working.

"Can we talk about the other night?" I asked.

"What about the other night?" *How could he not know what I'm referring to?*

"You know, with Avery."

"Sure," he said. "Give me twenty minutes."

After an hour he finally came inside. He grabbed the drawings of the backyard plans, sat down at the kitchen table, and unrolled the large sheet of paper in front of him. I set two glasses of water on the table for us and then took a seat catty-corner to him. But he stared at those plans like I didn't exist, and I watched for a few minutes as he reworked the sketches with a pencil and ruler, never once looking up at me.

"Jon," I said. But he remained speechless, as if my voice had been muted and he was in the kitchen alone. "Jon," I repeated as my pulse quickened and my body trembled. I was awash with adrenaline.

"Jon!" I yelled finally. "Why are you ignoring me?" He didn't budge. "I'm scared. I'm sad. You hurt our son."

And still nothing. He didn't even lift his head.

"Where is my husband?" I asked him. "Who are you?" I stood up, pushed in my chair, and grabbed my water. I'd only made it up a couple of stairs before I turned around. His body still in the chair, transmitting a cold of Antarctic proportion. He seemed impervious to my feelings and I was desperate to be heard. "Jon!" I shouted one last time, and then, with his back still to me, he said three words I'll never forget.

"You psychotic bitch."

I didn't recognize his voice. It was cold and hateful. He'd never said anything like that to me before. I was afraid of him and infuriated at the same time. I looked down at the pint glass in my hand. I held my breath and walked toward him. He didn't see me coming. I emptied the glass of water over his head. He stood up immediately and turned to me with water dripping onto his shoulders and the same ferocity he'd directed at Avery earlier that week. I finally had his attention. He was taller than me, but he wasn't overly muscular. His power didn't come from a broad chest and cut biceps, but from rage. I dropped the glass on the carpet and stopped breathing.

He reached across the short distance between us and grabbed me hard above the elbows. I looked into his dilated pupils for the man I thought I knew, but he was gone. Before I could react, he took hold of my wrist and twisted my arm behind my back until my knees buckled and he shoved me onto the floor. I turned to face him, but was too afraid of what might happen if I stood back up so I stayed put. I just lay there on my back beneath his glare.

"Don't. You. Ever. Do. That. Again." There could be no doubt he was threatening me. Then he walked away. When I heard the groan of the garage door opening I knew he was leaving. I remained on the floor, supine, and alone. Then I screamed into the emptiness.

Jon returned hours later. He was sullen and quiet. The boys were already asleep.

"You can't be here anymore," I said with surprising directness. I was no longer angry or scared. I was barely sad. I said it as the matter of fact that it was.

"I know," he replied and started to cry.

His anger had often been a gateway to his tenderness and I loved when he was tender. He looked different to me, like the lines on his face had softened. I could still feel his hot hands tight around my arms, but I was suddenly worried that in his tears I'd lose my nerve to leave him. In those few seconds I worried that my caretaking impulse would kick in and I'd tell him to stay. Because maybe he'd never lay an angry hand on us again. Maybe he'd get help and everything would get better—ultimately, he would. But I couldn't know that then. I couldn't be sure that the following day or week or year he wouldn't do something else to one of the boys and what if I no longer had the clarity or strength that I had right then? I couldn't risk it. Tears or no tears, we had to be over.

"Is everything all right?" Dee asked when she answered the phone. That was often her first question when I called.

"I told Jon to leave," I said. "He left."

Lesson 8

HOW TO LOVE A WITCH

Wicked opened at The Gershwin Theatre on October 30, 2003. Dee was starring as the misunderstood green witch of Oz, Elphaba—affectionately referred to as Elphie—in a musical adaptation of Gregory Maguire's novel *Wicked*. The theater boasted close to two thousand seats, the most on Broadway. Before me hung a formidable dragon that spanned nearly the width of the stage and hovered over the first few rows of the orchestra. The dragon appeared to be made of armored scales layered together with steel pins like medieval suits of armor. He was a massive puppet, a marionette, with visible strings that held up his batlike wings, claws, neck, jagged teeth, and crocodile snout. Behind him hung a massive parchment map that depicted the Lands of Oz, with the Emerald City at the center lit up in a green spotlight. The innards of a giant clock, its cogs and gears, surrounded the map, suggesting an emotionally deadened, manufactured landscape.

I sat between Mom and Dad, as I so often did for Dee's performances, and as I had almost eight years earlier for the opening night of *Rent*. I felt those eight years; I felt older. There had been an innocence in me, an idealism back then that was now elusive as I sat before the stage and admired the set design. A couple of months had passed since I'd asked Jon for a divorce. I'd lost fifteen pounds—if the gentleman in the seat behind me had sneezed, the force might have sent me flying into the front row. At night when I lay in bed asking the universe for guidance, whatever divine portal had once brought me access to my purest inner voice had shut. I'd once believed people when they said, "God never gives you more than you can handle," but it was starting to smell a lot like *bullshit*. I'd believed "If it's meant to be, it's meant to be," *bullshit*. "Everything will be all right," *bullshit*. But the truth was that things could be worse. In fact, if someone had said, "It could be worse," I wouldn't have called bullshit. I was jaded. I knew it. And I didn't like myself that way.

But some things never change, like those potent minutes before Dee makes her entrance onto the stage. Mom's hand in mine, Dad's wide grin and glassy eyes, the heightened awareness of my heartbeat, and the way I shiver, a product of air-conditioning and anticipation.

I pictured my sister in her dressing room a couple of hours earlier, in the tiny bathroom with the toilet a mere foot or two from the plastic curtain of the standing shower. I imagined hearing her sing scales of "Ave Maria" in the steam, just like she had when we were children, back when I drew hearts in the fogged bathroom mirror.

This time her makeup artist would be there to greet her when she emerged from the shower. Dee had explained to me the lengths to which the makeup artist had gone to find the best way to transform her into the green witch. Initially there was experimentation with airbrushing, but then, after much trial and error, it was concluded the best option was to use a just-add-water green makeup by Mac. He used a wide brush with soft bristles from Japan, I'm told. Like he was painting with watercolor, he would dip the brush in water, then the flat paddy of makeup, and gently paint Dee's face, then her ears, neck, hands, and wrists like she was a work of art.

The lights dimmed. The orchestra began. The ensemble celebrated the "death" of the Wicked Witch, and then a bedazzled Kristin Chenoweth as

Glinda shimmered as she descended over the stage in a bubble-like contraption. She greeted the theater, "It's good to see me, isn't it?" Then, after an ensemble performance of "No One Mourns the Wicked," Glinda began to narrate the story of Elphie. Soon, Dee emerged from backstage, a bespectacled green girl in a dark blue beanie, her black braid draped over one shoulder. She wore a matching blue blazer, knee-length skirt, and combat-like black boots. She held a vintage briefcase. Everyone cheered. I wondered which was more exhilarating, to be Dee and take that first step onstage or to be me and watch her do it.

Her first song was "The Wizard and I." By opening night, I had already heard her sing the song a handful of times—once at the San Francisco tryout and a few more times during Broadway previews. But the first time I'd heard her sing it was so early in the creative process that she'd barely sung it before and it was still being shaped. We were in *Wicked* composer Stephen Schwartz's apartment. I'd never been there before, and in fact was quite shocked to be there at all. Stephen had written *Godspell* and *Pippin* and I hoped he wouldn't ask me about either show because, while I knew of them, I hadn't seen either.

We arrived at Stephen's door so casually he might as well have been my neighbor and I might as well have asked him to borrow an egg. But my stiff grin belied my anxiety. *Holy shit, I'm in Stephen Schwartz's apartment!* I tried to hush this thought at the risk of actually saying it aloud. Inside, I saw his black grand piano shine like patent-leather Mary Janes, standing regally against floor-to-ceiling windows, its lid propped open wide like a giant mouth.

After introductions, I became the proverbial fly on the wall—I literally leaned against the wall, my eyes wide. Stephen—I'll call him Stephen, but I didn't assume we were on a first-name basis—sat on the piano bench, and Dee stood next to him. He handed her sheet music. From a short distance away, I could see the music staff, the suggestion of a time signature, and notes sprinkled across the pages. Since my childhood piano lessons I'd retained little to no ability to play, except for the first few measures of the boisterous

"Spinning Song," which I found odd to have remembered of all the songs I'd played. Stephen played a chord or two, gently setting his right hand over the keys, the way you'd put a hand on a friend's shoulder. Dee started to sing, tentatively at first, tiptoeing over the notes of a relatively new melody. The tempo picked up and Stephen's left index finger bounced steadily over an ivory key and Dee began, "When I meet the wizard, once I prove my worth." Dee stopped occasionally to confirm or correct herself, at which time Stephen sang the part for her, and repeated the measure or verse for clarification. He wasn't a singer—his singing lacked beauty—but he had pitch and managed to land on each note accurately, even the ones he strained to reach.

I wondered what it must be like in Stephen's head. To hear the melody and to have chords play spontaneously from your hands. For a piano to be a living, breathing part of yourself. And to be a creator, to know the whole composition and define every fraction of music within it. To place Dee's voice at the heart of his art.

Dee gained confidence as the song progressed, but she wasn't perfect. When she came to the lyric, "No father is not proud of you, no sister acts ashamed . . ." the melody unexpectedly changed a bit and she tripped over it. He played the part again, but this time he omitted the chord and struck each note of the melody individually for emphasis.

Every now and then, they stopped and talked about the song. He was animated and spoke similarly to the way he played. He moved his hands through the air in sweeping motions or fingered an imaginary keyboard. Sometimes he rested his hands casually on top of the piano the way one might rest an elbow on the arm of a chair. I stood quietly, not wanting to chime in and say something stupid that I'd perseverate about for the next month. But mostly I was mesmerized. Before me were two enormous talents converging into a fixed point in the center of the universe—or, more accurately, the center of New York City.

The tempo slowed again, and Stephen's fingers lightened on the keys. He repeated the same notes over and over, a circle of sweet, twinkling notes, and then Dee sang, "Unlimited, my future is unlimited." The music had a magnetic quality. Dee's voice was crisp and lucid. Nothing hides in her voice. It's as if every emotion has a wavelength and she projects each one.

That night, apart from Stephen, I was the sole member of her audience, and I liked it that way. I felt special. Sometimes I struggled to be just one of Dee's many fans; though I wanted the whole world to be a fan of Idina Menzel, occasionally I felt possessive. There was still a little girl in me who wanted her big sister all to herself. But my selfishness was easy to override because I was proud of Dee. I knew she was meant for the masses. She was meant to be heard. How could you sing like *that* and not be heard?

Dee finished the final verse and turned to me: "What do ya think?" I wiped a fresh tear and said with a smile, "It sucked."

Back in the Gershwin Theatre, Dee was once again singing about how her future was unlimited. It was hard not to be aware that the fictional character looked and sounded exactly like my sister—even green paint can't conceal the broad sweeps of Dee's eyebrows, her dramatic cheekbones and jawline, her full lips. As I listened I remembered when my future seemed unlimited. A time when I had a long braid, wool socks, and was proudly counting the days since my last shower. I remembered how I used to light up with perpetual optimism. I felt young Elphie's optimism that night—if only briefly—and I missed the girl I'd been.

I squeezed Mom's hand as Dee plunged into the final verse, her voice growing into an explosive crescendo. I looked over my shoulder for a second and followed Dee's voice over a dense forest of darkened faces and into the mezzanine, then back to the stage where Dee stood, arms outstretched, like she held the entire audience within them. She was captivating. She delivered one final extended note that traveled through the crowd, leaving chills in its trail. I couldn't have been more proud. *That's my sister,* I wanted to shout through the subsequent uproar. *My sister!*

At the end of Act I, Dee sang the show-stopping power anthem, "Defying Gravity." Again, my mind drifted away from Elphie's story to my own, to remember Avery and Jacob and a future waiting at home too opaque to trust. "Something has changed within me, something is not the same . . ." Dee sang. "If I'm flying solo, at least I'm flying free . . ." I could relate.

As I listened to Dee, I realized that I was more comfortable with her when I was a member of her audience than when I was next to her just the two of us. The crowd that surrounded me mollified the tension I often felt when alone with her. I'd always wanted Dee to pay more attention to me, and yet it was so much easier when she didn't, when I could focus on her without having to work for her approval. From the stage, Dee understood me. From the stage, she inspired me. And when she rose over the stage and sang, "No one is ever gonna bring me down!" she silenced the victim in me. Through Elphie, Dee took my breath away and with it my grief and failure—at least temporarily—as only a sister—and Idina Menzel—could do.

Act I ended and members of the audience were still applauding as the lights came back on. Some people remained seated, some stretched, and still others squeezed through aisles toward bathroom lines and concessions. Mom, Dad, and I eavesdropped on a conversation between two women in some seats behind ours.

"That girl," the first said.

"Which one?" the second asked.

"Well both, but I meant the one who plays Elphaba."

"She's unbelievable, right? What a voice."

Dad stood up, rested his hands in his pockets, and scanned the crowd, hoping for an opportunity to boast about Dee—I knew his tricks well. This time he didn't wait for the opportunity, instead he turned around. "That's my daughter," he said to the women.

"Who?" they asked.

"The green one," he answered and then introduced himself. "Stu, Stuart Mentzel." Then it was awkward to keep our backs to them so Mom and I turned around and introduced ourselves, too.

I was proud, but embarrassed. I preferred covert spying during intermission, especially on the ladies' bathroom line.

I looked at Mom. "I'm heading to the bathroom. Did you need to go?" Mom knew this was code for *Do you want to come spy and see what people are saying about Dee?*

"Yeah, I was just thinking that," she said to me. "So nice to meet you," she told the women as we scooted out to the main aisle. Then Mom and I rushed toward the bathroom without a word, sweeping up fragments of conversations and as many Idina Menzel compliments as possible along the way.

Wicked was a triumph—in every way it exemplified the best of Broadway. From the costumes to the lighting and set design, the music and the performances, *Wicked* was fabulously entertaining.

That night, I was well aware that Dee was literally flying at a career high, and I didn't even have a job. I was aware that Dee's purpose had been reaffirmed, while my purpose was waiting for reinvention. And it's true that seeing how high someone you love can soar does magnify just how far you've fallen, even when you try not to look at the disparity between the two. I felt both inspired and inadequate at the same time. I wanted more for myself and I expected more of myself.

I don't remember feeling envious; with Dee, envy never had a sharp bite. I've always assumed that was because her happiness meant as much to me—if not more to me—than my own. The way my boys' happiness was more important to me than my own.

I remember Dee telling me that because the green makeup was prone to getting trapped in the folds of her ears and the creases near her nose, she'd negotiated biweekly facials into her *Wicked* contract. I was desperate for self-care and relaxation, hot steam, the smells of lavender and apricot, someone's gentle fingers tracing the orbits of my eyes and circling my temples. One facial would have been spectacular, biweekly would have been a dream. And so, while I'd been curious about the glamour and attention of fame, I was mostly envious of those facials. Relaxation and clean pores had far more appeal to me than fame.

It was a tough Christmas. I overcompensated for the boys' difficult autumn with a mountain of guilt gifts for Jacob and Avery: a book titled *Moon*, filled with black-and-white images of the moon, K'Nex Big Air Ball Tower, Snap-Circuits, bristle blocks, new train tracks, Hershey's Kisses, marshmallow Santas, gelt (leftover from Hanukkah), and Jacob's favorite toy, toilet paper. His preferred pastime was to sit under the toilet paper dispenser and unroll the tissue until he sat in its pile like it was his personal cloud.

My guilt was heavy during those months. I felt as though I'd been swimming in a down coat. I wished I could convince myself that finishing a relationship and failing at one were different experiences, but with Jon they felt the same. I'd failed at family.

One morning Avery told me what he'd do the next time his dad tried to hurt him. "I'm gonna go like *this,*" he said, and pulled his knees against his chest, tucked his head between them, and locked his arms around himself. "See?" he added, the word muffled because his face was still wedged between his knees. I told him he was brave but that he didn't need to worry because keeping him safe was my job. I told him that I'd messed up, but I wouldn't mess up again. "Okay, but just in case," he concluded and then uncurled himself and stood up with a big smile. He was proud of his plan.

I decided to go back to CU to earn my elementary-education-teaching certificate. The program was only a year-and-a-half long, and according to my lawyer, I'd likely get two years of alimony. Between alimony and the opportunity to take out student loans, there seemed no better time to return to school full-time and pursue a career as an educator.

It wasn't the first time I'd considered a career in education. A lot of my childhood role-playing involved teaching; I used to give spelling tests to my stuffed animals. I'd set them up in a semicircle on the floor around my chair and read that week's spelling list to a frozen, fluffy audience with unblinking plastic eyes. As an adult, I often thought that once the kids got a little older,

I could take some education classes. Dee really wanted me to. She was always coming back to that time I was a T.A. "You're a natural," she liked to say. "Why aren't you teaching?" I'd enjoyed the little bit of teaching I did in college, and I was good with kids. Teaching had been a "down the road" prospect, and suddenly that road wasn't as long as I'd thought it would be.

Also, Avery had struggled in preschool and the first half of kindergarten—and let's face it, no child should struggle in preschool and kindergarten. At the behest of the school, Jon and I had taken him for some testing and learned that he was a twice-exceptional student. The psychologist explained that in Avery's case, "twice exceptional" meant that he was gifted. "He hit the ceiling on the IQ test," the doctor explained to me, but he also had severe ADHD. The gifted part of his assessment wasn't a shocker. But having read more than a handful of articles on the overdiagnosis or misdiagnosis of ADHD in children, I was reluctant to believe the doctor. I still had a preference for alternative medicine and didn't trust what I deemed a mainstream medical diagnosis. "He's like a Ferrari without the tires," the doctor further explained. I appreciated the simile, it was helpful, but I was also offended by it. I didn't want anyone suggesting that my five-year-old was missing anything, especially "tires." Avery was too young to be confined to a label.

But diagnosis aside, it was evident that Avery would need an advocate at school and I wanted to be fully equipped to advocate for him. Becoming a teacher meant I'd be able to see behind the curtain of the public-school system. I'd learn what services were available to Avery, how to get those services, what role the classroom teacher played in supporting him, and so on. I wanted to know everything, official and unofficial. I wanted to help Avery and other kids like him.

In the more than four years I'd attended the University of Colorado as an undergraduate, I'd never set foot in the School of Education building. It was located on the western edge of campus off one of Boulder's main thoroughfares, Broadway, and across from the heavily student-populated Hill, with its student rental apartments, tattoo parlors, taco and pizza joints, and the Fox Theatre.

Eight years had passed since I'd graduated, and I was terrified to return. I worried that what I'd once excelled at, academics, had changed. That I'd show up with a pencil and a notebook and everyone else would be diligently typing notes on laptop computers. I worried that there would be a class of tanned and toned, blond and blue-eyed ski bum girls talking about the drinking they'd done the night before, and as the eager, older, single mother, I wouldn't belong.

Jon and I had only recently purchased our house, so it had no equity, and Dee, with a little help from Mom and Dad, gave me the ten thousand dollars I needed to sell it. I was relieved. I was ready to move on. But I was also grieving. I loved my home. I loved that I could watch the boys play in the backyard against the jagged skyline of the Rockies while doing the dishes, that the park was a two-minute walk away. I loved the tall ceilings and how the light found new windows to enter throughout the day so the house was bright until the sun went down. I loved knowing that I slept in the same room where Jacob was born. It was unbearable to imagine another person sleeping with our most intimate memories within those bedroom walls.

The ten-thousand-dollar price tag for my freedom was humiliating. Of course Dee wanted to help, but taking her money felt awful. Maybe it was paranoia, maybe intuition, but I still sensed that as happy as she was to be in a position to help me financially, I'd become one more thing she had to deal with, a phone call she was reluctant to answer, a tiresome rescue mission. But I needed her nonetheless. It would have been okay to need her for a hug or a pep talk, but *not* for money. Internally, I berated myself. I called myself a spoiled girl from Long Island. I called myself naïve and lazy. I wondered what other women in my position did without a sister to rescue them. Did they stay with their soon-to-be-ex indefinitely until there was a better offer on the house? I didn't know. I didn't *need* to know. I had Dee, and I was shamefully eager to take her money and be done living in limbo. Needing Dee's

Right: In my big sister's arms, 1974. This picture was taken a few hours before I was admitted to the hospital.

Below: Happy kisses.

Above: Family photo taken by Dad using the self-timer feature. One of many self-timer pictures from that period featuring his bearded chin.

Left: Sisters in footsie pajamas from Dad's work.

Above: Horseback riding at The Brickman.

Below: Dorothy (Dina in fifth grade) a long way from Kansas on a Long Island driveway. (Mom can be seen through the car's rear window. I can just hear her saying, "Stu, take a picture before she gets in the car.")

Left: "Tis Mabel." Dina in fourth grade.

Right: Dina, Syosset High School talent show.

Below: Dina with Mr. Roper in Baylis Elementary school.

Me, tap dance recital.

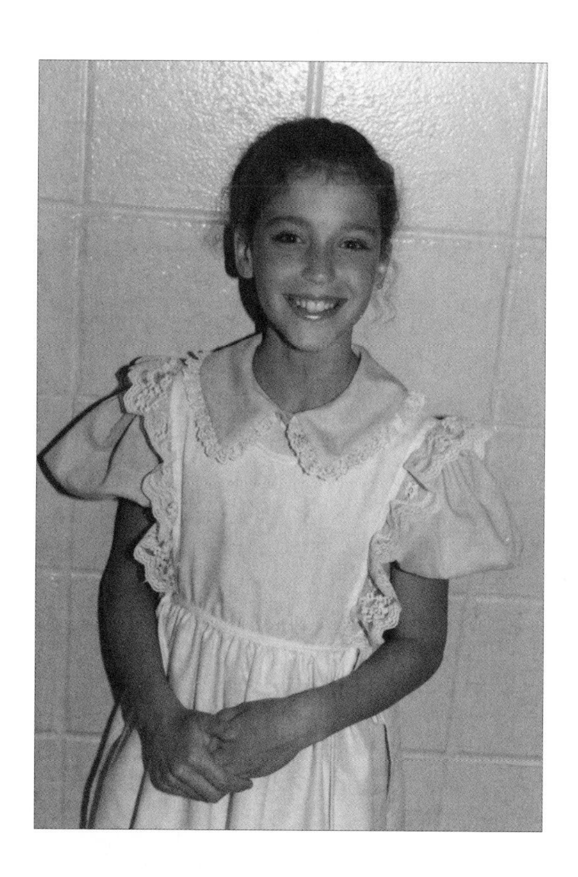

Me in my milk maiden costume for *Oliver*. "Any milk today, monsieur?"

Teenage Cara taking herself very seriously, clearly unaware that the cotton crotch of her Lycra tights is visible beyond her leotard. Classy.

Left: Dressing in our "coolest" digs for a trip into Greenwich Village.

Below: Dina and me after my Syosset High School graduation. Class of 1992.

Right: Rollerblading on the CU Boulder campus, 1993.

Below: *Rent* opening night party at Chelsea Piers. (From left to right: me, Dad, Dina, and Grandma Sylvia.)

Mom, Dad, and me on my graduation day, CU Boulder Class of 1996.

Left: This is what snuggles look like all grown up. Mom's couch, Thanksgiving, 1998.

Right: Karaoke, Montego Bay, 2003.

Above: In San Francisco for the pre-Broadway tryout of *Wicked,* 2003. (From left to right: Mom, Dee with Jacob, me, and Avery.)

Left: Auntie Cara with scrumptious little man Diggs.

Below: Colorado's gorgeous Red Rocks Amphitheater. Idina Menzel's Barefoot at the Symphony tour, 2011. (From left to right: Mark, me, Jake, Avery, and my stepson Oscar.)

Backstage after Dee's Oscar-night performance of "Let It Go," 2014.

The better—if you can believe it—of two poor photos taken of me in Dee's and my borrowed Oscar-night diamonds. (I'm trying to keep a straight face for my wannabe Sophia Loren glamour shot in the dark Escalade.)

Oscar-day glamour prep.

money was the ultimate admission of failure. Any empowerment that I'd gleaned from leaving Jon and making a fresh start evaporated whenever I remembered who was footing the bill.

Yet, thanks to my family, the boys and I were able to move into a two-story, two-bedroom rental at one of the University of Colorado's family-housing developments with a name that mocked me every time I drove past the sign: Smiley Court. When I first drove up all I saw were asphalt parking lots, concrete sidewalks, and brick buildings. Everything appeared cold and unforgiving.

Our unit had a two-step stoop and a fenced patio in the back. It was an end unit with a view and very likely the nicest one in the complex, but that didn't say much. I unlocked the door and was greeted by white cinderblock walls, the stinging smell of bleach, and a steep staircase that made my stomach flip when I pictured Jacob trying to climb it. There was a tiny kitchen, a lane barely wide enough to open the fridge, and a living room at the end of a small hallway. Upstairs, two bedrooms were set apart by one dank bathroom that had rubber moldings, and I couldn't help but wonder how many times a filthy mop had sloshed against them.

I looked into what would soon be the boys' room and tried to find a seed of optimism inside myself. I remembered my rationale for moving there. There was childcare for Jacob and a bus that could take both Avery and me to our new schools, his conveniently located right across the street from mine. The rent—though not cheap enough—was cheap. But the new place felt more like a shell than a home, holding only the stale memories of its previous residents.

I stared at the white wall in front of me and pictured a mural. In our house, I'd painted a mural on the wall in Avery's room. He slept under outstretched branches, like open arms, of a beautiful tree with leaves painted in warm browns, reds, and even cool, muted blues. I was proud of that mural, and as I looked at the blank canvas in front of me, I wanted to paint something for the boys, somehow.

The rental was a downgrade—no question—and I couldn't bring the boys there until I was able to face our new reality myself. I headed back to my car like a zombie and then sobbed in the parking lot—I sobbed in the parking lot of Smiley Court, and then, because it was too soon to appreciate the irony, I secretly renamed the complex Self-pity Court.

The last few weeks with the boys in our house were especially difficult. I was back at CU, acclimating to school as a grown-up and trying to get the house ready for the new owner. Packing was a challenge with a one-year-old. Jacob thought it was funny to drop little treats into open boxes of our belongings where I might never track them down again: keys, the garage door opener, the Candyland gumdrop card, a Sharpie without a cap, numerous pacifiers, and the occasional carrot stick or soggy biscuit. If I packed when Jacob was awake, my progress—or lack thereof—was dispiriting.

But packing at night, when theoretically the boys would be sleeping, was problematic, too. Avery wasn't feeling well. I woke to him screaming nearly every night. The first time, I raced into his room and found him curled up in a ball on his bed, crying. "My stomach. My stomach," he said. "It hurts, Mommy." The pain was recurring, so rather than get in and out of my bed all night, I stayed with him. I spooned him and stroked his hair off his forehead. He screamed during the day, too, suddenly doubled over in pain at the top of the slide or waiting with me for a table in a restaurant.

Two weeks after Avery's stomachache began, he was still struggling with acute pain. I'd taken him to the ER and to our family doctor. But no one could find anything physically wrong with him, and no homeopathics, herbs, or other alternative remedies worked either. Avery was suffering from an ailment that had no physical explanation, and Avery, of all the children I'd known, thrived on explanation. Even before his mysterious stomachache he'd been intrigued by the digestive system. At four years old he sat with me at the table finishing up dinner and he said, "I know there's only one tube from my mouth to my stomach, but sometimes I really think there's two."

"What makes you say that, boo?" I asked.

"Well, because I think there are two bellies—a protein belly and a sugar belly. Like right now, my protein belly is really full, but my sugar belly is empty."

One night after one of Avery's screaming episodes, I couldn't fall back to sleep. I made myself a cup of tea and sat down at the empty kitchen table. I looked up at the angles of our vaulted ceilings, then over the railing that I'd dusted daily, and then into the living room with the chartreuse accent wall—it took Jon and me weeks to choose that color. It occurred to me that the boys and I were moving soon and they knew too little about where their kitchen table would sit, where they'd watch TV, sleep, or bathe. I'd been remiss. Amid my tornado of a to-do list, my resistance to change, and my fear that the boys would be disappointed when they saw their new home, I'd left them in the dark.

The next morning I mentioned Smiley Court to Avery. I explained that our next home would be smaller and that he'd share a room with Jacob. I hoped he was too young to know that it was less desirable to share a room with your little brother than to have a room of your own, and thankfully, he was. I asked him what kind of mural he wanted in his bedroom and he told me he wanted to sleep in the clouds.

"Can you paint clouds, Mommy?"

"Sure, I can paint clouds. How 'bout a rainbow, too?"

"A rainbow!" he responded, the words so big he needed to throw his arms into the air to properly transmit them.

Motivated by Avery's enthusiasm, I took secret trips to the apartment to get his blue sky with clouds and a rainbow just right. Avery was still screaming about his stomach, and I was still leery of disappointing him and his brother, when I took them on an overdue visit to the town house.

"Boys," I announced. "We're taking a little field trip to our new home." They lit up. We loaded into the car and drove the twenty minutes from Erie into Boulder.

I pulled in to Smiley Court, slowed down for the speed bump, and made the first left turn into our parking lot. Avery hopped out of the car first.

"Which one's ours?" he asked, already running down the sidewalk off the lot.

"Keep going, keep going," I instructed, and walked around to Jacob's side of the car to free him from his car seat.

"This one, Ma? This one?" Avery shouted as he pointed to each one on his way to the end of the row. He responded to Smiley Court the way he responded to a visit to a new friend's house where he'd get to play with all new toys. The toys weren't necessarily better in someone else's home, but they were different and different was exciting.

Jacob followed after Avery and I shouted, "That one! The last one. That's it, boo. Wait there for Mommy."

We used our new key and the boys helped me open the door. We walked into the kitchen. It was filled with balloons that I'd secretly planted earlier. The apartment was still sparse, but with the boys there I started to see its potential. I pictured where I'd put the couch and television, Avery's train table, and all the toys and bicycles that would clutter the patio.

"Alrighty!" I declared with a clap and surprising enthusiasm. "Let's check out upstairs." I let Avery go ahead of me. I held Jacob's hand as he took his time with each step, looking up periodically to try to keep up with his big brother. When we walked through the door to their room, I saw the rainbow in the fluffy clouds; it looked good, really good. I gave myself a little pat on the shoulder as Avery said, "Mom, it's wrong."

"What do you mean it's wrong?"

"The red goes on the top. The purple goes on the bottom," and in that split second I realized he was right. *How in the world could I screw up a rainbow?* ROY G. BIV (red, orange, yellow, green, blue, indigo, violet), ROY G. BIV, I'd said to myself over and over as I painted. I'd been so focused on the order of the colors I'd neglected to pay attention to whether the sequence started at the top or the bottom. I did the only thing I could think to do, lie.

"No, sweetie. The violet's on the top, the red is on the bottom."

"No, Mom," he said, and if I didn't know better, I'd have thought my five-year-old was being condescending. "I can't sleep under a scientifically inaccurate rainbow," Avery insisted—and that's a quote.

I rubbed my eyes and temples and lied again. "I'll fix it." I had no intention of repainting the rainbow; I didn't have the time.

I walked to their closet and changed the subject: "Look, boys! A movie theater," and then stuck my head in the closet. To the left, two large steps were built on the slanted floor from the adjacent stairway, and spanned the width of the closet. The closet's profile reminded me of a mini-auditorium.

"Come on in here," I said and they stepped into the partially lit closet. I gestured to the opposite end. "We'll put your video player over there on the little end table, and set up pillows over here on those steps like seats. If you want it dark you slide the doors shut." I could see the pink creeping into Avery's cheeks and Jacob was already busy climbing to the top step.

Then we discussed the layout of the room. Where should the crib go, the bed, the dresser? Jacob, with his limited language and his tendency to follow his brother's lead, was amenable to all the arrangements. And so it was there, in front of a fucked-up rainbow, that the three of us stood together making plans, and I knew we'd be okay.

We talked about our new place the full twenty minutes it took us to drive home to the old house. When we walked in, I took out the chocolate cupcakes and ice cream sundae fixings, the colored sprinkles, whipped cream, hot fudge, and even the red dye number 40–ridden maraschino cherries. I gave the boys one index card each and colored pencils. Avery and I drew lots of townhouses that resembled our new place. I helped Jacob color in a house, then I cut out the houses, wrapped them around toothpicks, and stuck them into our cupcakes. We set each cupcake in a bowl and added all the fixings of chocolate decadence. Avery and I happily stuffed our faces until the remnants lay like mud in the bottoms of our bowls, while Jacob spread the slop all over the tray of his high chair and periodically tried to take fistfuls of cake and shove them into his mouth, his fingers splayed as he licked the palms of his hands.

Just when I felt sick to my stomach, Avery casually announced, "My stomach feels better, Mom." I looked up at him, chocolate covering his mouth and the greater part of his cheeks. "I think my sugar belly was feeling really angry, and it's not angry anymore."

I sighed and resisted tears.

"I'm so glad, Aves," I said, and then hoped to please my angry sugar belly with one more big spoonful of sludge from my bowl.

We'd lived in Smiley Court for a couple of weeks when I was saved by the charcoal sky of an afternoon thunderstorm. A double rainbow reached across the horizon and I noticed that its colors were inverted.

"Avery, look!" I shouted and pointed at the sky. "*That* rainbow has purple on the top."

"It's a double rainbow, Mom. The second one always has purple on the top."

"Well then, that's the kind of rainbow in your room." He looked at me as if to say "you have a point," then declared, "My rainbow is scientifically accurate after all!"

"Yep!" I confirmed with a sigh of relief.

I lay in bed that night and thought of my boys. I started to cry. This time it felt good to cry. When the tears dried, I fell asleep to echoes of my favorite lullaby, "Rainbow Connection."

Lesson 9

HOW TO *WANT* TO WIN

Dee wore a lavender gown with a deep V-neck and ruched bodice to the 2004 Tony Awards. Her hair was sleek, swept to the side across her forehead and pulled back into a bun. She was nominated for best actress in a musical for her portrayal of Elphaba in *Wicked*. She earned it.

The Tonys took place inside Radio City Music Hall, where, a decade earlier, I'd seen the Rockettes' famous kick line in the Christmas Spectacular. I was there with Mom, Dad, and my beaming grandmother. From my seat, the stage looked like the Looney Tunes insignia, a series of arcs, one within the other. The lighting was golden, and opulent scalloped curtains hung above the edge of the stage. Dee sat near the front with Taye, in a cluster of other nominees and their dates. We sat a distance behind them in the front row of a section toward the back.

Needless to say, it was a big night for Dee. She was a performer and a nominee, a common coupling at the Tonys except that Dee would be in full costume for her performance. This meant that she would spend hours with her stylist, hairstylist, and makeup artist for her walk on the red carpet. Then, only shortly thereafter, she'd rush to a dressing room backstage and undergo a full transformation into the green girl for her "Defying Gravity" performance with Kristin, who was nominated for the same award as Dee that night. At the conclusion of which, she would quickly—that is, before her Tony category was introduced—return to a dressing room and retransform into the beauty in lavender. If she won, Dee would be onstage that night as both Elphaba and Idina. It seemed the perfect way to honor both her and her work.

Hugh Jackman hosted the Tonys that year. I watched him kick higher than a Rockette as Peter Allen in *The Boy from Oz.* I watched him pelvic thrust for a few minutes in gold lamé pants with Sarah Jessica Parker. On any other night, the thrusting would have been the highlight of my evening. But alas, my sister was nominated for a Tony, and I couldn't sit there without reflecting on how hard Dee had worked for her nomination.

She had been starring as the third replacement for Amneris in *Aida* for months when she auditioned for *Wicked*'s Elphaba, and she needed a new job. More important, Dee was excited about the possibility of originating a role again and being part of a new production, like she'd done with Maureen in *Rent.* She loved collaborating and playing an integral part in the development of an interesting character and show.

Dee prepared for the Elphaba audition. She read Gregory Maguire's novel (I read it too). She wore green lipstick and a black pointy hat and she sang the stirring and melodic "I Know the Truth" from *Aida.* At the callback she'd prepared "Defying Gravity" but botched the high note. As the story goes, she went to hit the note and her voice cracked, at which point she shouted "Fuck!" Then she took the line again, this time without piano accompaniment, and nailed it. I've heard Joe Mantello say that's when he knew he'd found his Elphaba. But from the thrilling moment when Dee was given the role, she worried she'd lose it.

Becoming Elphaba had been a challenging and at times a grueling process for Dee. In the months between the San Francisco pre-Broadway tryout of *Wicked* and the Broadway opening her self-esteem and fortitude had been tested in a way few other experiences had tested them before. I understood Dee's struggle from conversations she had with Mom, Dad, and me.

During that time, the creative team worked hard on rewrites to build a stronger, more active Elphaba. Among other things, the green girl needed a sharper wit and a bigger heart. But that meant a lot of trial and error for Dee as new script pages arrived and she needed to perform them on the spot. She didn't feel cold readings were among her strengths, and the team's sense of urgency put a lot of pressure on her to get things right the first time.

Even without a changing script, Dee would have described her creative process as messy. To craft a part, she liked having time to digest her lines independently and to explore them in character with the cast. But that summer she was chasing a moving target, which made her process messier and more time-consuming. Sometimes she sat on the floor in rehearsals amidst a spread of new script pages. "I don't just feel like a mess," she said to me one day, "I literally look like one."

And yet Dee's feelings of inadequacy drew her closer to Elphaba, who struggled with similar worries. In fact, Dee and Elphaba were alike in many ways. Like Elphaba, Dee was afraid and ashamed of her temper. She hated that she could be hurtful, that she'd say things in anger that she could never take back. Like Elphaba, Dee's greatest strengths sometimes made her a target. Dee wasn't ostracized for being green or for her magical powers, but growing up she'd been bullied. Her voice was a threat to many a faltering ego—that of a girl named Laura Wellen, in particular. Laura was a year older than Dee and an aspiring singer. They attended the same schools from elementary until Laura graduated from high school. Laura's claim to fame was performing the national anthem at an NHL game. For Dee, getting a solo or a leading role, or just generally being exceptional, meant getting bullied by Laura. For Dee, doing her best—being her best—meant spitballs, name calling, and mean girls following too close behind. Dee may have been competitive, but like the rest of us—and like Elphaba—she also wanted to be liked. She was a fiercely loyal friend and worried that her talent, something she loved about herself, had the potential to alienate her from others. Dee's and Elphaba's greatest desire was to be their biggest, best selves and still be loved. (And let's not forget that Elphaba had her younger sister, Nessa, and Dee had me. They were caretakers.) In so many ways, they were kindred spirits.

But Oz didn't like Elphaba, and as Elphaba, Dee became a target again. It didn't matter that she was acting, it wasn't easy to have people shouting "Kill the witch!" at her repeatedly in rehearsals. And the first few times Elphaba got teased for showing up to the dance at *Wicked*'s Shiz University wearing a pointy witch's hat, it wasn't easy for Dee to dance surrounded by Elphaba's bullies, who also happened to be professional Broadway dancers with impeccable posture and enviable foot arches. (Despite years of tap, jazz, and ballet Dina didn't consider herself a dancer.) Dee felt as self-conscious and uncomfortable as Elphaba did. By that point, her self-esteem was so tattered she could barely tolerate fictitious rejection from a cast she knew and loved.

"It's like I have no defenses," she told me one night in tears. I wanted to hold her, but we were on the phone.

"But that's how he wants me to be," she added. She was referring to Joe, her director.

"I don't understand, Dee. What do you mean?"

"He wants me to be raw and vulnerable all the time. But that means my guard is always down and when he—or whoever—is hard on me, or questions my approach to a scene, I can't handle it. I end up in the bathroom, fuckin' crying." She paused and I couldn't tell if she was crying right then, but then she added, "I try to cry it all out so I can get back and focus again, hopefully."

To me, Dee had always been the embodiment of strength, from her athletic build to the way she persevered. But just then I couldn't imagine there was anything I could say to revitalize the strength I'd always seen in her.

"I'm so sorry." I could imagine how awful she felt, but I couldn't come up with my own words of wisdom so I offered up someone else's. "I have one of those cheesy inspirational cards on my bulletin board right now," I told her. "It says, 'If you're going through hell, keep going.' "

"Nice," she replied.

"You just have to keep going, Dee. And you can. You're the strongest person I know." It seemed all I had to offer were clichés.

"Thanks," she said.

In search of better counsel, I dug deeper.

"The thing is, if you have to draw on Elphaba's vulnerability, then can't you also draw on her strength, you know, when you're having trouble finding your own?" My advice seemed hokey and analytical, but it made sense and I was a little proud of it. "You are, after all, the girl who defies gravity."

"Maybe," she answered. By her gentle tone I gathered that Dee thought my idea was worth consideration, which brought me some satisfaction.

"Dee, if you can't pull this off, nobody can." *Ugh. Where were all the clichés coming from?*

"Pfft. Right," she said.

"I sound like Mom, huh?" I admitted, and she laughed. "You'll get there, Dee. I have no doubt you'll get to the other side of this and it will have been worth it."

"Part of me knows that," she said.

"Well, when you doubt yourself, know that I'm over here with the clarity you may not have, and I can see audiences falling in love with the fierce yet delicate green girl who can sing the roof off a theater."

"Thanks, lovey," she said.

"You're gonna kick ass. I'm sure of it."

Dee wasn't favored to win the Tony, and she felt conflicted about the possibility of winning. I remember Mom had told me about a meltdown Dee had had on the phone with her in the week before the awards. Dee had squeezed a blackhead on her chin and it left a crater—"a *huge* crater," Dee had said, in tears. Apparently some green makeup was stuck in it. It had been days and

Dee still couldn't get the makeup out. The stress snowballed and Dee was sobbing, "I'm ugly. I'm literally a witch with a big green wart. I shouldn't want to win. I'm too competitive. But part of me really does want to win and I'm scared to want it. I'm scared to write an acceptance speech. I don't want to be let down."

On this point, Mom offered some of what Dee deemed her best advice.

"There's nothing wrong with wanting to win. And there's nothing wrong with planning for it. How could it hurt?" Mom asked. "What's wrong with living in that joyous place and dreaming? If you don't win, at least you enjoyed the process instead of negating it the whole time."

The thing is, Mom and I were certain Dee would win. In one of her dreams Mom had seen Dee onstage with the Tony. But a little insurance couldn't hurt, and Mom also believed that positive thinking and imagery could sway fate. "See it as you want it to be," she often said to us, and sometimes Dee and I would scoff and roll our eyes. Mom believed that her prophetic dream paired with nightly visualization was the winning combo for the Tony. Not only for Dee but for all of us. "See the announcer say her name, Cara," she said to me. "Just keep picturing it in your mind." And so I did. Every night for weeks. It was easy. For me, Dee's Tony win was already a fact, a truth just waiting for time to catch up with it.

Dee speaks affectionately about Taye being very supportive during that time, too. One of her fondest memories of him was the night before the awards ceremony when he listened to her share her mixed feelings about winning and helped her prepare an acceptance speech.

Dee was flawless in lavender again, as if she'd never transformed into the green girl. She and Kristin had performed and were back in their seats when Renée Zellweger, who had recently starred in the movie adaptation of *Chicago* with Taye, and Rob Marshall, the director of the movie, walked out onstage to present the award for best actress in a musical.

I had my legs crossed tightly, as I'd recently been made aware that my gauzy black dress was transparent in flash photos. (Some people learn the hard way that nude undergarments are preferable to black ones when wearing black.) The top of my dress was a wraparound halter. I made sure that I crossed my hands over my knees, and covered as much of my breasts as possible with my upper arms. Excited and tense, I sat like a knot—legs crossed, wrists crossed, fingers crossed.

"This has been an extraordinary year for women on Broadway . . ." Renée began.

Mr. Marshall read the nominees from the teleprompter: "The nominees for best performance by a leading actress in a musical are . . ."

Suddenly I started to question myself. *What if she doesn't win? Picture her on that stage, Cara.* "Kristin Chenoweth, *Wicked*," he said. "Stephanie D'Abruzzo, *Avenue Q*, Idina Menzel, *Wicked*."

When he said Dee's name, the crowd cheered markedly louder than they had for anyone else, a good sign. I saw her face on the jumbotrons. She sported an uncomfortable smile. Mom untangled one of my hands and gave it a good squeeze. I peeked at Dad. I think he was holding his breath.

Mr. Marshall finished, "Donna Murphy, *Wonderful Town,* and Tonya Pinkins, *Caroline or Change*."

It was Renée's turn again: "And the 2004 Tony for best leading actress in a musical goes to . . ." *Idina Menzel Idina Menzel Idina Menzel.* Renée opened the black-and-gold booklet and lifted it so Mr. Marshall could see. *Idina Menzel Idina Menzel Idina Menzel.*

"Idina Menzel, *Wicked*!" they announced in unison. I was already sobbing when Mom and I launched out of our seats. Dad took an extra few seconds, clearly in shock. He covered his face with his hands, then helped Grandma up. Horns burst from the orchestra and played an instrumental excerpt of "No One Mourns the Wicked." A female voiceover said, "Idina Menzel takes home her first Tony Award . . ."

I watched Dee's reaction in the jumbotron. She absorbed the shock and maintained her poise. She leaned over the seat to kiss Kristin, who sat in the seat in front of her. Then she kissed Taye and made her way to the stage.

Ours was a loud row. We shouted, screamed, hugged, and proudly lost all our composure (so what if my Doogie Howser longtime crush was right over *there*). I clapped with my hands high in the air the way I did whenever I wished I could make them clap louder.

Is it possible for the best moment in someone else's life to double as one of the best in your own? Because that's how I felt at that moment. I was blathering-idiot happy. With the exception of holding my children for the first time, I'd never been happier.

Dee took the stage, and this time was different than other times I'd seen her onstage. She didn't perform. She wasn't in character. She was Dee. Gracious, humble, and beautiful Dee. She managed to remain composed. I managed to wipe the snot from my upper lip without anyone seeing.

She stood in front of the mic, the Tony between her hands. She wiped a tear from the corner of her eye and said thank you. Before she could say anything else, someone in the audience, an audience that by now was unabashedly cheering, shouted, "We love you!"

"I love you too!" Dee shouted back and swallowed. "I, I, I . . . am so proud to be in a musical that celebrates women. That celebrates their strengths and their differences . . ." She alternately held her hand over her heart and held it up by her head to help her pull from her memory the names of people she wanted to thank. She stammered, she giggled a nervous, overwhelmed giggle, she gasped for air, she cried. She was an elegant mess, and I loved her desperately.

With actors it can be hard to tell what's real. But onstage that night, with the Tony in her hands, the world saw my sister in her truest form. The woman who was still trying to tease apart humility and insecurity. The woman who wanted to win, but didn't want others to lose. Who was genuinely grateful and gracious. A woman brave enough to take the stage with no facade. I think people knew then—if they didn't already—that it was Dee's authenticity that came through and made her a good actress, and not good acting that made her appear authentic. Dee was more beautiful than ever that night because when she accepted the Tony, she accepted both her talent and her imperfections, her strength and her vulnerability, and in doing so she set an example for all women. I'd never been more proud.

She continued, ". . . and my mother, my father, my sister Cara, and my grandmother . . ." I heard my name. A few syllables in a run-on sentence filled with many names, but the sound of "my sister Cara," from her mouth, sent an extra spurt of adrenaline through my body. It was a big deal that she said my name. And I get that maybe it shouldn't have been. That I should have known she loved me and she was thankful for me without her saying it on national television. And I *did* know. Still, the honor of her acknowledgment on such a grand scale was significant. Hearing my name helped validate the pride I felt in her accomplishment. That I was a meaningful part of Dee's life. That it was okay I felt like I'd won, too, because of course: I was a part of her, and she was a part of me. And vicarious or not, it felt good to win.

Lesson 10

HOW TO MAKE MISTAKES

To a good girl from Woodbury, nothing says rock-bottom like a mug shot.

Jon and I had an altercation. Apparently, if the police are called to the scene of a domestic dispute in Broomfield, Colorado, where he lived, by law one of the parties must be arrested. I was at my wit's end juggling school, student teaching, and nearly full-time parenting. Winter break was around the corner and was supposed to be my saving grace. It was Jon's night to pick up the boys. He'd planned to come straight from work, but had forgotten the car seats. He asked if I could do him a favor and bring the boys to his apartment, a twenty-minute drive.

"I'm worried if I bring them to you, you're going to bring them into the apartment," I said. "And I don't want them to get sick."

Jon's brother was visiting from out-of-state and was ill. "My throat feels like it's covered in sores," he'd said to me on the phone earlier that day. But we still wanted the kids to see their uncle, so Jon and I agreed they'd go out to dinner instead of being together in the apartment, where the germs had been congregating for days.

Jon promised me that if I brought the boys to him, they would not go into his place. But the minute I dropped them off, he started to walk them straight in.

"It'll just be for a second," he said. "Don't worry about it."

"I am worried about it," I told him. "Because I'm the one who takes care of them when they're sick and I can't have two sick kids over winter break. I just can't."

"It's only gonna be a minute," he reiterated, then turned away.

So I waited in my car. And I waited. I took a drive around the block and then waited some more. I waited at least a half hour, my eyes alternating between his door and the squared digits of the car's clock. My jaw tightened a notch every time I saw a minute pass. When I could wait no longer, I walked up the flight of stairs to the landing in front of his condo door and knocked. I was trembling and as angry with him as I was with myself for taking him at his word, and so when he opened the door, I got straight to the point.

"Give me the boys."

"Uh, no." He raised an eyebrow and glared at me. I knew the look. It was the "you're crazy, you're overreacting" look.

"Why are you all still here?"

" 'Cause we're not ready to leave yet."

"But you promised." I felt powerless. He'd dismissed my frustration and ignored our agreement.

"It's no big deal. We're gonna leave in a minute."

"Give me the boys," I insisted. I'm guessing he didn't like me telling him what to do, because he got pissed.

"They're in *my* custody now," he said and tried to slam the door in my face. Instinctively, I put the toe of my sneaker and then my upper torso in the way. He drew the door wide open, grabbed me by the shoulders, and forced me backwards until I could feel the outer railing against my waist. My anger quickly turned to fear and I needed to get away from him. Without thinking, I freed my arm and slapped him across the face. When he stepped back,

I saw the kids in the kitchen and realized that they might be able to hear us, even see us, and so I gave up.

I drove home and sat in the car, in the dark, in the parking lot of Self-pity Court trembling. My anger and fear were inseparable, filling every hollow in my body, every corner, every crevice.

I was taking deep breaths, trying to purge the adrenaline in my system and calm myself down when my cell phone rang.

"This is Officer So-and-So from the Broomfield Police Department."

His voice roused a new kind of fear inside me. Not about my own safety, but about a loss of control, a fear of being more powerless than I already felt. He asked me to come down to the station. My voice caught in my throat.

"Do I need to be worried about something?" I asked.

"Your ex-husband gave us a call and we just want to ask you some questions," he answered. I was naïve. I'd forgotten all about the episodes of *Law & Order* I'd seen, the primary takeaway being, if you're ever arrested, ask for an attorney and then shut up. It only made sense to me that I could tell the officer what had happened and everything would be all right, that *I* could never be seen as the perpetrator. A sudden nausea suggested otherwise and I remembered something my divorce attorney had once said. He explained to me that I could have been arrested for pouring water over Jon's head a year earlier. When it came to the law, it didn't matter why I was upset with him, my actions were considered aggressive and whatever altercation we had that night would be deemed my fault.

I showed up at Broomfield's new police station around 8:30 P.M. After some questioning and writing a statement, Officer So-and-So arrested me. Apparently, Jon's passive-aggressive behavior was not a crime and I was culpable for our interaction because *I* was at *his* place. I put *my* foot in *his* door. The officer and his partner put me in handcuffs and a five-by-five-foot holding cell; I recognized the cinder-block walls from my apartment. An hour later they moved me to "processing," in another location. The space looked like most police stations on television and film. A long and extra-tall counter ran the length of the rectangular room. Some chairs were grouped together in a U shape off to the side and reminded me of a dentist's office waiting room. One officer shuffled papers and typed on the computer using only his index finger.

I waited in a mauve fabric chair with a monstrous headache, certain that my pain resembled what it would feel like if large screws were twisting through my temples and my skull was cracking at its sutures. I didn't want to cry in front of the officer, though he'd hardly notice. He'd barely looked at me since I'd arrived. Holding in my tears exacerbated the pounding in my head, and the fluorescent lights stung my eyes. I rotated my head slowly in an effort to loosen my neck and control my headache. I closed my eyes and tried to focus on my breathing, but it was too hard. I was destroyed. After half an hour, I stood up and stretched toward the ceiling. When I let my arms fall to my toes, the officer finally looked up from his desk. "Ma'am," he said. "Ma'am," he repeated, and I stood up to meet his eyes. "There'll be no yoga in here. Ain't no yoga allowed in here." He definitely wasn't from Boulder. Any Boulder police officer would know the difference between a P.E. stretch from elementary school and a sun salutation.

Instead of holding back tears, I was suddenly holding back laughter. I was a lunatic, ready to sob and still cackle at the top of my lungs. I sat back down and put my hand over my mouth until I was certain I'd swallowed my laughter. Arrested? It was laughable. Hyperbole. It couldn't really be happening. *Not to me.*

Eventually the officer "processed me" and reality couldn't have been clearer. I didn't know what "processing" meant exactly, but I quickly learned. I was checked for bruises—I didn't have any—fingerprinted, and photographed. "Don't smile," Officer Yoga said before taking the picture. *Really? He must be the life of every party.*

When I was allowed to make a phone call, I called Dee, who—this time—literally bailed me out. I remember nothing of the conversation. By that point I couldn't see straight. Even my thoughts moved in crooked lines. My head was splitting. And all I wanted was to be home with my boys, who, to no one's surprise but Jon's, ended up sick for the whole of winter break.

In addition to my bail, Dee paid for a high-powered attorney, the same one the Broncos hired to handle their domestic disputes. Hiring him was like hitting a fly with a frying pan, but I couldn't afford to accept even a deferred sentence. There's a tiny box on the application to school districts that asks if you've ever accepted a deferred sentence. If I checked the box, I'd never be a teacher. My record needed to be expunged, completely. And so, the frying pan. Dee saved my ass, again.

Having to enroll in anger-management class pissed me off. It was a small price to pay for a clean record and a career as a schoolteacher, but it was a waste of time, time I didn't have. I drove to some seedy building off the interstate surrounded by fast-food restaurants and gas stations. The designated room was filled with about twelve people. A few high school girls who had been in one too many catfights. A couple of drunks who got out of hand at the bar. A guy with meth teeth. A couple of "too cool for school" college-aged jocks. The teacher, a heavyset man with a full, dark beard and an irritating boisterous demeanor. And me. *Me.*

I tried to make the most of the class and think of something other than the circumstances that had put me there. I figured if I was going to be there, I might as well try to learn something. *We could all use a little help managing our anger,* I acknowledged. But the class was no place for my optimism. The highlight of the experience was the thirty-minute break midway through, just after we'd learned how to breathe deeply and count to ten. I decided to embrace the part of court-ordered anger-management pupil, so I picked up some Burger King, bummed a cigarette off one of the catfight girls, sat on the hood of my Subaru, and watched the busy highway.

The debris from those awful months lasted years; it still shows up sometimes. Occasionally, I wish I'd asked to keep a copy of my mug shot before they closed my file. I could have made coasters or calendars with the image—better yet, thank-you cards. It seemed there would always be something I could thank Dee for.

I couldn't stay in family housing once I'd finished my full-time studies. I'd been searching for a job and rental I could afford. I was pretty discouraged by my options. Then Dee called.

"I just got off the phone with Burt," she said, referring to her business manager. "I want to buy you a house." Dee fascinated me sometimes. She'd only recently insulted me for not having cable TV.

"You've never seen *Six Feet Under?*" she asked one day.

"I can't afford HBO, Dee," I answered, a little embarrassed.

"It's only like fifty dollars a month or something."

"Yeah, I know. I can't afford that. Besides, I don't have a lot of time for TV right now."

And yet, there we were on the phone again, not three months later, and it was clear to me that she definitely understood the extent of my financial struggles. I didn't know what to say to her.

"Dee, I can't let you buy me a house. I told you, I can't be a charity case. And I already am. You've done too much."

"I get that, Cara. I do. But you're not a charity case. I'm getting paid a lot to sing for a couple of hours at a bat mitzvah. I want to put the money in a Cara Fund," she said.

"A Cara Fund sounds a whole lot like charity."

"I guess, but that's not how I mean it. I mean that it'll only take me a couple of hours to make sure you and the boys are comfortable for the foreseeable future. It's not like I'm buying you a mansion or something, just a comfy little house."

I thought about the lowly thirty thousand dollars I'd probably make that year, before taxes and only *if* I found a teaching job.

"I guess they're paying you more than you used to make to sing at bat mitzvahs," I joked.

"Yeah, you have no idea. It's crazy. But look: I want the boys to have stability and a yard. I want them to have a home."

I started to cry.

"I want that too, more than anything," I told her. I covered my eyes and held my face in my hand.

"Then let's do this: I'll buy a house there as an investment, you'll calculate how much you can afford each month—I don't care how much it is—and then you can pay me rent. Does that feel better?"

"Yeah, it kinda does. But I know myself, I'll constantly be wondering if it's okay to buy this or that. I'll feel like I have to justify every purchase."

"You don't have to do that. I trust you."

"Maybe," I said. "But I'll worry about it anyway. And no matter what you say, taking your money gives you a voice in my decision-making and that makes me uncomfortable. You don't always like my decisions."

"Well, whatever. We'll figure that out later. I can't bear seeing you in a shithole." I couldn't be sure, but I thought I detected some impatience in her voice, and I felt bad. She was excited about her plan, and I'd put a negative spin on it. And that must have been hard on Dee. I imagined that if you're going to buy someone a house, you'd like it to make them happy. So I changed my tone to match her excitement.

"It *would* be nice to have a bedroom door that locks," I offered.

"I bet it would!"

"That's not what I mean," I answered, offended that she'd think I'd hide a lover in my room while the boys were home. "I don't do that when the boys are with me! The lock is for time-outs," I continued, "*my* time-outs. You know, like when one of the boys takes scissors to my ponytail when I'm squatted down in front of the dryer—and yeah, that's happened. Sometimes I need a place to escape so I don't scream or throw something."

"Well, that's that, then. You need a home," she said, "a home with locks."

"I know. And you couldn't be more generous. I'll start looking."

"Make sure it has a yard," she added. "A good school. And stop crying. I *want* to do this."

"I love you. I love that you want to do this."

"Love you too. Keep me posted," she finished.

I found a home in a town called Louisville, just east of Boulder and one of the top ten places to raise a family in the country. It was a good investment for Dee. It was a four-bedroom tri-level with a fenced-in backyard, on a corner lot. The neighborhood elementary school and local park were only a couple of blocks away. The only downside was the fake front lawn. When the pine needles fell from the evergreens it was easier to suck them up with a Shop-Vac than rake them. This made for a couple of embarrassing fall mornings with my neighbors.

Two weeks before the 2005–06 school year began, I found a job teaching third grade in Boulder. I'd have thirty students in my class that year. I was as overwhelmed as I was ecstatic. As inexperienced as I was determined. On the first day I locked us all out of the building by accident. A few days later at recess an untimely wind blew my skirt up to my waist. "Maybe you should get some skorts," one of my students suggested. "They're on sale at Target." And a few weeks later, I made yet another mistake.

I had an "open classroom." It looked like an unfinished rectangle with an eight-foot-wide opening in one of the walls. Through the opening, observers, parents, other teachers, other children, and administrators could watch everything my students and I did. They were afforded a good look at my blackboard and me, but only the backs—the bedhead, braids, and ponytails—of my third-grade boys and girls.

I was in the middle of a math lesson. We had deviated slightly from our unit on money to learn about the origin of the word "cent." I had just posed the question, "How many pennies in a dollar?" when three adults approached the entrance to the classroom. I recognized the first gentleman as the superintendent of our district, the woman next to him as my principal, and the last woman, whom I didn't recognize, I later learned was a board member in our district. I'm pretty sure my stomach was trying to climb out of my throat. Without warning, I was being watched by my boss, my boss's boss, and my boss's boss's boss. I was a bug under a child's magnifying glass. I didn't know if I was being examined or if I was about to get burned.

Lots of students had their hands raised to tell me that there are one hundred pennies in a dollar, but I called on the one student who liked to raise her hand even when she didn't know the answer.

"Alana, how many pennies in a dollar?"

"Uh . . . uh . . ." she started.

I grabbed a plastic penny, set it on her desk, and reframed the question.

"How many of *these* make up a dollar?"

She was a sweet girl who took her sweet time and by the absent look in her black eyes, I suspected we were a long way from an epiphany. Nonetheless, I knew that good teachers resist the urge to cut off students' thinking. Ample "wait time" is key to good instruction. So I waited as long as I could bear and then tried to move things along without making Alana feel bad.

"How 'bout asking one of your friends for help? Your neighbor Zach, maybe. It looks like he would love to help."

Zach sat there with his hand stretched high in the air and his butt like a bouncy kickball unable to stay seated. Still, Alana didn't want give in.

In the time she took to ponder the answer, my sons cleaned their rooms, my mother finished leaving me a voice mail, and teacher pay doubled in the United States.

"Zach, help a girl out," I said, finally caving.

"One hundred. There are one hundred pennies in a dollar," he answered correctly.

"That's right, Zach. There are one hundred pennies in a dollar, or one hundred cents. One hundred. That's what cent means," I concluded.

I would have loved to discuss a century or a centimeter, but I didn't get the chance. By the time I had another opportunity to subtly check on my visitors, they had disappeared. I let out a big sigh and turned back to face the board. I froze. Smack-dab in the middle of my blackboard, in large letters that could only have been formed by the most careful of elementary school teachers, was the word "penis."

Gulp.

A little later in the day I was hustling down the hall to the front office on an errand, and still shaking my head about my phallic faux pas, when I spotted the superintendent in front of the cafeteria. I had just determined there was no escape route when he approached me and said, "I saw your interview in *The Denver Post* this morning. You must have been very happy when your sister won the Tony."

I'd forgotten all about the interview and it took me a few awkward seconds to remember as he stared at me, waiting for my reply. The national tour of *Wicked* had arrived in Denver that week. Dee wasn't a part of the production, but days before my fateful math lesson, a reporter had called me to get a quote for an article he was working on about the show. I obliged.

"I was. I am," I stammered a little. I couldn't hear my own voice. All I could hear was "penis, penis, penis, penis" inside my head. "It was one of the best days of my life," I added and hoped he couldn't see through the huge superficial smile that disguised my relief.

The superintendent and I parted ways and I felt lucky. Dee could rescue me without even knowing it, without even being there. And thank God. As I walked into the front office I heard a little Bing Crosby playing in my head and I thought, *I guess sometimes clouds really do rain penis from heaven.*

Lesson 11

HOW TO MAKE HELLO DOLLIES

A few months into the school year, my grandma died. I loved my grandma.

Sylvia Mentzel didn't fit the grandma stereotype. She wasn't the gentle, petite woman with a falsetto voice full of princesses, parties, and lollipops. She wasn't fond of spoiling or doting. She was tough, tall, and big boned, and her voice was loud and nasal, with more attitude and New York accent than affection. Her feet were a size eleven, but that never stopped her from putting one of them in her mouth. She could be abrupt and insulting and had bad habits of eavesdropping and judging people harshly. She was more Bea Arthur than Betty White. She had almost superhuman hearing, but could say, "What?" louder and more frequently than most. And sometimes she shared things I wished she hadn't, while at other times she didn't share things I wished she had.

Grandma had been a consistent part of our childhood. Dee and I spent school holidays at her eighth-floor apartment in the Banyon building in Pembroke Pines, Florida, back when Grandpa was still alive. It was in their den that Dee and I watched *As the World Turns* by day and Pat Sajak on *Wheel of*

Fortune by night. It was there that we channel-surfed, punching the single row of buttons on a brown cable remote the size of a thin-mint box. It was there that we read our books and played Spit. There that Grandma brought us sandwiches for lunch and made us egg creams with U-Bet chocolate syrup. There that Dee and I slept together on the sleeper sofa, where she repeatedly insisted *I* had the softer skin. There that, left to our own devices on New Year's Eve, we snuck Manischewitz out of the fridge and shared a glass—rebels. And it was there, on the wall over the den couch, that she hung framed photos of family generations. The old-fashioned scalloped edges and blurred black-and-white photos of her parents, stunning photos of her and my grandpa in their youth, a series of annual picture-day photos for each of her four grandchildren, Andrew, Evan, Idina, and Cara—every lost tooth, new tooth, pimple, and hellish haircut memorialized on her wall for visitors to admire.

I had a few favorites. There was a pair of pictures, junior high–age Dee with teal eyeliner and third-grade Cara with an oversized pair of front teeth, both sporting matching checkered blouses with ruffled collars. And there was an eleven-by-fourteen-inch photo of my sister in an elaborate gold-leaf frame. She was probably five years old and posed preschooler-style with her hands folded over an open picture book, her silky pigtails accentuating the corners of her smile. When I thought of that den and those pictures, I knew there was more to Grandma than her prickly exterior.

Grandma would sit on a lounge chair out at the pool in her retirement complex and watch Dee and I play in the chlorine. We did handstands and counted to see how long we could keep our legs up in the air. Sometimes we stood in the water and stretched our legs apart as far as we could, while the other dived underwater and tried to swim through the triangular tunnel without touching. We also played lifeguard. "Help! Help!" I'd holler and Dee would jump in, pull one arm across my chest and wedge it under my armpits, then dig the other arm into the water to help her swim back to the pool's edge. Grandma watched and talked to her neighbors; "Those are my granddaughters. They're in town from New York," she'd say.

Dee and I used to give Grandma manicures. One time when Dee was around seventeen years old and I was fourteen, she painted Grandma's nails while I styled Grandma's hair—a daring proposition for Grandma in the late 1980s. I gave her a side part and used a curling brush and a hair dryer to feather her bangs across her forehead. I teased the hair by her temples out and back a bit for added volume, then I placed my hand over her eyes and sprayed one too many squirts of Stiff Stuff hair spray around her head to keep each strand in place.

An hour or so later, Grandma, Dee, and I were in the elevator with our towels heading down to the pool when in walked two silver-haired ladies, friends of Grandma's. After a brief greeting, Grandma motioned to her hair and proudly said, "Look what a great blow job my granddaughter gave me!" To which I spat a laugh at their distressed faces and slightly peed in my bathing suit. At least sixty years spanned their age and ours, but in silent milliseconds we came to a collective understanding about the meaning of "blow job." Dee and I locked eyes for the remainder of the elevator ride, as if that were the key to containing more laughter. When the elevator door slid open, we smiled stiffly and ran out to the pool. For the first time, I jumped in without first feeling the temperature with my toes.

When I started attending the University of Colorado at Boulder and the regular trips to Florida ended, I reached out to Grandma by phone. Sometimes we connected through her recipes. Her cooking represented heart and heritage to me. The family favorite was Hello Dollies, and the recipe was like a highly sought-after family heirloom. This is one of the few baked desserts that is better out of the freezer than the oven, and Grandma always kept plenty of batches in the kitchen for when her grandkids were around. She sent me the recipe, along with a handful of others, handwritten in her perfect script on yellow legal paper. Grandma was fluent in graham cracker, sweetened condensed milk, chocolate, coconut, and walnuts, all substitutes for the affection that eluded her.

We also connected through my writing. I had started writing in the quiet, nesting time of pregnancy with Avery and had since enjoyed journaling about my experiences as a mother. The first piece I wrote, "The Masterpiece," was anything but. The title referred to my unborn child and not my prose. To my surprise, a New Agey magazine, *The Tide,* wanted to publish the piece. *The Tide* was a local publication riddled with advertisements for massage therapists, hypnotists, herbalists, and, my favorite, an over-the-top horoscope section that I perused weekly even though I gave it as little credence as a tabloid. But I wasn't picky. I was happy—shocked, really—that they liked what I wrote.

"The Masterpiece" was about how babies build themselves from scratch with a divine knowingness in each cell. I suggested that if we can work with spirit in our own creation, we can certainly heal ourselves as we grow older. "There's a sweetness to healing," I wrote, "that comes when you experience yourself as divine."

I read the piece to Grandma over the phone. She wasn't a spiritual woman; she liked to cook the Passover Seder, and that pretty much summed up her relationship with God—at least as far as I knew. Yet, she was a generous audience. She listened in silence as I read every word of the article to her from the clipping I'd cut out of the paper. She never interrupted to say, *What?* or *I don't get it.* I didn't know if she liked the content, the sound of my voice, or that I had called and paid attention to her. But she attended to every word I read. "Beautiful," she said at the end. "That was beautiful, Cara." She looked forward to subsequent stories. I looked forward to making her laugh, and wrote some funny ones for her. Making her laugh felt like an achievement in its own right. When she laughed with me it was as if seventy years had evaporated and she was all child, all playful.

I tried to call Grandma the night she died. She was in the hospital in New York where she'd been a lot that year—for surgery, a host of tests, and once because her ICD (implanted defibrillator) went off in a restaurant. It knocked her out of her seat, stiff as a board, and frightened everyone, herself the most of all.

With each visit to the hospital Grandma seemed less likely to leave. And she knew it. She was fading, one willowy layer of existence at a time. Her voice grew quieter. Her movements slower. Her body thinner. And even her feelings became lighter, her brusque disposition softened.

I tried to call her in the hospital several times. The line was busy. Lines were never busy anymore. People had cell phones. They were either answered or sent to voice mail. I had a bad feeling. I was in the car on the way home from work—or maybe I was in a coffee shop, or picking up groceries for dinner—in any case, I was someplace inconsequential when Dad called. "She passed," he said in a voice so thin it bordered on unfamiliar to me. He held his breath to control the sobs, but it didn't work. He was still crying when he asked, "Will you write her eulogy? You were close to her. You're the writer."

"Of course," I answered automatically, as if he'd asked me to fetch him a tissue. My pat response hid the complexity of my feelings. *Grandma is dead? She was a phone call away an hour ago. And Dad wants me to write her eulogy?* I had never considered writing her eulogy when she passed, or writing any eulogy for that matter. "You're the writer," I heard Dad say again, in my head, and the words stuck with me. I'd only ever sent him e-mails of my short stories, stories of the boys that I thought he'd appreciate. I enjoyed writing, but that didn't make me a writer any more than my love of singing made me a singer. I'd never been "The" anything. Dee was The Singer, The Actress. I was a mother, but no one says, "This is my daughter, The Mother." And I hadn't been a teacher long enough to hear myself referred to as The Teacher. When Grandma died, I expected Dad to ask Dee to sing at her funeral, not to ask me to speak. Yet he did ask me. Within minutes of Grandma's death, I became Cara, The Writer. I didn't a hundred percent believe the title was appropriate, but I liked it.

Writing Grandma's eulogy was tough—tough like Grandma. I'd continued at CU for my master's in education and literacy, so not only was I a brand-new teacher and a single mother when she died, but a part-time master's student. Getting out of town for her funeral would be a miracle. I was also worried about writing the eulogy. I had to write something worthy of my father's trust and my grandmother's memory. I didn't have time to grieve. Unlike the stories I was used to writing, this one had a deadline. I was accustomed to deadlines on research papers and could hammer those out with the best of 'em, but writing and grieving, childcare and travel, and substitute notes and sleep deprivation made my presence at a podium at two o'clock on a Wednesday afternoon feel more like a crapshoot than a foregone conclusion.

In the early A.M. I stared at my pillowcase and formulated my thoughts. I thought of how much I loved her. I conjured memories and feelings, threads of Grandma, but nothing that tied together. In brief moments throughout the day I jotted down notes, but it was like writing with a pen that kept quitting—I had a thought, but couldn't capture it before it slid away. In the airport I had time before boarding. I sat alert, ready to get it done, but nothing came—plenty of ink this time, but no ideas. I told myself it would come together. *Please* let it come together.

On the plane, in a window seat, every thought lulled me nearly to sleep, my head giving in toward the window, but I resisted. I sat in near darkness, mine one of only a few overhead lights still on in the cabin. I stopped trying and instead let myself miss my grandmother. I hadn't seen her in almost two years, since the Tonys, but now that I would never see her again, I missed her in a way I hadn't before. I thought of her size and how diminished it was the last time I saw her. How happy she was tucked into a booth at a party after Dee won the 2004 Tony. I thought about the stuffed cabbage she taught me to make, and all those handwritten, stained, and wrinkled recipes that her hand had touched—that I could still touch.

I tried to cry quietly, privately. I held the sadness in my throat and let the tears loose. I liked that Grandma was abrupt sometimes, that after a long day she probably didn't go to bed worried what everyone else was thinking of her—the way I always did. I liked that in her eighties she still found occasion to put on lipstick. I liked that she was generous with her time and her cooking and that she never forgot my birthday. I liked that she'd faced her last years with grace. I liked *her.* Her sometimes-coarse nature made her a tricky woman to write about, but I decided it was okay with me that she was imperfect. I didn't need to make her perfect to write her eulogy. I would honor her with honesty.

I started to write. I wrote through the descent into LaGuardia. I wrote in the car. I wrote before bed in the strangeness of her apartment surrounded by partially packed boxes of her belongings. I revised in my head in the shower, made last-minute edits on the way to Gutterman's Funeral Home. I reviewed it in my head in between nods, hugs, and thank-yous, the words weighing heavy on my diaphragm while I wove through relatives, strangers, and friends.

More and more people arrived; could it be over a hundred? Two hundred? We all milled around while a shell of my grandmother lay in her dark, closed casket. I took comfort in the familiarity of extended family, my aunt and uncle, my cousins. My cousin Andrew would be sharing his thoughts first.

We sat down, Dee and Taye, my dad, his wife, Susie, and me. Andrew got up to the podium, read from his paper. He was choked-up. He talked lovingly about the attributes of driving with Grandma, and how back when he was a teenager, she used to listen in on his phone calls, and once found his pot and flushed it down the toilet. His voice grew distant even though I sat in the front row right in front of him. It was almost my turn.

The rabbi said my name. I thought instantly I would cry. I walked behind the podium. I used a shaky hand to set my papers down. I looked up at a crowd that filled more pews than I could quickly count. I fixated on the faces in the front row, Dee's and Dad's especially. I began.

I reminisced about everything from the stationary bike in Grandma's apartment that no one ever rode, to the afghans she generously knitted for her family and friends as she neared her death. Then I told my favorite Grandma story, my favorite because it said as much about her as it said about my father. And maybe because it said something about me, too.

Grandma never said "I love you"—at least I never heard her. I asked my dad once and he confirmed it, she'd never told him she loved him. Grandma and I had been talking regularly for years, and at the end of each conversation I made a point of saying "I love you" before we got off the phone. I'd say each word deliberately so she couldn't help but hear it, each word like I was baiting her, luring her into my comparatively lush emotional territory. But all she'd say back was "All right, hon," or "Okay, then," her polite way of avoiding the sentiment.

Until one day, she slipped.

"I love you, Grandma."

"Love you too," she said before she could stop herself. I was stunned. I didn't want to bring it to her attention and risk making her self-conscious, risk never hearing her say "love you too" again. Instead, because it was a breakthrough worthy of a celebration, I called the one person I knew would appreciate it most.

"She told me she loved me!" I said to Dad.

"Well that makes one of us," he joked with his squeaky laugh like a short series of hiccups. But I felt sad for him. The dad who used to sing me to sleep and scratch my back, let me dive off his shoulders in the swimming pool, and reliably shared his chocolate-covered almonds at the movies deserved an "I love you" from his mother. I was determined to make it happen.

Grandma's breakthrough wasn't a fluke. From that initial conversation, she reliably told me she loved me at the conclusion of every phone call. Eventually, I decided to push her a bit.

"Grandma, you're getting old," I reminded her candidly—as if she didn't know. "You need to tell my dad you love him."

"What?!" she said. The word climbed up an octave. "Ya fatha knows I love 'im."

"It's one thing to know, Grandma. It's another thing to hear your mother say it to you." She quickly changed the subject. I didn't want to make her too uncomfortable, so I let her. Then we got off the phone.

It wasn't but ten minutes from the end of our phone call that my phone rang.

"I guess you spoke to Grandma," Dad said, and I knew what was coming. He was already laughing.

"Oh, God," I said with my hand over my mouth. "What'd she say?"

He did his best Grandma impression and said, " 'What's wrong with you? You don't know that I love you?!' " We were in stitches, laughing so hard our stomachs hurt. That was the best Grandma could do, and for my dad, it was good enough.

From the podium, I said my final goodbye to Grandma. I'd decided to write part of the eulogy as a letter to her, what I would have said if she'd answered the phone the night she died. I shared the letter aloud. It ended with the following:

I've heard it said that we get to stand on the shoulders of those who came before us. We are afforded a better view, a deeper understanding, a clearer picture. Grandma, you knew I was standing on your shoulders, and though in some ways you had settled into the comfort of what was familiar to you, you had no problem holding me up. For that, for indefinitely lending me your shoulders, for being a model of strength, and for the tender, loving man that is my father, I will be forever grateful. I love you.

I looked up, finally able to take in the rows of faces, tissues, futile female efforts to save their makeup. I wiped my eyes and stepped back to my seat. Dee stood up to hug me. "You were so good up there," she whispered. Then she shook her head from side to side as if to say, *I'm speechless.*

Apart from my Bio Psych lesson in undergrad, that day was the only time I could remember her watching *me*. It felt like the only time I stood on a stage and she heard *my* voice, *my* words, strong and clear, despite my grief. Even though we were in the shadows of sorrow, my grandmother's casket several feet behind us, Dee saw me in a new light. In some ways, she saw me at my best. She saw me do something, well, right.

I was grateful for the solid pew behind us because my legs felt like pudding. Before the seat could save me, Dad hugged me. He was pieces of his typical self, and while his arms were all that held me up, I worried that my arms were all that held him together.

"Thank you," he whispered and cried. "That was perfect. I can't begin to tell you . . ." My hands were on his back, my head against his shoulder, and his breathing was choppy against my chest. With my arms full of his sadness, I had a strange awareness of a change in myself. A renewed sense of dignity. Finally, I wasn't the needy one. I wasn't the one leaning on others, at least not how I had been. I had something to offer. I'd given something meaningful to my father.

I sat down between Dad and Dee and I stared at the casket until its sharp edges blurred. I thought about Grandma, how we were a couple of hours from entrusting her body to the cold earth. How somewhere in that earth was moisture and nutrients and potential and maybe a seed that managed to sprout in its darkness. And I thought of my darkness, my failures, and my solitude. Everything that had died with my marriage: my hope and idealism, my faith and pride. I thought about all I'd been grieving, including Grandma. And it occurred to me that a part of me would be in the earth with her. That in her end was my new beginning. That she would be proud of me. Proud and still loud.

The service concluded. A distant cousin—my name for any relative within ten years of my age—pulled me in for a surprising bear hug.

"Have you any idea how many years of therapy you saved me?" he asked, with a big smile. I had the sense that I was getting taller. Like somehow I existed in a way I hadn't ten minutes earlier. Stuart's "other daughter" had a name and a face and left an impression. I felt like I'd earned a place at the grown-ups' table. That by acknowledging one void—the loss of Grandma—I began to fill another. The void within me.

How to Make Hello Dollies

Melt a stick of butter and pour it onto the bottom of a 13×9–inch shallow baking dish. Then crush a package of graham crackers into crumbs and pour those over the butter. Cover the graham cracker layer with semisweet chocolate chips, and drizzle a can of sweetened, condensed milk over them until the tops of the chips are sticking out like the bobbing heads of children in a swimming pool. Add a layer of coconut and a final layer of chopped walnuts. Bake until they're golden brown, gooey, and the layers glom together, about thirty minutes. Let them cool before you cut them and then store them in the freezer.

Hello Dollies are best when enjoyed poolside, during prime-time TV game shows, and after blow jobs.

Lesson 12

HOW TO ENVY

Dee bought me my first first-class ticket. She was starring in *Wicked* at the Apollo Victoria Theatre in London. I flew to visit her and to see the show. Mom and then Jon would take care of the boys while I feigned jet-setter, leaving Annie's Mac & Cheese, late-night reflective papers about my teaching practice, and my petri dish of a classroom behind. I looked forward to seeing Dee and to the time away. The kids at school and the boys at home had me feeling like a bag of dirty laundry. Perhaps that's why my first thought was what I suspected all good Jews from Long Island wondered when they got their first first-class ticket: *What should I wear?*

I refused to go the Ann Taylor route like I'd seen other women do on airplanes—tailored black pants and a pastel camisole under a cashmere cardigan. I never understood traveling in heels or beautiful fabrics that would wrinkle after sitting in them for hours or, worse yet, would get ruined when turbulence shook coffee or red wine off the tray table. I opted to prioritize comfort over style, and splurged on a lavender velvet Juicy Couture sweat suit that I believed befitted my brief stint as a first-class passenger. It was smooth and luscious like sorbet and for a brief moment I considered licking it.

I borrowed an ugly, kelly-green suitcase for the trip. It was one of those Samsonite hard-side retro suitcases popularized in the seventies, and since then more often seen in movies or TV shows than on baggage carousels. But it was hardy, with lots of organizational pockets inside and a four-digit steel combination lock for added safety. (The latter, of course, was completely unnecessary since I had already planned to wear the most expensive item I owned.) In short, the bag was a beast. The lender provided complete training on all of its attributes, how to open it, close it, all the latches, the bells and whistles, and the combination to the lock. I dry-cleaned my sweaters and stocked that doozy full of all my favorite clothes and boots.

I boarded the plane looking forward to my book, my window seat, and the fact that for nine hours no one would need anything from me. A friendly gentleman took the aisle seat next to me. He had a rugged appeal, was probably in his late forties, and quickly referenced his boyfriend. We enjoyed a glass of champagne together. When he inquired about the purpose of my trip, I was simply too excited to withhold the information. I gushed, my disposition like the champagne, bubbly and effervescent.

"My sister's starring in *Wicked* on the West End."

"Oh, really? Who's your sister?" he asked.

"Idina Menzel."

"Wow. She's terrific. How exciting."

"It is. I can't wait to see her."

He didn't seem overly impressed and I quickly learned that he much preferred to talk than to listen. He really liked to name-drop, apparently he was BFF with Emma Thompson—one of my all-time favorite actresses—and for a split second I worried that after meeting me, maybe he would say he was BFF with Idina Menzel, too.

What he liked more than talking or name-dropping was drinking red wine. By the time dinner was over, his animated arms were swinging around as he told his loud stories. I lost track of how much he had to drink. The flight attendant kept looking over to check on me, but I was trapped, sandwiched between his flailing arms to my right and the window to my left. Inevitably, he knocked over his wine—yes, on the velvet.

He bobbled out of his seat, flagged down the stewardess to ask for a rag, apologized several times, and, while he was at it, requested another drink to replace the one that was currently in my lap. Fortunately, the stewardess refused to give him any more. He then tried to complain about her to me and I pretended I was asleep until, indeed, I was asleep.

I was relieved when my hungover seatmate and I were able to go our separate ways at the baggage claim. Fortunately, my green suitcase was one of the first bags on the luggage carousel and stood out like Elphaba at Shiz. I made a quick exit to the curb before my seatmate could suggest we share a cab. Dee had ordered a car to meet me at the airport and take me to her place and I wasn't about to bring him along.

She was staying in an apartment, part of an extended-stay hotel-type establishment. After a short drive and more roundabouts than I'd seen in my lifetime, the driver opened my door and helped me out. He was kind enough to walk my suitcase up a long flight of stairs to the second-floor apartment, where Dee had the door open for me.

"Hey!" she said and gave me a hug. "I'm not gonna kiss you. I might be coming down with something."

"Oh no."

"How was your flight?" she asked.

"Great! Thanks for the ticket. They gave me an eye pillow and earplugs, even my own toothbrush!" I said nothing about the wino. The stewardess and I had worked diligently with a rag and seltzer water to minimize the stains. I didn't want Dee to know that first class had been tainted by her new best friend—and Emma Thompson's. I followed her into the apartment and she gave me a tour.

There were three bedrooms and mine had two twin beds in it. There was a stately living room with a long, floral-printed couch with claw feet, end tables, lamps, and a large coffee table. I could hardly imagine Dee needing that much space, but she'd be there for a total of six months and was expecting guests periodically. On the way to the kitchen there was an elegant dining table with room for ten settings, and Dee had a few things piled on the corner, mostly paperwork, including a script lying on a large manila envelope. The kitchen was impressive, with marble countertops and all the fixings of a remodel, but apart from the hot pot for Dee's tea, it looked largely unused.

We both went down for naps. We usually napped together, but given that she was trying to avert a sore throat and was waiting for the doctor to call her back, we decided to sleep apart. I shut the blinds over my window, pulled back the crisp white duvet cover, and slid into the fresh sheets. My mind was racing for a few minutes, wondering what the plan was for that evening, when I would see the show, if we'd go out after for a bite with the cast, and if Dee would feel better. Any respiratory infection was stressful for Dee. She once explained to me how she knew which notes she'd be able to sing depending on where the mucus was building up and where she was swollen. With high accuracy, she could determine whether or not she would be able to modify her performance or if her understudy would need to go on in her place. I had no idea she could map out her voice with such precision and I was thinking about how it all worked when I fell asleep.

I woke up disoriented. It took a second to remember where I was, and I had no idea how long I'd been sleeping. I'm sure it had something to do with jet lag. With the blinds shut I couldn't tell whether it was day or night and whether I'd been asleep for one hour or whether it was the following morning. I opened my door and didn't see Dee. I walked through the kitchen, noted the time on the microwave, nearly 4:40, and judging by the light in the apartment it was 4:40 P.M. I moved toward her bedroom door, but it was closed. I didn't want to wake her so I opted to unpack.

Back in my room, I approached my suitcase, then knocked it onto its side. I rotated the little golden numbers with a fingernail until they read the correct code. I pushed the button and pulled the silver latch. Nothing happened. I tried the button and the latch at the same time. Nothing happened. I fiddled with the numbers a little to make sure they were perfectly aligned, tried a different code, and called back to the United States to confirm the code. Nothing happened. The suitcase wouldn't open.

I was pissed. I never liked to be an imposition when I visited my sister, especially when she was working. Every performance was important to her. She hated to miss a show and let her fans down. She kept a strict schedule. She slept well, drank tea, took steam showers, and depending on how she was feeling or how many shows she had to do in a given week, she was often on "vocal rest," meaning she barely talked. Over the course of our lives she'd made exceptions for me and we'd had a handful of brief, whispered conversations over the telephone. I liked to think of those chats as tiptoe talking. But I still worried that when I visited Dee while she was working, she felt responsible for entertaining me. Of course she wasn't. Mostly, I traveled to see her perform, to snuggle with her, and to hear her siren. The latter was one of my favorite things about her. She'd roll her voice from low to high and back down again—out of the blue. Occasionally she'd apologize for the loud, unexpected sound, as if she'd burped at a dinner table. Sirens were classic Dee and always endearing.

But there I was in London with my big green problem. I called the front desk and described my dilemma. A kind female voice with a British accent said, "We'll send someone right over." I thought that perhaps this wasn't the first time they'd been called to an apartment to help open a suitcase. Within fifteen minutes a maintenance man showed up with a big red toolbox. He was a bulky chap who clearly took pride in working out his biceps before he went to work in the morning, and he had a sympathetic smile. When the front desk said they'd send someone, I'd thought someone would show up with an elegant gold master key or pick. But he set his toolbox on the dresser with a clunk and took out a crowbar. He was focused on the suitcase so he couldn't see how my eyes widened when he withdrew that hunk of metal and took it to the luggage. I wasn't sure if he was going to open the bag or whack it until it cracked. He wedged the crowbar into the slit between the metal lock and the plastic case, like a knife in a stubborn clamshell. He rocked it back and forth, back and forth.

He pried that bag open in under a minute. (Funny thing, I hadn't once considered that the damn suitcase wasn't mine.)

"Well there you go," he said, back on his feet, standing over the bag.

At that moment, I was grateful for two things. One, that teaching elementary school had given me plenty of practice holding my tongue when I wanted to shout a string of cuss words. And two, that the look of shock on my face could easily be mistaken for delightful surprise. I was too embarrassed to let him know that he'd just broken into someone else's suitcase.

"Nice work!" I said and forced a smile. "Thank you so much."

I couldn't get him out of the apartment fast enough. I closed the door behind him and then stood over someone else's floral dresses, underwear, scarves, beige pumps, and bras with cups so big I'd need a third breast to fill even one. Still a little foggy with disbelief, I got down on the floor and sat cross-legged in front of it. I nudged a pair of light pink classic briefs to the side with the backs of a couple of fingers. The possibility that someone else on my flight owned the very same suitcase was unbelievable to me. A black duffel bag or a floral set with rollers, sure, but this beast, no way. And yet it was true. The frickin' bag wasn't mine.

I learned that Dee wasn't napping behind her closed bedroom door when she called from the theater to check on me. I was scared to tell her about my luggage and felt a familiar twisting in my gut. I didn't want to hear her reaction, the irritated sigh. The "Ca-ra." I didn't want to be a problem, so I decided not to tell her until I'd called the airline and worked out a plan.

According to the airline representative, I needed to get the bag safely shut again, take a train back to the airport with it, and lug it to some special customer service/baggage-claim desk where they'd swap one ugly green bag for the other. Then I'd hop back on a train with my real suitcase and return to Dee's.

Dee's reaction was as I had suspected. She stood in the doorway of my room where the evidence lay untouched—apart from one pair of underwear.

"Ca-ra."

"I know. I'm sorry," I said. "But did you see my bag? Who would have thought it had a twin?"

"I just don't understand why these things happen with you," she started. "How you can take care of two boys by yourself, pull off camping trips every summer, and chaperone thirty third-graders on a field trip, but take the wrong suitcase?"

"I know. I mean, I don't know. I was rushing. I didn't double-check. I'm sorry."

Another sigh.

"It's no biggie, though," I assured her. "I'll hop on the train and take care of it tomorrow."

"No, I'll take you. I don't want you traveling around London by yourself."

"Seriously, Dee. I don't need an escort. You don't feel well. I'm a grown-up. I may have taken the wrong fuckin' bag, but I can certainly return it on my own."

"You don't know the city. I'm coming with you," she insisted. And because arguing with Dee would only annoy her more, I complied.

So, I sat in that room feeling like a child in need of supervision, rather than a thirty-two-year-old woman and mother of two. The old insecurity returned and, like I'd done many times before, I pondered the irony—that the strong, confident woman she wanted me to be, I was more likely to be in her absence.

I wished I could believe that Dee insisted on joining me for the round-trip excursion to Heathrow because I'd flown over the pond to be with her and she wanted to take advantage of every minute we had together. But I doubted that was true. I felt sad and lonely, very likely the opposite of how

Dee wanted me to feel. I wanted to be Dee's equal, to take care of her as much as she took care of me. I imagined tickling her arm, making her tea, and finding us a good movie to watch. Instead, we'd be schlepping that stupid bag back to the airport when she should be at home resting.

The next day we boarded the train to the airport. I set the suitcase against the scuffed wall by the window seat and we sat down. Dee scanned the train car looking for evidence that we were on the right one. When she spotted a conductor on the platform, she hopped up, tossed her purse on my lap, and popped out the door to verify the train's destination.

The doors shut behind her. Of course they did!

Dee didn't actually say *You've got to be kidding me* as we stared at each other on opposite sides of the glass, but I'm certain that's what went through her mind. That and, *Fuck! Cara has my purse and my phone.* If I wasn't the pain-in-the-ass little sister before, I definitely was then.

London swept past through the windows. A rhythmic *foomp, foomp, foomp* sounded beneath me. And I hoped that not too far behind, my sister sat on another train watching the same landscape race by. It seemed I was destined to screw up with Dee every time. Like somehow my anxiety created static interference around me, a blip in my personal natural order. I wasn't quite myself with her and I didn't know how to change that. With Dee, I became the sister with the problems, and she became the sister with the solutions. Suddenly, I felt certain that had she not been a part of that trip to London, had I gone simply to visit a friend, I would never have taken the wrong bag off the luggage carousel. Nothing was Dee's fault, of course, but it was clear to me that she and I had grown accustomed to the roles we played in our relationship, and we'd yet to figure out how to escape them.

I tried to remember a time when I took care of Dee. It was the last time she was green. Dried tears had left tracks in her Elphaba makeup. She was in the emergency room. It was the afternoon of her third-to-last *Wicked* performance on Broadway after nearly two years as Elphaba. I'd come into town to see her last show.

Eight times a week during Act II a trapdoor opened in the stage floor. Dee took three steps sideways in the dark, stepped on the plank, and descended—"melted"—beneath the stage. After hundreds of successful performances, the trapdoor opened too soon. It lowered beneath the stage without Dee. She stepped in the dark into the hole that remained and fell through the floor until she caught herself by the armpit and elbow. According to Dee, the fall knocked the wind out of her. She couldn't breathe. She thought she was dying.

There was a flurry of activity in the lobby of St. Vincent's Midtown Hospital. The check-in area was filled with her managers, agents, friends, her dresser, Joby, Taye, Mom, and me. Some paparazzi loomed outside the ER's sliding doors.

When Dee first arrived, there had been a kerfuffle removing her costume. The value of her black Act II dress was estimated at sixteen thousand dollars. Dee was in excruciating pain and could barely move. She wanted the dress cut off her, the way street clothes would have been under different circumstances, had she fallen as Idina Menzel and not Elphaba. But there was a consensus among the staff at the hospital and representatives from the production that they should try to save the dress. Dee lay on a gurney in her wig and shoes, her microphone and its wires still taped to her bra, while a gaggle of people fussed over her to remove the dress.

By the time Mom and I sat next to Dee in the ER, she was in a hospital gown, her hair a flattened mess with a couple of loose bobby pins, and she still had green hands, wrists, nails, ears, neck, and face. We sat with Dee unamused as a few distracted and giddy nurses spoke in shout-whispers just beyond her cot to tell each other, "That was Taye Diggs!"

Dee had broken a rib and could barely take shallow breaths. Until the morphine kicked in, she tried not to move. She was devastated. She was looking forward to her final performance the following day and it was evident she wouldn't be able to perform. She was also due to begin filming the *Rent* movie in two weeks. She would need to perform "The Tango Maureen" and could hardly imagine being up to the task. She was angry, worried, sad, and traumatized . . . and green.

"I'm still fuckin' green," she said, her voice scratchy but soft and her eyes full of another round of tears. I borrowed a couple of hand towels and a small basin of warm soapy water from the nurses. Mom and I took turns gently wiping Dee's face.

"It's no use," Dee whispered to us. "For some reason, it only comes off with a full shower and Neutrogena soap."

"We'll get it off, most of it anyway," I told her as Mom pulled Dee's hair out of the way and I dipped a white towel in the warm water, folded it like a compress, and lay it across Dee's forehead. After a minute I wiped what I could from her temples, brows, and forehead. By the look of the towel, it appeared I'd removed a significant amount of makeup, but she still had a green glow and there were traces of green makeup that had collected around her brows and the orbits of her eyes. It crossed my mind that in removing the makeup I was helping Dee say goodbye, one layer at a time, to the green girl she'd loved so much.

"Close your eyes," I said softly. I wet the towel again and ran it over her brows one more time, then down the bridge of her nose, pressing the covered tip of my index finger into the crevices along her nostrils, and then, finally, under the tip of her nose into the sloping valley above her upper lip. I couldn't remember a time when Dee had needed me. I hated that she was wounded, but I took pleasure in taking care of her and I felt a little guilty about that.

Taye had joined us when the doctor approached and said it was okay for Dee to put her clothes back on and head home.

"Uh, my wife arrived in a witch's costume, remember?"

Dee left the hospital high as a kite, in oversize scrubs cinched loosely at the drawstring, with several of us huddled around her to keep paparazzi at bay.

The following day, Dee agreed to make an appearance at what was supposed to be her final *Wicked* performance on Broadway. She could barely move or project her voice, and was on painkillers, so Taye went shopping to find something loose and comfortable Dee could easily get into and wear to the theater. He returned home with a red Adidas tracksuit. Mom and I helped pull Dee's hair into a tight ponytail and put a little makeup on her.

I still don't know how Dee managed to get on the Gershwin stage that night, but it doesn't surprise me that she did. Maybe she did it because she felt pressure from the producers, or didn't want to disappoint her fans—some of whom had flown hundreds of miles to see her—or maybe she did it for herself and the cast and their sense of closure. Knowing Dee, it was for all those reasons.

I watched from an aisle seat in the audience as Dee took the place of Shoshana Bean, the understudy, and stepped out onstage in her red tracksuit to perform Elphie's last scene in the show with Fiyero, her good friend and New Kid on the Block Joey McIntyre. The audience instantly rose to their feet with thunderous applause, whistles, squeals, and shouts of "We love you, Idina!"

I clapped and cheered with them, tears streaming down my cheeks and down my neck because I couldn't stop myself from clapping for even the second it would take to wipe them. The standing ovation was long. Every time the applause waned, someone shouted and initiated a new round of cheers. It must have gone on for over five minutes. The theater was filled with gratitude and love and it was all directed at my sister.

Dee and Fiyero finished their scene. Dee was stiff and cautious, but that made her all the more lovable. As generous as it was of her to climb out of bed and get on that stage, the night was less about what Dee had to offer and more about the gratitude her fans and peers had the chance to show her. For sixteen months her portrayal of Elphaba had helped marginalized people of all ages feel strong and significant, and they loved her. I understood how they felt. In that huge packed theater, there was an intimacy, people bonded together in their affection for Dee. It was a crazy, ridiculous moment. She should have been in bed. Instead she was onstage. She was in a red tracksuit—in itself a random selection. She was transparent, both Elphie and Idina. And most notably, barely able to speak—no less sing—she was almost without the voice that had brought her there. I was one of two thousand in the theater that night who loved Dee, but shortly I'd be in a car with her, headed back to her place. I'd settle her back into bed, get the icepack, the medicine, and the remote. "What do you wanna watch?"

I was holding Dee's black leather purse and the busted green bag when the train arrived at the airport. I waited on the platform for her. In less than five minutes she stepped off the next train and ran a hand across her forehead.

"Here," I said and handed her the purse.

She shook her head and finally smiled. "Let's get this over with."

The suitcase was an exact match for the one we returned—apart from the damage I'd done to the lock. The whole mess took only a few hours—albeit a few hours too many.

After the suitcase fiasco, my time in London with Dee improved. I saw the show—which was, in my opinion, of equal caliber to the Broadway production. Dee and I went out with the cast a couple of times for food and drinks. Once we were rejected from a nightclub because Lindsay Lohan was partying inside. Helen Dallimore, the West End's original Glinda, and a new, dear friend of Dee's, looked at the bouncer and said something like, "Lindsay Lohan? Pfft. Do you know who *this* is?" and gestured toward Dee, at which point Dee got embarrassed and we moved on. Dee and I spent a lovely afternoon at the National Portrait Gallery together. We shared tea and scones and clotted cream with a view of Trafalgar Square, the Houses of Parliament, and Big Ben. We talked, a lot. Our lives were complicated. Things were good in London, but she and Taye were dealing with the challenges of a long-distance relationship. I loved my job and my boys but was hopping from one unsuccessful relationship to the next. The good and the difficult were ceaselessly twisted together. Rarely was there a moment of pure ease or joy. Yet we both had so much to be grateful for, including the fact that—even if only briefly—we were together.

When it was time for me to go home, I packed up *my* suitcase. Could it have been a more glaring symbol of my relationship with Dee? I wondered. It was, after all, baggage. It was a symbol of every time I sought Dee's attention or approval, when I rehearsed with her for my first audition with Mr. Roper, when I sat with the *Rent* script on my lap, unable to interpret its metaphors, when I sang "Rainbow Connection" to Avery and she overheard. That monstrosity of a suitcase was wedged between us. It symbolized the time it took Dee to return phone calls, the miles between Denver International Airport and LAX or LaGuardia, and the distance between the stage and my seat. It represented our caretaking dynamic, the residue of her resentment and my shame. That suitcase was a cataclysmic reminder that with Dee I was the little sister, I'd always be the little sister. Whether I liked it or not, I couldn't help but play the part. Against all evidence of my independence and competence, despite Dee's admiration and love, I'd always feel littler than her. What is it about family dynamics that they persist no matter how we evolve or our lives change around us?

As if that bag weren't hard or heavy enough, it was goddamn green! Not just a green reminiscent of Peter Pan's ragged clothes, or Elphaba's skin, but green like envy. There was lots one could envy about Dee—a standing ovation, for instance, had to be pretty fuckin' great—but in the end, what I envied was the way she always seemed to be the strong sister, the successful sister, the save-the-day sister, the sister I rarely had the chance to be.

I wanted that chance.

PART IV

LETTING GO

Lesson 13

HOW TO LIVE

Life was full during the 2008–09 school year. The boys were growing up. Avery was ten and Jacob was six—he'd recently decided he preferred to be called Jake. I had a few years of teaching under my belt. I'd moved on from misspelling "pennies" to this:

"No, it's not "h-a-p-p-y-n-e-s-s," one of four multiple-choice options. "You have to drop the 'y' and add an 'i.' " Then I wrote the correct spelling on the overhead projector for my class and said, "See, 'ha-PEE-nis' " as I ran my pen under the word, emphasizing the second syllable. The giggles started immediately and I realized my mistake, but it was too late. Garret, with whom I couldn't get away with anything, embellished my mishap: "Miss Mentzel just said 'happy penis,' " and everyone laughed. *What is my problem with penises!* Like any skilled teacher, I sent my class straight out to recess instead of continuing the lesson. I could barely keep a straight face and didn't know how much longer I could behave like the adult in the room.

I was also no longer a seasoned online single. I'd met match.com's Mark—he "appreciates good grammar and sweaty sex." He had provided ample photos, one with his twelve-year-old son on a San Francisco hill with skateboards, and another shooting pool with a cigarette hanging from his lips. I wasn't interested in dating a smoker, but something about that cigarette was sexy.

He showed up in my driveway with flowers, a gift bag filled with socks, and his infectious smile. The socks were a reference to one of our phone conversations during which I'd been on a fruitless search in my house for a pair of matching socks without holes. Mark was a classic "tall, dark, and handsome," and he wore a wool cap. During dinner I couldn't help but ask what the cap was hiding. I might as well have introduced myself as Cara the jaded bitch. Fortunately, Mark had a better impression of me. He grabbed the bill of his hat, lifted it a few inches over his head, and then ran his fingers through his thinning hair with the other hand.

"Just a little male-pattern baldness," he admitted, then flashed a grin that filled my stomach with butterflies.

Dee kept busy, too. She'd played a supporting role in a film called *Enchanted*. She recorded "A Hero Comes Home" for the end credits of Angelina Jolie's blockbuster *Beowulf*. She released a new album, *I Stand,* on which she sings one of my favorite songs, one she wrote with Glen Ballard called "My Own Worst Enemy." It's edgy and has a Native American drum beat that makes it impossible not to bounce your head. She toured with the album, entertaining fans with her charisma, disarming sense of humor, and anecdotes from her days as a wedding-band singer. She also performed with Josh Groban in *Chess in Concert,* where she got to wear a black bustier-type top with black slacks and looked as hot—though classier—as she did back in her "Take Me or Leave Me" pleather-pants days.

It was sometime around *Chess in Concert* and Happy Penis that Dee called me.

"Hey, Sis. Can you go somewhere no one can hear you?" she said.

"Sure," I told her and walked from the kitchen up into my room. "I'm here. What's up?" I took a seat on the edge of my bed.

"I think I might be pregnant."

"Really?" I said, my voice swinging up at the end. She and Taye had been trying.

"Yeah, but I need to know what you think 'cause I'm not sure."

"Why not?"

" 'Cause the window of opportunity was pretty small. Taye and I were barely in the same place last month."

"It only takes one time, Dee," which of course we both knew, but I knew all too well—I swear I could laugh too hard in front of a man and end up pregnant.

"I know, but still . . . am I ready for a baby? Will I be able to balance motherhood and my career? Do you think it's the right time? What if I have a girl and she calls me Mommie Dearest?" The sudden influx of doubt was a clear indication of her racing heart and the nearness of motherhood.

I laughed. "Just don't show her the fuckin' movie."

She laughed. "Good point."

"Dee, you're ready. You're going to be an amazing mother." I paused and then asked what I deemed more pertinent questions. "Have you taken a pregnancy test? What's the stick say?"

"Yeah, they all came up positive."

I always purchased the double-pack of supermarket pregnancy tests—one positive or negative dipstick had never been convincing enough for me. But I wasn't sure what Dee meant by "they *all* came up positive."

"How many did you take?" I probed.

"Five, I think."

I stifled a chuckle. "And they all came up positive?"

"Yeah," she answered, and I couldn't help but laugh out loud a little. I was familiar with the denial and shock of even a planned pregnancy and I was glad that Dee had sought my advice. But it didn't take an obstetrician to know she was pregnant.

"What do you think?" she asked again.

"I think congratulations are in order," I said, and then I squealed, "You're gonna be a mommy!"

That was the confirmation she needed. We were instantly giddy. I ran to my dresser drawer and grabbed my pregnancy wheel so I could calculate her due date. I'd held on to the wheel for years, the way I was holding on to the prospect of having a third child. According to the wheel, I was going to be an aunt in August or September. I had enough energy to run around the whole neighborhood and tell everyone my sister was having a baby, but my sister was Idina Menzel and the baby's father was Taye Diggs. Unless I wanted it to show up in *In Touch* magazine, I couldn't share the news with my neighbors or in the teachers' lounge over leftover Valentine's Day cupcakes. My sister's pregnancy was *actual* news.

I was as elated about Dee's pregnancy as I would have been about my own. Part of what made it so exciting was my hope that in motherhood there was potential for a closer relationship with her. I knew things she couldn't know yet. She'd look to me for guidance. She'd come to understand the choices I'd made: home birth, co-sleeping, maybe even kiss-feeding. And we'd finally be mothers together.

Even six-year-old Jacob—Jake—and ten-year-old Avery had knowledge they wanted to impart to their aunt Dee Dee and uncle Taye. They starred in a gripping how-to video that we filmed as a pregnancy gift, using Jake's teddy bear as a prop. Part I: How to Change a Baby's Diaper; Part II: How to Hush a Crying Baby; and my favorite, Part III: How to Feed a Baby. For Part III Jake held the teddy bear against his chest and Avery said, "Always remember to put your boob back when you finish." Clearly, Avery recalled a choice maternal moment I must have forgotten.

But after that initial phone call from Dee about the pregnancy tests, we didn't talk as much as I would have liked. I didn't have the chance to coach her through her first-trimester nausea or to explain why it was better to take a liquid iron supplement than a pill. We didn't discuss perineal massage, yoga stretches, or helpful meditation to prepare for birth.

I was thrilled when Dee invited Mom and me for a weekend with her at a spa. I learned that she had a doula, a birth companion and advocate, and that she'd considered home birth but ultimately opted to have the baby naturally in a hospital. I remember being envious of the doula, as if my experience with birth and my status as Dee's sister made me better qualified for the role and I'd been slighted. At the same time, I was relieved that Dee would have someone she trusted to support her, especially in a hospital. My hurt feelings seemed selfish and unreasonable—I lived in another state, for crying out loud—so I cast them aside like I did with the other less-than-honorable thoughts and feelings that sometimes wormed their way into my consciousness.

Dee and Taye learned they were having a little boy, and the summer before he was born, they rented a house on the beach in Malibu where they could enjoy the final stretch of couplehood before parenthood. Mark and I joined them there for a long weekend. It was a special couple of days. Dee met Mark for the first time and I got to feel my nephew squirm about in her belly. Then, at Dee's request, I photographed her very pregnant silhouette in the light of the floor-to-ceiling windows of the beach house.

When I returned to Boulder I made a habit of wearing my phone in the back pocket of my jeans and made sure I was prepared to bolt out of town in an instant. I'd already written notes for a substitute and made plans for Jake and Avery so that I could leave them home and be in Los Angeles with Mom within hours.

My planning paid off. The call came in the middle of the school day. Dee was in labor.

Within a few hours my ass sat comfortably in front of a tray table at thirty-five thousand feet while Dee labored in a hospital bed. It seemed unfair that I should be sipping sparkling water with lime and enjoying a break from children when Dee was a few states away and breathing through contractions. I empathized with her, but I wasn't worried about her. Dee was fierce. Birth was intense, but it was no match for my sister.

At some point during the flight, I realized I had a big, stupid grin on my face, but was talking to no one and staring off at nothing. I'd remembered a babysitting experience Dee and I shared back when she was still Dina. Back then I was too young to babysit alone, but with my big sister, I could capitalize on her age and she could capitalize on my domestic strengths, like my diaper-changing expertise.

A gorgeous little boy named Aviv lived in our neighborhood. He was Indian and had skin like caramel. His eyes were so brown I could barely distinguish his irises from his pupils, an attribute that accentuated their roundness and made me want to squeeze him like a puppy. He and his parents lived around the corner from us at the base of a large hill.

One night, when Aviv was about two years old, Dina and I babysat together. She was thirteen at the time and I was about ten years old. Aviv was potty training. His parents gave us a rundown on the potty-training protocol, which was, essentially, to check in with him a lot and get him to the potty quickly if he said he had to go.

It was mid-evening and we were all on the living room floor with a wooden puzzle when Aviv said, "Go potty." Aviv's bathroom was upstairs, so Dina squeezed his pudgy hand like a wad of Silly Putty and started up the stairs with him. "Go potty," he repeated, "go potty."

"Go, go, go," I said, waving my hand behind them as if pushing the air would move them along more quickly. Dina scooped Aviv up into her arms and started jogging up the stairs. I followed behind, taking two steps at a time. In our race to get him to the toilet, we overlooked the step stool and cushioned potty seat with built-in deflector that leaned against the bathtub. Instead, we sat him directly on the standard ceramic toilet seat, where he gripped the sides tightly and tried not to fall in. Dina bent down on her knees in front of him.

If Aviv had needed a French braid or pigtails, we were the girls to do it; a lanyard cobra-stitched bracelet or beads threaded through his shoelaces, we were the girls to do it; a wannabe-Broadway-star performance of "It's the Hard-knock Life," we were the girls to do it. But help him pee on the potty . . . not so much.

And so, with a smile full of teeth like mini Chiclets and his penis at a ninety-degree angle to the pot, he proudly began urinating everywhere except the bowl—including, but not limited to, the opposite wall, the floor, part of the tub, and, of course, us—especially Dina.

"Ahhh!" I shouted.

"Tip him over!" Dina shouted back, and she steadied him on the potty as I gently pushed his shoulders toward his knees to redirect the stream into the bowl. He tilted his head up at us, his earlier smile now a small dash above his chin. We all froze in place and listened to his last bit of tinkle hit the water and I stared at a streak of urine across the front of Dina's gray sweatshirt. Then we helped him down and he stood before us with his Smurf underwear and pj's scrunched around his ankles. Dina and I looked at each other, unsure what to do next. Aviv's little Lincoln Log–size penis was the first we'd ever seen and we were two sisters who knew how to do only one thing when we finished peeing—wipe. I shrugged and then handed Dina a single square of toilet paper. She looked at Aviv's puzzled expression and then tapped the droplet of pee off the tip of his penis like it was a bug that might bite. Afterward, we cleaned up and put his nighttime diaper on, wrapping the sticky tabs across his belly with great relief.

Dina and I said nothing to Aviv's parents when they arrived home that night, but we laughed under the streetlamps all the way back to our house, and again as we took the stairs up to our bedrooms. And over thirty years later, on an airplane, I was still laughing.

It was hard to believe how much time had passed since that experience with Aviv. Hard to believe that I was a seasoned parent, well-schooled in the ways of potty training little boys. And that Dee would soon be, too. It was even harder to believe that two sisters from Long Island were about to be outnumbered by our male offspring, and wouldn't be painting a little girl's fingernails or pinning buns into place for ballet class anytime soon.

I had barely stepped through the doorway to Dee's delivery room when she spotted me and said, "We have to talk. You did that *twice*?"

She caught me off guard. I knew I'd be proud of her when I saw her for the first time as a mother, I was already proud of her. But I didn't know that she'd be proud of *me*. Her acknowledgment made me feel like I'd achieved a higher ranking in her book, as a woman and as a sister. I nodded my head in confirmation. "Yeah, twice."

Dee lay in the bed, her brown hair pulled back into a loose knot. A slightly exposed breast. A glare of shock still in her eyes—birth can do that—and her child cradled in her arms. I walked toward them until I could see the baby better. His hair was slick and black, his lips plump and heart-shaped like his mommy's. His dark eyes peeked at me through swollen slits, with the essence of both innocence and enlightenment. It was easy to love Walker Diggs.

Dee and I finally had motherhood in common; and a few hours later, as I watched her nurse Walker, I wondered if we'd had more in common than I'd realized. If maybe we'd shared a strength I'd overlooked because I'd struggled to see it in myself.

Mom and I stayed for a couple of days and then boarded a flight home from L.A. I sat down in my aisle seat while she got situated across the way. As I used my foot to shove my backpack a few more inches under the seat in front of me, I caught Mom eyeing my seat belt.

"Is it tight enough?" she asked as she reached across the aisle and tugged on the strap a couple of times for me.

"Mom, what the fuck? I'm thirty-five years old. I know how to fasten my own seat belt."

"Sorry," she said with a shrug. "Once a mother, always a mother."

A gentleman squeezed past us toward the back of the plane. Then Mom leaned toward me.

"You know, I can't help but think about you when I'm in a hospital with little babies." She didn't have to say why. I knew she was referring to those weeks I'd fought The Whoop.

"I know, Mommy." She loved that even as adults, Dee and I still called her Mommy sometimes. Every now and then I did it on purpose to make her happy. "I look at little babies, how vulnerable they are, and I can't imagine how unbearable that time must have been for you."

"You always think about that," Mom said, "the vulnerability. I know I was overprotective sometimes when you were growing up—"

"Or now," I interrupted. After all, she'd just tightened my seat belt.

"But I hope you know I was overprotective because I was afraid. It was *my* fear. *My* trauma. It wasn't because I thought you couldn't handle stuff."

"I never thought that, Mom."

"But you should know, Cara. People die from pertussis. Babies died from pertussis. Especially thirty or forty years ago."

"I know, Mom."

"No, look at me," she insisted with a new shade of seriousness and teary eyes—she could never talk about The Whoop without crying.

"What?"

"You. Lived."

I don't know what came over me. I started to cry, full-on scrunched-up face, ugly crying. I couldn't help myself. People were still moving about the plane. A flight attendant was walking by, shutting the doors of full overhead compartments. And I was having A Moment.

"I never thought you were weak," Mom continued. "Quite the opposite. You were a fighter, a survivor." And then she said it again: "You lived, Cara. There's nothing weak about you."

"Thanks, Mommy, I know," I said, but I was wholly unconvincing, given the crying and all. Part of me must *not* have known, *not* have identified as a fighter or a survivor, because those tears came from a hole so deep inside me I'd long forgotten it was there. In that hole I was still a baby:

Cara, so little, so weak.
Cara, so fragile.
Cara, who needs to be rescued.

Mom took my hand from across the aisle and gave it a squeeze, and I regained my composure.

Lesson 14

HOW TO MAKE A MARK (OR MARRY ONE)

In 2010, Dee was invited to perform at the White House as part of their music series, *A Broadway Celebration*. I proudly announced on Facebook, "My sister's singing at the White House!" and then, to my horror, I realized the post had suffered an unfortunate autocorrect and it appeared that Dee would be singing at the "whore house"—another kind of gig altogether. Around that time, Dee also scored a role in the popular television show *Glee*. Fans of both the show and Dee noted the resemblance between her and one of the show's stars, Rachel, played by Lea Michele. Dee was given a recurring role as Rachel's mother, Shelby Corcoran. As exciting as it was for Dee to be a part of a television series where she could act and sing and still have time to be a mother to Walker, being cast as the mother of an actress fifteen years her junior stung a little bit—or maybe a lot.

While *Glee* fans saw a resemblance between Dee and Lea, it wasn't long before Walker noticed the resemblance between Dee and *me*. He was almost three. I hadn't seen him nearly enough in those first three years and I missed him. I went to visit them in their home in Los Angeles. Walker and I were sitting on the living room floor with a large sampling of rubber dinosaurs. He looked up at me with his dark eyes, long lashes, and broad brow, cocked his head to the side a bit, and then said, "You look like my mom."

I smiled. "That's 'cause we're sisters," I told him. "You look like your mommy too."

"I do?" he asked, wide-eyed.

"Yep. You do."

He smiled.

That was also the year, 2011, that Mark and I celebrated a Late Christmas together, the Christmas we have every other year when our kids get back from celebrating Real Christmas with our exes. We sat around our tree with Mom, the boys, and Mark's teenage son, Oscar, among the crumpled paper and collapsed boxes and Styrofoam. Mark asked everyone for their attention, then lowered himself onto one knee and professed his love for me. He withdrew a small black box from his pocket while explaining that he'd ordered a ring that wasn't ready yet—not a diamond, because I didn't want a diamond—and also, because he wanted to propose during the holidays, that he'd gone to the store to buy a temporary ring, an understudy to fill in in the absence of the real one. He lifted the lid and revealed a beautiful emerald-cut amethyst. Before I could respond, he scrambled to pull another ring out of his pocket, explaining that he couldn't decide which temporary engagement ring to get me so he bought me two and I could choose my favorite and he liked the funkier one with the rubies, but thought I might prefer the more traditionally cut amethyst, but also that I didn't have to choose, I could keep both and that would make him very happy.

I loved that my typically suave man was fumbling and reduced to rambling.

"Wait, what?" I said. Was this a proposal or a magic trick? Would he pull another ring from his ear? Was there another up his sleeve? I wanted to say yes to his proposal, but it had been a full minute or so since he'd gotten down on his knee and I couldn't remember if he'd even asked me to marry him yet. Mark slowed down and took a breath.

"You're my world," he said. "Marry me?"

"Of course," I answered and kissed him.

Then I wiped a happy tear and added, "I'm keeping both rings."

A few weeks later, I had a triumvirate of engagement rings: a ruby, an amethyst, and a green sapphire. I wasn't just engaged, I was *really* engaged. I was lounging on the couch, my feet up on the coffee table, admiring my new sapphire in the noon light when Dee called with another proposal I couldn't refuse.

"I have three shows to do on a cruise ship. It'll be like forty-five hundred gay men. Wanna come?"

Duh.

In February 2012, I overheard someone say the *Allure of the Seas* was the largest cruise ship in the world. I'd never been on a cruise ship and I'd only seen a few from a distance off the shores of Mexican beaches. But as I stood at the *Allure*'s side it seemed to lie on the ocean like Superman had tipped over the Empire State Building and set it afloat. It was preposterous that any amount of water could support its brawn.

The trip would be short. Dee and I would hop aboard in Cozumel for the last two and a half days of the cruise's seven-day tour, giving Dee just enough time to rehearse and perform. Those two days were busy and spent largely apart. Dee had shows scheduled; she needed to conduct business, rehearse, warm up, find her sea legs—it's hard to stand in platform heels when you've only just boarded a cruise ship. I was equally busy, overloaded with problem-solving tasks. I had to figure out how to eat using a fifteen-piece place setting, how to determine the time zone—easier said than done—how to use the bathroom at the spa when both rooms were designated Men's, where to look when taking the shortcut through the poolside Dick Deck, and how to walk from one end of the ship to the other during the Speedo contest without accidentally swiping too many hard bodies, or, conversely, ensuring that I swiped every possible hard body (on this point, I felt conflicted). I was busy.

On the last full day on the ship, Dee and I finally had an uninterrupted hour together that wasn't spent sleeping. The spa arranged for a private steam room where Dee could warm up her voice. It turned out to be less like a room and more like a shower. The shower was tiled in mosaics the color of the Caribbean, and attached to the wall on either side hung a large white chair that struck me as a disparate cross between the chair Jane Jetson would sit in while watching TV, and a urinal. We giggled a little, trying to figure out how it all worked, and finally sat down in our towels.

I spoke up quickly. I told Dee I'd been depressed. Even with Mark and the boys and the way my life was coming together, sometimes I still felt distant.

"Atheism suits Mark well," I told her. "Me? Not so much."

"What do you mean?"

"Well, he grew up Baptist, pretty much *Footloose*-style. No rock music and stuff. He was always trying to figure out God's will instead of his own. For him, atheism is liberating. For me, it's lonely. My spirituality was like . . . this is gonna sound so corny . . ."

"Just say it."

"It was like a witness, a kind one. Then there was all that blood when I hemorrhaged with Avery and all the craziness with Jon and now it's gone."

"You don't have to go from believing in God to believing in nothing, Cara," she said, and I knew she was trying to help—ever the big sister. But I realized that I hadn't brought up such a serious subject because I wanted her to help me. I brought it up because I wanted her to *know* me.

We always told people we were close. If that was true, wouldn't she know my deepest thoughts and feelings? Living in different states, Dee and I had to work to have meaningful experiences together, like lots of siblings living at a distance from each other had to contend with. But there were other aspects of our relationship that weren't so common, and that added to my sense she didn't know me as well as I wanted her to. In magazines, on television, the Internet (I googled her several times a week to see what was new), and movie screens, I could see Dee and hear about her life—albeit mostly her professional life—far more than she got to see or hear about me. It wasn't like I could broadcast my classroom once a week and she could watch and say, "Great job teaching Colorado history today, Sis! I had no idea top hats were made out of beaver pelts." So sometimes our relationship felt lopsided. I wondered if I knew her better than she knew me. I think that's why, in an odd little shower somewhere in the depths of the *Allure of the Seas*, I attempted to close the gap a bit. What better way to do that than with a lighthearted conversation about God and depression?

"I can't force myself to believe in something just because it makes me feel better," I told her. "I wish I could."

"I know. I get that."

"I feel like my idealism and spirituality were bound together, and as one eroded, so did the other."

"Well, things got pretty ugly for you. You were in survival mode," she said and then paused. Her hair was soaking wet and she adjusted her ponytail. "You know how much I admire you and how you handled all that, right?"

"Sure," I said.

"You've always been such a wise soul."

"Oh, whatever. Pfft." I shook my head, unable to accept the compliment. It was sweet of her to say and made me think of a song she'd written for me. About six years earlier she wrote "Rise Up." When she performed it in concert she told the audience about a prophet named Devorah, whom she described as a judge, a general, and a poet—the mother of Israel. Then she told them about the time she overheard me sing to Avery, and how my voice was beautiful. She told them that I'd had a rough time and was a single mom. And that to her, I was the poet, the warrior, and the mother. "Sing to the world, my sister," she sang, "rise up"—I cry every time I watch it on YouTube. The crazy thing was, I didn't remember ever seeing Dee perform it live, but she was as certain that she'd performed the song for me during one of her concerts as I was certain that she hadn't.

Dee continued. "Cara, you're the first person I call when I need advice.

Remember Howard Zabinski? You're the one I called when he broke up with me. You're the one I called when I thought I was pregnant."

"I think maybe my brain has selective memory or something. I mostly remember the shit about me needing you, not you needing me." I wondered if Dee had performed "Rise Up" for me after all and I'd simply forgotten about it, just like I'd forgotten about Howard Zabinski. Why is it that the times when I felt most diminished made sticky memories and the times when I felt valued made slippery ones? It hardly seemed fair.

"Well, you're the one I call," Dee repeated and took a swig from her water bottle. When she set it back down she smiled and said, "But now you have to get the fuck out of here, 'cause I need to warm up." We laughed.

We'd been in the steam for over forty-five minutes when I left Dee and decided that the closest thing to God on a cruise ship had to be an endless view of the ocean.

I dragged my dehydrated, starving ass (thanks to Ship Time, Dee and I had overslept and missed breakfast that morning) up the elevator to the pool deck. I was determined to have a piña colada with the theme to *The Love Boat* playing in my head. I arrived to a slate sky that—had I been at home—would have been an excuse for a movie and Raisinets. But even with gray skies, I was able to fulfill my cruise-ship dream with a couple of added perks—cigarettes and drag queens. I bummed a cigarette, downed my drink in under fifteen minutes (a personal record), enjoyed the fashion and makeup of a couple of gorgeous drag queens, and ordered a second beverage.

Just moments after ordering my second drink, the fun came to an abrupt end. A cold sweat made its way across my face and down my back, my ears started to ring, my vision darkened along the edges, and my drink appeared to sit at the end of a tunnel. I couldn't keep my head up and so I let it fall to the bar, thinking, *Oh my God, I'm the slovenly drunk in this story.* With my forehead against the bar I visualized the path back to my room. I needed to trek across the pool deck to the elevators, get in the elevator, hold myself together for the short trip to my floor, then make it down the hallway to my room, where it would finally be safe to collapse. But first I needed to mind my manners and take the drink the bartender had just made for me, lest he be insulted or, worse, learn of my embarrassing condition. My drink was filled beyond the rim, nothing but surface tension preventing the imminent spill. It jostled in my hand as I used what little focus I had to steady it. My mantra—"Elevator, fifth floor, hallway, bed. Elevator, fifth floor, hallway, bed." I made it to the elevator doors. No one else was there. My head was a bowling ball and my legs stood no chance beneath its weight. I slid down the adjacent wall and onto the floor. Then, I vomited so vehemently that I also lost control of my bladder. It was mutiny.

Feeling about as far from the "strong, successful, save-the-day sister" as I could possibly be, but also feeling a hair better after vomiting, I climbed to my feet. I backed away from the puddle of vomit and the curiously damp spot off to the side of it. I folded my arms and looked off in another direction. Soon enough, a few people collected around the elevators. One casually noticed the drink and the vomit. I hoped he attributed it to the late party the night before and fixed my eyes on the shut elevator doors of the slowest . . . elevator . . . in . . . the . . . history of elevators. When it finally arrived I pushed the button for the fifth floor, and secretly hoped that my jeans were dark enough to render the wet spot that spread down the center of my thighs undetectable. When the doors opened I power walked myself back to my room, where I peeled off my pants and flopped onto the bed. I briefly debated placing an anonymous call to the operator requesting a "cleanup on deck 8" but gravity was unrelenting—I couldn't even turn my head. All I felt was the coolness of the sheets against my body.

I stared at the ceiling and had a paranoid vision of my semiconscious moments on the floor near the elevator. I imagined a video camera like a big eyeball high on the wall recording my episode and a small secret room filled with a group of shirtless men with waxed chests and six-packs, all watching me on the screen. One of them says, "Holy shit! Is that Idina Menzel's sister?" Another one adds, "Ew! She threw up. And left it there."

And yet another one adds, "Hey! I wonder if she can sing."

I lay on the bed, grateful. I'd been lucky to fly under the radar that day. After all, I was a rarity on the ship. One-of-a-kind. A female lightweight with a weak bladder and a famous sister. A famous sister! I remembered that Dee was rehearsing on a stage somewhere in that huge ship and I started laughing. How different our afternoons had been. She was preparing to be glamorous and the center of attention, and I was in bed, sleeping off one beverage and one cigarette—cheap date—and relieved that no one was watching a recording of my indignity.

I was surprisingly reflective, given my condition. There was something to be gleaned from the previous two hours of my life—the conversation with Dee in the steam room and my drunken catastrophe on the pool deck. It's true that anonymity had been a blessing for me, but ironically, it was feeling seen—even at my worst—that was precisely what I wanted more of in my relationship with Dee and what I missed when I no longer felt a divine presence in my life. When it came to spirituality, there was something about having a gentle witness that made me feel more significant and gave weight to my existence. Instead, even with the good fortune of a job I loved, family and friends I loved, and the ability to laugh at myself—which I was exceptionally good at—I felt like a ghost sometimes. The kind that floats around without even holographic feet on the ground. I felt like I was writing my life with an invisible pen, going through the motions, but leaving no mark—except near the top floor elevator of the *Allure of the Seas,* of course. And even that mark was temporary!

In some ways, Dee had the opposite problem. Parts of her life were documented and couldn't be erased if she wanted them to be. There were songs she'd released that she no longer liked. Hairstyles immortalized in magazines she'd prefer to forget. And off-the-cuff statements she'd made in interviews that she couldn't retract. I remember being with Dee at her apartment in Manhattan after she performed "Defying Gravity" on David Letterman's show. We were watching a recording of her performance on her huge television. "Oh my god! My eyes are crossed. Do my eyes cross when I sing? Are they always like that?" and she paused the screen so that the two of us were staring at a close-up of her green face, wide-open mouth, and eyes ever so slightly . . . crossed.

When it came to fame and relative anonymity, Dee and I were occasionally able to empathize with each other. Once, we even agreed to trade places for an evening. It was at our cousin Evan's wedding back in 2007. Evan, who, as a teen, enjoyed too much Manischewitz on the high holy holidays and played a decent game of air hockey on the table in his basement. He was all grown up and the last of us to walk down the aisle. I'd already been married *and* divorced, Dee and Taye were hitched, and Evan's brother, Andrew, had married Andrea years earlier.

Dee, Taye, and I drove to Long Island together from the city. We hadn't seen Dad's side of the family much since Grandma died. We talked about our expectations of the wedding. Not the bride's dress or the flower arrangements. Not the ceremony, or steak or fish, but how the evening would unfold socially. Dee didn't look forward to having to account for the last two years of her career, of lower-profile projects—no starring roles or platinum albums—and having to answer tactless questions about why she hadn't been on the *Today* show for a while. "What are you up to these days?" people would ask. For my part, I wasn't looking forward to the more banal, courtesy questions about the weather in Colorado, but hoped someone might ask about the boys. Uncle Marty still liked to remark about how "big I'd grown," so there'd probably be that, too.

Our extended family was always well intentioned, but more often than not their interest was directed at Dee and I felt peripheral, more like a sidekick. Dee knew how I felt and it upset her. She didn't want any part in making me feel bad, but she couldn't help it. With her at my side, people seemed less interested in me, even disinterested in me. Their attempts at conversation bordered on obligatory. On our way to the wedding, neither Dee nor I was interested in playing our parts, not the superstar, not the sidekick.

"We should totally pretend to be each other tonight," Dee said from behind the steering wheel. "You can field questions about what the hell I've been up to—heck, just make shit up. And I'll talk about the boys and the mountains."

"You think anyone would fall for it?" I asked. I couldn't tell if she was serious.

"Who cares?"

In our thirties we looked more like sisters than ever, but we were far from spitting images. We shared similar bone structure, strong cheekbones, broad eyebrows, dark hair—hers was a little darker—and light eyes. But we also resembled each other because of our smiles and our demeanor. We carried ourselves similarly and during casual conversation we often shared similar mannerisms, intonations, and expressions. Furthermore, we were both prone to malapropisms and had a self-defecating—whoops, self-deprecating!—sense of humor. It was safe to assume Dee and I were related but clear that we weren't identical twins. To accentuate our differences at the wedding, Dee would have the beautiful Taye Diggs on her arm, whereas I would attend single—another possible topic for discussion that I didn't look forward to. It would be another year before I met Mark.

Dee and I continued to joke about trading places. Taye thought it was a genius idea. He loved practical jokes. Dee would pretend she was me, I'd pretend I was her, wouldn't it be fun? With his slick suit and bow tie, Taye egged us on (or, as I used to say, edged us on).

True to form, early on the day of Evan's wedding, Dee took me shopping. She bought me a Diane von Furstenberg shimmery gold minidress that made me feel elegant and sassy, like my boots were made for walkin'. I didn't know the difference between Diane von Furstenberg and Diane Keaton at the time, but in that dress, with my hair pulled off my face and knotted high on my head, I felt ready to face Long Island and my relatives.

As the guests at the cocktail party waited for the reception doors at the temple to open, a vaguely familiar relative approached me. I should have known her name. I was certain I'd shared a table with her at Rosh Hashanah, or Yom Kippur, or Passover at some point in my life. I held a glass of champagne that sparkled like the gold in my dress.

"I-dina!" she exclaimed with an emphasis on the phonetically long "i" sound, as in Long *Island.* She wore foundation that was a couple of shades too dark—more like a tanning solution than makeup. Mascara was caked on her lashes and left remnants above her lid and beneath her bottom lashes (no doubt from removing her glasses to put on her makeup). Her lipstick suffered a similar fate, applied beyond the lines like the crayon in a toddler's coloring book. I guessed that the vision that made it difficult for her to apply her makeup was the same vision that led her to mistake me for Dee.

Before I could stop her, her mouth was off and running: "How are you, dawling? I saw you in *Wicked.* You were marvelous. I went to the show with your second cousins and your grandfather's brother's cousin and we had dinner at this place on the corner and it was all right but we went backstage and you were so gracious and thank you so much for . . ." I didn't interrupt, though I probably should have. I hadn't intended to deceive her, but I knew my silence was akin to lying. I felt guilty, but the coincidence was too perfect and I thought Dee would find it funny, maybe even commend me for having the balls to go through with our plan.

The woman rambled on in her starstruck excitement and I lost track of the conversation. Instead, it occurred to me that this must be what it felt like to be Dee. A person stands in front of you, gushes over you, and you wish you could remember her name. And after a little while your smile starts to feel stale because you're tired of the subject matter, but you're grateful for the love because you know it's partly that love that made you successful. I listened with a sense of Dee's struggle. She could never take a day off. She couldn't attend the wedding, or for that matter go out for dinner in New York City, or grab a coffee at Starbucks, without having to be on her best behavior. I realized that Dee didn't have a choice. She had to attend the wedding as Idina Menzel, Broadway star, and couldn't simply be Evan's cousin.

Still, I drew a parallel to my own life. In my own way, and obviously on a smaller scale—like a microscopic one—I was famous. At Foothill Elementary, kids shouted my name out the bus windows as they arrived in the morning, and ran to me with big hugs in the hallways throughout the day. I couldn't go to the grocery store in my pajamas, sneak a rare cigarette on the Pearl Street Mall on a Saturday night, or pick my nose at a Stop sign. Someone might recognize Ms. Mentzel.

The woman was still talking. I snapped out of my stupor. I nodded intermittently and squeezed in a few spontaneous thank-you's. Eventually, we parted ways. I gave her a big hug and one last thank-you.

Half an hour later, Dee and I were back together. It's no surprise really that the woman approached us and turned to Dee: "And who are you, dawling?" The jig was up!

"I'm Idina," she answered. Then, of course, the woman said, "No, *she's* Idina . . ." and then stared at me through her clumped mascara and searched my face for confirmation. Instead, she saw the truth in my guilty grin.

"I'm Cara," I admitted. "So sorry. *This* is my sister, Idina."

"You played a trick on me," the woman said and generously cracked a forgiving smile. Then, before I could feel too bad, she looked at Dee and began all over again: "How are you, dawling? I saw you in *Wicked* . . ."

Later on in the evening, the bride asked Dee if she'd be willing to sing a song with the band. Dee wasn't sure how to respond. If I had a voice like Dee's I imagined I'd sing anywhere and everywhere, but Dee didn't feel the same way. She wanted to be generous, but she also wanted to be a normal guest, a normal guest like me. I was standing with Dee near a table with a small numbered table tent when she turned to me.

"Hey, *Idina*," she said in her best Long Island accent. "Why don't *you* get up there and do it?"

"Ha. Ha." *If only I could.*

Another time, instead of pretending to be Dee, one of her fans pretended to be me. And I didn't like it. Not too long after my fiasco in London with the green suitcase, I received an e-mail from my old boyfriend Ken.

"Congratulations on your wedding. I had no idea you remarried."

As I was then very single, you can imagine my surprise.

"I had no idea either!" I wrote him back. "What made you think I remarried?"

Apparently, I had a Myspace profile. I searched my name and sure enough, there I was.

To my horror, in the top left corner there was a photograph of my sister with my mom and me, our hair blown out stick-straight at the same salon, on either side of her, taken back when Dee was starring in *Rent*. To the right, equally horrifying, were a few erroneous facts about Cara Mentzel, including my marital status, that I didn't have any children, and that I lived in New York. Below the basic profile was a squat little paragraph inundated with exclamation points. I winced as I read, "My sister Idina Menzel is the coolest sister evah!!! We're totally gonna hang out soon . . . I'm just sooooo proud of her!!!!!!!" I knew that if there was a way to dot the exclamation points with hearts, this imposter would have hearted each one. This page was public. Not only could ex-boyfriends view the profile, but my students and their parents could see it, too. Moreover, my sister might see it. I didn't want Dee to think I would exploit her like that. (I also didn't want her to think I was a shit writer.)

There were a few more pictures of Dee and me pasted off to the side of the text. Some were the very images I had on my fridge. With my hand over my eyes like this was of *Nightmare on Elm Street* proportion, I examined the rest of the page through my fingers. I recognized the writing as the fiction of a young teen, clearly a big fan of Dee's. While this teenager (let's assume she was female) had been diligent about finding actual photos of my family, she felt no obligation to tell the truth in her writing. She didn't care about my divorce, Avery or Jake, or that I was an elementary school teacher. She'd taken my name and rewritten my life as if nothing about me was important except for my sister. As if I didn't matter. She didn't want to be an exhausted single mom tinkering around on match.com at 1:00 A.M. with a bag of popcorn. She wanted to be Idina's sister.

I was hurt, hurt by some stranger who was probably half my age with *Rent* and *Wicked* posters on her walls, and maybe even Dee's signature on the cover of a playbill. Regardless of the writer's age or innocent intentions, my space—or Myspace—had been violated. I was pissed. I wanted to call this girl up and say, "You wanna be me? You gotta take the divorce and the bills, and the laundry, and the stomach flu, and the piles of grading. You don't get to pick and choose what part of Cara Mentzel works for you!"

My hurt was real, but I knew I was overreacting and that I shouldn't take the page personally. I understood Dee's overzealous fan. I knew what it felt like to be an Idina fan, and what it felt like to want to be closer to her. Still, I couldn't leave the page online. I had a professional life, one that—among other things—included teaching kids how to use periods and commas and the occasional exclamation point.

I was trying to figure out how to reach customer service at Myspace when I noticed a chat function at the bottom of "my" Myspace page. Fraudulent Cara was chatting with Dee! My stomach did a flip. I didn't want Dee to accidentally disclose personal information to an imposter.

I called Dee in a frenzy and explained the situation. I assured her that I would never share personal information online. She interrupted me.

"That's not me," she said calmly.

"What do you mean that's not you?" I asked.

"Whatever Myspace page you're looking at, obviously isn't you, and it isn't me either. It's someone *pretending* to be you, talking to someone *pretending* to me."

"No. Stop it," I said.

"Really."

I raised my voice in astonishment. "Who would do that? Why would someone do that?" I wasn't sure which was more inconceivable, that two frauds would knowingly engage in conversation in character or that I was so naïve I actually believed one of them to be Dee.

"Welcome to *my* world," Dee said.

I let out a big sigh.

"In this world of yours, is there someone who can get a Myspace page taken down for me?"

"Yeah. I'll take care of it."

The glamorous *Allure of the Seas,* packed with loyal Idina fans, was also a part of Dee's world and it was there that I finally woke up from a two-hour nap and took a long shower. (Note to self: do not drink *anything* alcoholic when the orange slice and maraschino cherry garnish will be the only thing with it in your belly, and when you're dehydrated from nearly an hour in a steam room.)

I enjoyed dinner and Dee's performance. We spent the A.M. hours together at a crowded piano bar for Honolulu comedian Matt Yee's vulgar sing-along show—some of the most fun I've ever had. Back at the suite, Dee and I fell asleep in side-by-side lounge chairs on the balcony. And then, in true diva-style, unable to hear the telephone, we overslept and delayed the disembarkation procedure for the entire ship. With over four thousand paying cruise goers waiting on Idina Menzel, it sure was nice to be the anonymous sister.

Lesson 15

HOW TO JUMP

In November 2013, Dee was in Washington, D.C., rehearsing for the trial run of a new Broadway show, *If/Then,* and only weeks away from the Thanksgiving release of her latest movie, Disney's *Frozen*. She would star as the towheaded Scandinavian queen, Elsa—the towhead part was something only animation could pull off. With a new show and a new movie you might think Dee was happy, yet when I answered the phone, she was in tears.

"It's over," she said. "Taye and I are getting a divorce."

Mark and I were minutes from going to bed. He was reading his book by the only light on in the room, the small lamp on his end table. I sat up.

"Oh, Dee. I'm so sorry." Mark put his book down and looked over at me. I pointed to the phone against my ear and mouthed "divorce." He looked at me with sympathetic eyes and I resumed the conversation.

"Are you okay?"

"I guess. I don't know."

"What can I do?"

"Nothing . . . I just don't want this for Walker." Her voice cracked and I guessed her tears were falling in a steady stream. I pictured her in a dim hotel suite, away from home, a new theater family nearby, but still very much alone.

She continued. "I don't know what this'll do to him. He's so little. I wanted to give him the perfect family. To do everything right for him." I knew her pain firsthand. I knew that the end of a marriage, especially when children were involved, was pretty much an emotional clusterfuck.

"If you're okay, Walker will be okay too, Dee. I promise. He'll adjust." I wasn't surprised that Dee's main concern was Walker. Since he'd come along, she was a mother before all else.

"Try to take one step at a time," I added. "What do you need right now?"

"I just have to get through rehearsals. There's so much going on. I don't have time to think or make any plans."

"Would it help if I flew out there? I can hang out. You can do what you need to do, and I'll just be there to keep you company."

"No. You have school and the boys and so much going on. I'll be fine," she replied.

"I know you'll be fine, of course you'll be fine." Mark and I locked eyes for a second. A confirmation of what I'd say next. "But I'm going to come anyway." It was in Dee's most difficult moments that she reached for me and I wouldn't miss a chance to be there. I glanced over at Mark, who had already pulled up some flight options on his phone and was pointing to them for me.

"You sure?" Dee asked.

"Yep. I'll be there tomorrow, probably late."

"All right."

"One more thing, Dee, this isn't a failure. You and Taye were together for the better part of eighteen years. Try not to beat yourself up. After that long, there's blame to share." The latter statement, "there's blame to share," was a quote from *Wicked*'s "For Good" and entirely unintentional.

"I know," she said, but her voice was hollow.

That night, I went to sleep next to Mark, my husband of over a year, thinking about how my marriage to Jon and Dee's to Taye had been different, the details of hers not mine to share. But the differences in our marriages didn't matter. When it came to divorce, I always felt the ingredients were the same. There was self-loathing, usually spousal loathing, regret, guilt, sadness, some relief, and, eventually, the odd pairing of fear and excitement. Fear of the unknown, and excitement about new possibilities. Being able to identify with each other had often brought Dee and I closer, and I enjoyed that, but not once did I hope we would bond over single motherhood.

In D.C. I mostly played tagalong, hung out at the theater, and loafed around in bed with Dee in front of the TV. Initially, I harbored a similar feeling to the one I had when I read the *Rent* script decades earlier, anxiety brought on by a desire to say the perfect thing, and a fear of saying the wrong thing. And yet I knew that sometimes emotions run too high for words to reach, and this was very likely one of those times. I realized that what Dee needed from me was easy to give: time, understanding, and love.

I watched the dress rehearsal of *If/Then*. Dee played Elizabeth, a woman on the cusp of forty moving back to her beloved New York City for a fresh start after a bitter divorce. The story wasn't an exact replica of Dee's recent life, but it still hit close to home. Also, with a plot that followed Elizabeth through two different lives—one as Liz, who falls in love and starts a family, and one as Beth, who pursues a high-powered career—it wasn't hard to draw parallels between the different paths Dee and I had chosen. Eventually, the show would be billed by the *Los Angeles Times* as ". . . two Menzel's for the price of one!" I watched Dee inhabit her roles with an emotional rawness drawn straight from her personal struggles, offering her audience a rare intimacy, another chance to witness her derive strength through her acceptance of vulnerability. The secret to her powerful voice, and the secret to her magnetism. A truth best expressed toward the end of the show when she belts the riveting ballad "Always Starting Over" and leaves the audience breathless.

By December, *Frozen* was growing in popularity and the terms of Dee and

Taye's separation were taking shape. She was worried about Walker and wanted him to be with family, so we planned a New Year's trip. Dee and Walker, Mom, Mark, the boys, and I took a vacation to a villa in Anguilla.

The villa was a five-bedroom, two-story house with cathedral ceilings, part of only a handful of homes on Shoal Bay West in Anguilla. Reviews of our accommodations noted the villa's otherworldly modern architecture—stark white, massive wide-eyed aliens on a foreign beach. It stood at the foot of the seashore, facing the southern Caribbean, with walls of windows and sliding glass doors that, according to *New York* magazine, ". . . court the seascape from every corner . . ." The kids gave us no time to unpack. We arrived at the villa, walked straight through the front door, over the terra-cotta-tiled floors through to the beach, and in no time at all had three boys in wet clothes.

Walker clawed at the waves velociraptor-style, bared his teeth, and growled as they jumped toward him. Jake dived right in fully clothed like he'd just arrived at a frat party with a pool. And Avery greeted the water with his pensive gentleness, observing the coral and his new turf, surf? Welcome to paradise.

There were minor shuffles as Mom, Dee, Mark, and I took turns watching the boys and grabbing our beach necessities—books, hats, sunscreen, towels, and non-necessities like champagne and strawberries—from inside the villa. Eventually we toasted to family, then collapsed on our lounge chairs. We'd arrived.

In my experience, a kitchen table is often the stage for classic family drama, whether it's nestled in an alcove of a Long Island town house or in shouting distance of a child's train table in Colorado's suburbia. The table in our Anguilla villa was no exception. It was a long wicker oval set to accommodate ten diners (and Walker's innumerable rubber dinosaurs), situated near a wall of windows that overlooked a shaded strip of beach and bushes—a hospitable residence for many hermit crabs, our own private beach-life terrarium.

At breakfast on our first morning in Anguilla, the family drama began. Tanzania, one of our chefs—I'm a little embarrassed to admit that we had chefs for breakfast—brought yogurt to the table and Jake noticed the label said "probiotic." I'd previously taught Jake that probiotics were healthy bacteria that lived in our bodies. I'd explained that because he'd been taking antibiotics, medicine that killed "bad" *and* "good" bacteria in his body, he'd need to supplement his diet with probiotics. Jake had clearly remembered this conversation when he posed an interesting question at the breakfast table: "Why are probiotics healthy, but yogurt and dairy are supposed to be bad for you when you're sick?" Honestly, I'd often wondered the same thing (and later learned it was a myth). It seemed counterintuitive that healthy probiotics should be part of a food that isn't healthy to ingest when fighting a respiratory infection. I attempted to explain the relevant pieces of information to him: mucus, pH balance, and intestinal bacteria. As I said "intestinal," Dee interrupted.

"Cara, hear how your voice goes up, there? It's a sign of insecurity, a lack of confidence when you're speaking." Tears welled in my eyes but I stayed them with the mind control of a sci-fi villain. A lump of sadness crept up the very throat that wasn't speaking deeply enough, the very place Dee wanted my confident words to rise from, and I swallowed hard, sending my sadness back to a safer place.

It had been a long time since Dee had last pointed out the weakness in my voice, but she'd referred to it enough times throughout our lives that I knew the criticism well.

"When you speak lower," she added, as if she were making the observation for the first time, "from your chest, like you do sometimes, you sound more confident."

"I don't know why I do that," I managed to say in a voice neither high nor low—but fuck if I could tell the difference at that point.

"You're brilliant," Dee added. "You should speak with confidence." But the compliment disappeared under the weight of the criticism. Mark, Jake, Avery, Walker, and Mom were all around the table, listening and watching. My insecurity on center stage, I felt impotent, envious of the shelled privacy of the nearby hermit crabs.

Maybe I wasn't as successful at hiding my tears as I'd thought because then Dee added, "I'm sure nobody else notices it. It's just me, 'cause I pay attention to these things—I have to." *Don't. Cry.* I flashed Dee a quick smile and replied, "I know. I get it." *Swallow those feelings, Cara.* I noticed my coffee patiently waiting askew on the bumpy wicker table. *Swallow them with some coffee,* I thought and lifted my mug to my lips.

I went upstairs following breakfast and put on a bathing suit. It was a cheap black one from Target with fringe that hung from the bandeau top. I stood in front of the mirror and stared at the fringe as I tried to recover from breakfast. Somewhere inside me there was a wound and I was reminded of it every time Dee commented on my voice—speaking or singing voice—or noted my nervous laugh. I didn't know what it would take for it to finally heal, but I needed it to. I wanted resolution and I wanted it right then and there because the dynamic was old and tired and made me feel old and tired too. And because I knew no other way to force a change, I forbade my nerves the same way I forbade my tears earlier, and went to confront Dee.

I caught her privately on her way to the patio. I was trembling.

"Dee," I said and started crying immediately. "Dee, why does that get me, bother me so much?" and there was a brief second where she searched my words for their context and then joined me in my memory, right back at the breakfast table.

She responded, "Because it's so critical and rude and I shouldn't say shit like that—people do that to me and I hate it." There was something confusing about her boomerang response, a response that turned the criticism around and directed it back at herself. I didn't want her to feel bad, but she clearly did. And so we stood there in our bikinis, wanting to take each other's hurt away.

"I know it's you protecting me, wanting me to be big and strong—" I said, and she interrupted, "Because I look up to you, Cara. Because that's how *I* see you."

"I don't know how to change it, Dee. How to feel stronger when I'm around you," and the tears that had slowed started up again.

"I'm projecting my own insecurities. It's my shit. Not yours."

She was sorry. I could see it in her face. I didn't know if acknowledging how bad we both felt would move us toward something different or just toward the next time the subject came up. I worried that acknowledging our pattern would only reinforce it, but I hoped it would take us somewhere new.

A couple of days later we took a day excursion in a private boat. We'd just arrived at a small beach where we saw a rock that rose an intimidating distance out of the cerulean water, a relatively short swim from the shore. In a vast Caribbean landscape, I guessed every distance was larger than it seemed from my seat on our boat; the distance from our boat to the shore would likely feel farther once I was in the water, and the rock might feel more like a cliff when standing on its crest. By my emotional estimation, the rock stretched high enough skyward to make me nervous, but not so nervous that I wouldn't let my boys jump from it. Our guide said it was approximately thirty feet high.

It was clear that many people had spent their day between that rock and its nearby shore. There were buoys marking acceptable places for boats to anchor, and at the top ridge of the rock were two two-by-four slats of wood vertically planted into its crust like a pair of hiking poles. On one end of the rock was a rope that hung from midway up its face and landed at the water's surface. I imagined many hands, large and small, had grabbed on to the end of that rope and pulled their way out of the sleek water and onto the rock's calloused skin.

My boys' hands would be next. They swam with Mark from the boat to the rope. Jake was first to grab hold of the rope, the strength in his skinny arms evident in defined mini-muscles. He pulled and climbed, carefully searched for footholds and handholds, and rounded the edge to the top within a few short minutes.

"It's a lot higher than it looks," he shouted. I watched him through the video camera, wishing I could protect his ego and his body simultaneously, trying to still the camera and distinguish the difference between his fear and my fear for him. But before I could overanalyze or beat myself up for letting him get up there in the first place, he jumped. He screamed with fear and excitement the brief way down to his triumphant splash. And he emerged giddy with pride and adrenaline.

Avery was next. I recalled our climbing trip to Moab only a couple of years earlier, where he spent four days rock climbing with his middle-school class. I was grateful for that experience, which was now helping him safely scale the rock. He appeared confident and I was proud of him. Just like Jake before him, he rounded the edge to the top within mere minutes and made his way to the launch. Unlike Jake, Avery examined his surroundings like a physics problem—if I step here first, then here, I'll have enough speed to get there and then I'll be able to clear the distance from that point over there, and I'll still land feet-first. Then he confidently took his hands off the two-by-fours and jumped as matter-of-factly as a wave to a friend across the street. We cheered. Jake, who had swum directly back to the boat, was next to me and I could feel brotherly pride when Avery braved the jump.

During a brief period of mulling around, offering towels, and opening soda cans, I decided I would jump off the rock, too. I'm not sure why. Looking back, the decision that I made in a split second had the force of years behind it. Apart from my feet during a few games of "run away" with Walker, in which we ran to the ocean and then ran away from it before it could touch us, I hadn't been in the ocean all week. There'd been intermittent rain, there was sharp coral in the water, there were strong winds, and there were waves that looked a bit like bullies. For whatever reason, I had opted not to go into the water in the days prior to our boat excursion, and I felt compelled to get into the water on the day of our boat trip.

I also wanted to connect with Jake and Avery. I'd been such a pain in the ass lately. My depression, though finally medicated, left our home life in overcast conditions and I was responsible. I hadn't been my usual fun, inappropriate self and I was developing the bad habit of nagging the boys rather than inspiring them. The days were all business—getting out of the house by 7:15 A.M., doing school, doing homework, doing dinner, and getting ready for bed. I wanted to be fun again. I wanted to give them the kick-ass mom I used to be. The one who would go to the top of the food chain and take down a teacher if he messed with my kid. The one who knew when they needed to be pushed harder and when they needed permission to say, "Fuck it." I used to be the mom who would cook a five-course Japanese meal from scratch because Jake requested it, or make a homemade Halloween costume of Max from *Where the Wild Things Are* without a sewing pattern. I wanted them to be proud of me, to like me again. I wanted to feel likable.

Sitting on the boat with my sister, I considered my strength. I was the flimsy, lanky sister, who got sick a lot. She was the athletic, strong sister, with the powerhouse voice. She loved sleepaway camp, and I was homesick. She fought with mom and I avoided conflict. She had direction, when I was lost.

The huge rock jutting out of the water was formidable and felt like an invitation to the formidable part of me. The Cara who birthed her boys at home, juggled single motherhood, and could pitch a tent with the kids in the twilight and rain. The Cara who sang a karaoke duet with her sister, who found a sense of humor in a holding cell and the word "penis" in "pennies." I'm strong. I'm fun. I'm in Anguilla.

"I'm gonna go jump." Once the words flew out of my mouth, there was no putting them back in.

As soon as I drew attention to myself, everything intensified. I belabored the jump from the boat to the water. Readied my bikini top and bottom. Tested the water with my foot, peeking over my shoulder to ensure no one would shove me in. I dived in before I could be pushed and the sea felt silky. It was smooth and crystal-clear, cleansing and refreshing. I began to swim freestyle over to the rock. Each time I lifted an arm out of the water and dug it into the sea, I felt my strength building—years of summer-camp swim meets in every stroke. I arrived at the rope quickly. I reached for the white, clean portion a couple inches above the algae-ridden end and pulled myself up. I was proud of my first few footholds, peripherally aware of the boat full of people watching my ascent. By the halfway point, where the rope ended, my momentum slowed and I was aware only of increasing height. I'd grossly miscalculated my fear of heights—as Avery liked to say, "You're not afraid of heights, Ma. You're afraid of landing poorly at a hundred miles per hour."

My once semi-graceful bikini-clad body became a clunky, awkward body, my crotch center stage for onlookers, my fingers clawing around the edge like a cat clawing out of a bathtub. At the top there was no happy place to plant my feet. Everything was steep and sharp. And it was high, really fuckin' high. In the air to the left of the two-by-four I imagined a large sign, JUMP AT YOUR OWN RISK. My legs started to shake as I made my way over the lichen and the ridges and bumps between the launch point and me. I took another step and the words on the sign blurred and faded, reemerging as CAUTION: PEOPLE DIE HERE, a statement for which I had no information to either confirm or deny. I made it to the imaginary sign and in its final state it read, YOU, CARA MENTZEL, WILL SLAM YOUR FACE INTO THE WATER BELOW, INCUR A NECK INJURY, AND LOSE YOUR BIKINI BOTTOM ALL AT THE SAME TIME, WHILE ONLOOKERS GASP AND GAB AT YOUR MISFORTUNE.

"Give us a pose!" Dee shouted from behind the video camera, and I managed to run my fingers through my wet hair and shove my hip off to the side. I thought of Halle Berry in 007's *Die Another Day,* standing on the edge of a massive cliff in her hot bikini, her back facing the open water. She flashed a knowing grin at Pierce Brosnan, brought her arms up over her head, and dived backward seamlessly into a tiny slit in the water below. On my comparatively little cliff, with my comparatively little boobs, and my giant-size fear, I hated Halle Berry.

I stood trembling between the two-by-fours. Though I have no recollection of Jake's being anywhere near me, he apparently leaped off the boat, swam to the rock again, climbed it, stepped in front of me, and jumped off the cliff a second time. His presence was eclipsed by my terror and known only to me through the video I watched that evening. In the time it took me to jump, someone a beach away enjoyed a grilled lobster and chardonnay, someone else napped in a sarong on a passing yacht, and yet another person discovered a functioning ATM in Anguilla.

I was wobbling, nearly naked, equally aware of my jiggling thighs as I was of the limited options to stop them: jump, or be the poor sap at the center of a humiliating helicopter rescue. I had to jump, but I was paralyzed. How had I gotten myself into this?

"Just jump, Mom!"

"Jump toward me, baby!" Mark hollered and threw in some inspirational whistles for good measure.

"The video camera's running out of space!" Dee shouted.

"Jump!"

And my personal favorite from four-year-old Walker Diggs: "Auntie Cara, you're boring me!"

In my hypervigilant state, I spotted a slight outcropping only a yard or two farther down the side of the rock. It would be debatably more dangerous to get to than to simply jump from where I stood, but looking at the small ledge the size of my two feet put together, I was able to imagine moving my legs again. I approached it with precision. Somehow I knew my party on the boat didn't like where I was heading; if I slipped, I'd be seriously wounded—if not dead. The rock had a couple of handlelike cracks in its surface and I wedged my right hand into one and steadied myself. I slowly slid my left leg down the face until it was inches away from the new ledge. I found a place for my left hand, and on my back I started sliding my right leg down to meet the left. I let go and felt my feet land safely on my tiny new spot. I could feel a collective sigh of relief from the boat. I examined my new, slightly modified challenge and was relieved when I realized the hardest part was behind me.

Mark jumped into the water and swam toward me. "Jump toward me, baby! Jump out this way." He whistled, they cheered, and I . . . jumped.

The water was kind to me. I kept my top and my bottom and, having landed properly, tolerated a surprising saltwater enema. I was relieved, but mostly indifferent. Was I proud or did I feel like an ass? Did my modified jump even count? Count toward what? Had I earned points toward the Fun Mommy Award of 2014, the Nearly 40 and Unforgettable Award? At least I was no longer the boring auntie.

I had aimed for brave, sleek, and swift. Instead I got terrified, awkward, and possibly cute. But I also aimed for memorable and I was fairly certain I'd achieved it. The swim back was a blur. I climbed back onto the boat.

"I'm proud of you," someone said.

For what? I thought. For thinking that pushing my personal limits would be rewarding, that it might help me occupy my life in a fuller way. Did I think that a thirty-foot drop would knock the depression out of me, that it would make me a better mom? That it might help me speak more confidently and improve things with my sister? Maybe I just thought I'd feel more alive.

The boat guy handed me a Ting and vodka and I finished drying off. Slowly but surely, perhaps thanks to the vodka, I felt a sense of pride. Maybe it was a twenty-five-foot sense of pride instead of a thirty-foot one. Maybe my bravery would be measured in percent of battery remaining on Jake's video camera instead of my free-fall distance. Maybe I ended up on a stage again, unable to perform as I'd hoped. Or maybe it didn't make a difference whether I jumped or not. Who knows? But I climbed that rock, stood on the edge, jumped, and I lived. That's got to be worth something.

Lesson 16

HOW TO LET GO

Frozen was a blockbuster and "Let It Go" was nominated for an Academy Award. Dee wouldn't only be attending the Oscars, she would be performing "Let It Go" live at the ceremony, and it was a big deal, the highest-profile performance of her career.

I wanted to go to the Oscars. I'd wondered what I would look like with a red-carpet makeover. I was curious to see how it would feel to be dropped into the heart of Hollywood in front of all those cameras and famous faces. Of course, I wanted not only to see Dee's performance live but to be the steady sister whose mere presence calmed her nerves. And even more than wanting to attend the Oscars with Dee, I wanted to be the one she preferred to take, not the logical choice that would save her from having to choose between Mom and Dad, or the default option because she was without a romantic partner. I wanted Dee to be as excited about taking me to the Oscars as I would be to go with her. And it was possible. She always wanted someone in the family to share first-time milestones with her.

I bragged to my colleagues and friends about Dee's pending Academy Award performance and they usually responded by asking if I would be going with her. "I don't know," I replied each time. "I'm sure there's a ton to consider." And there was. Dee had a million things going on both professionally and personally. More than I was even aware of, I'm sure. *If/Then* was slated to open on Broadway at the end of March. She was doing press for *Frozen* and performing "Let It Go" multiple times a week. And as always she prioritized Walker, focusing on him as her marriage continued to dissolve.

I waited for Dee to call for what felt like forever, but realistically it was probably a week or two from the time the nominations were announced. It took a conscious effort to prevent my hope for an invite from deteriorating into a fear of disappointment or, worse, entitlement. I wished I could be the kind of person—the kind of *sister*—who would pick up the phone and call or text Dee without giving it a second thought. I'd ask, "So what's the scoop with the Oscars?" and she'd tell me—no big deal. But I wasn't like that. I was a thoughtful sister—full of second thoughts and third thoughts, and then some.

Then Dee sent me a text. Simple. Direct. "Want to go to the Oscars?" I can't recall what I did first, sigh or scream. I was relieved and excited. I wanted to reply, "I thought you'd never ask," like a coy schoolgirl, but coy doesn't play well over text so instead I wrote, "Fuck yeah," which also accurately captured my sentiment. I sensed that Dee was proud. I don't know how I knew what she was feeling. It was only a text. There was no intonation, volume, or emotion to interpret. Still, it felt like Dee knew she'd made me happy and was proud that she was able to. She texted a laughing emoticon. I texted, "What do I wear?" She texted, "I've got it all taken care of. XO." I trusted she did. "XO."

A couple of weeks later, Dee explained that I didn't necessarily need to fly out to New York City for a fitting, that it was sufficient to send my measurements via e-mail to her stylist who, in turn, would send me pictures of possible gowns. But then someone mentioned that a personal fitting could streamline the process and Dee liked the idea because she thought it would be fun to try dresses on together. I didn't need any arm twisting. I wrote substitute notes for my class and a few days later I hopped on a plane to LaGuardia.

It was late morning the following day when Dee, her stylist, and I arrived at one of Vera Wang's studios and met a beautiful woman with long dark hair and even longer skinny legs. Every square inch of her was meticulously put together, so much so that I wondered if the few stray hairs that lay in front of her shoulder instead of against her back were intentionally placed, or if they'd simply lost their way during her walk to work. With her were two handsome gay men, designers of some sort. They immediately led Dee, the stylist, and me over glossy white floors, through a curtain, and into a dressing room. Then one gentleman rolled in several gowns that hung from a rolling rack, and referred to them as *her* dresses. Dee leaned in to me and quietly asked, "Are you all right if I go first?" which had evidently been the assumption.

"Of course," I said.

"It's my second fitting. It'll go fast," Dee added.

"Of course," I repeated. "I'm dying to see what they're working on for you."

With six of us in there, even the oversize dressing room was a tight space. I took a seat out of the way on a built-in bench that faced a three-way mirror. Dee stripped down to her thong without hesitation. Thanks to years of performing in theater, she was used to being dressed and undressed and too busy for modesty. I watched the men drape dark green fabric across Dee's chest and hips. The color evoked images of lush foliage and marshy waters, like a bayou at dusk. They adjusted the fabric, a little tighter here, a little lower there, and pinned it in place. They periodically stepped back to assess their work directly or in the mirror.

There was some oohing and ahhing over more dresses and one pink fabric that was "to die for," according to her stylist, Leslie; "Gawjus, just gawjus," she said. Leslie was an attractive middle-aged woman whose thick New York accent, slightly brusque attitude, and passion for the materialistic could make a room feel like a high-end New York nail salon.

After approximately forty minutes they finished up with Dee and it was my turn to try on dresses. Two of the ladies stepped out of the room and one of the gentlemen asked me to get undressed so he could take my measurements. Dee browsed the rest of the dresses on her rack. She pushed some to the side to expose a red gown and said to me, "This one's pretty, isn't it? You should try this one."

In the brief pause after Dee spoke, I heard conspicuous whispering beyond the dressing-room curtain and it made me uncomfortable. I was half naked when Leslie came into the room and explained that there had been a misunderstanding and no one had pulled any dresses for me.

"Oh," I said from the bench, looking up at her in my underwear.

"You can get dressed," the assistant added.

"Don't you still need my measurements?" I asked.

"We don't need them. You're a sample size."

"Can she try on some of the gowns on this rack?" Dee asked. She was in protective-sister mode. "You know, so you can get a sense of her figure and what kind of cut would look good on her?" But the assistant said no. I was embarrassed and I didn't know why. I'd done nothing wrong—though it didn't help that my leggings were still down around my ankles. What exactly did the woman think I was going to do in those dresses, throw a tantrum until they let me have one?

I felt tears well up, and I wished they wouldn't. I didn't want to make trouble for Dee. I didn't want to seem ungrateful. And I definitely didn't want to be the topic of discussion later in the day: "Oh my god, Idina Menzel's sister totally cried today because we wouldn't let her try on the couture gowns." Of course, the latter statement wasn't true. I didn't feel like crying because of the dresses, but rather because I'd been forgotten, or not worth considering, and because there was something about the earlier whispering and the subsequent tone of the assistant's voice that felt dismissive and insulting. I suspected that I was the favor someone had brokered; "We'll even throw in something for Idina's date," someone must have said. *That's probably how these red carpet things work,* I told myself. I was well aware that I wasn't a celebrity, but that didn't mean I was a nobody, and that's what I felt like. Nobody.

But when you're lucky enough to be Idina Menzel's sister, and you're going to the Oscars, and Vera Wang is going to let you wear one of her dresses, you don't get to be upset. You pull up your big-girl pants, keep your mouth shut, and smile amiably. *I* pulled up my pants, kept my mouth shut, and smiled amiably.

A few minutes later, Dee and I learned that *the* Vera Wang would be joining us for a post-fitting lunch date. Lunch with the ageless, hyperactive Vera in a fur hat with ear flaps helped soften the day's earlier blow.

The Friday before the 86th Academy Awards Ceremony, I arrived at LAX. It was after 10 P.M. when my driver pulled up to the entrance of the Four Seasons at Beverly Hills. A few patrons walked through the portico where tendrils of crystal chandeliers cast a shimmering light on the fronds of potted palm trees.

"I'm here!" I texted Dee.

"Come on up," she replied with her room number.

The driver pulled my roller from the trunk and I handed him a twenty-dollar bill. I didn't know if I was supposed to tip him or if the tip was included or if he was one of Dee's regular drivers and she'd take care of him. It seemed standard practice to tip a driver, but Dee's world wasn't standard and I wasn't certain how to navigate it, especially in Beverly Hills. And so I worried that my twenty-dollar bill was a lot like the five-dollar check Grandma used to send me on my birthday—cute.

I rolled my way over the lobby's marble floors, into the elevator, and up to Dee's room. A pretty woman in her midtwenties answered the door and beyond her I could see Dee at the end of the short entryway. She was partially clothed in a pink dress, her elbows out a little, while a man with just the right amount of product in his perfectly styled hair stuck pins in the fabric.

"Hi, Ca. How was your flight?" Dee asked.

"Piece of cake."

Dee turned to her guests. "Have you met my sister, the taller, skinnier version of me?" That's how she liked to describe me, like someone stretched her out from head to toe—even my eyes, nose, and lips were narrower.

I rolled my eyes at Dee for calling me "skinnier" and then smiled at the faces in the room. I knew a couple of them. Her manager Heather, her friend Shawna. I gave kisses and hugs. Leslie was there, too, with her assistant, the young woman who had opened the door.

"Are you hungry?" Dee asked. There was a platter of hummus, pita chips, and veggies on the round glass dining table along with a bottle of champagne.

"A little," I answered and ran a chip through the hummus.

"Take a look in the bedroom. You *have* to take a look in the bedroom." She pointed me toward it on her right.

I could see inside before I even stepped through the French doors. Heels of varying heights and in shades of white, black, nude, and blush lined the perimeter of the cozy room. Clutches, more than thirty of them, some beaded, some alligator skin, in bright colors and muted colors, with gold or silver finishes, mostly rectangular, but a few oval, were spread out in an orderly array of rows and columns over the whole of the king-size bed. Between the bed and the armoire was a rolling rack of gowns.

"Think you'll be able to find something in there?" Dee asked and cackled. (I love when she cackles.)

"Ya think?" I said, rifling through the dresses.

"Just wait 'til the jewelry gets here," Leslie added.

"The jewelry?" I popped my head out the bedroom door and looked at Dee, then Shawna. All three of us stopped in our tracks. Leslie explained that earlier in the week she had shopped the jewelry of several designers to borrow and the items she liked were being delivered to the room that evening so that we could decide which jewels looked best with the gowns. I took a sip of champagne. *This could be a long night,* I thought. *And I hope it is.*

In the hour that followed, three different gentlemen knocked on the door and delivered jewels, then waited outside our hotel room with security officers. We set a white terry towel over the coffee table for better viewing and so we wouldn't lose anything, and carefully laid out each necklace, earring, bracelet, and broach until the table looked like it belonged at the end of a pirate's treasure map.

I think Dee was first to ask about the value of the jewels in our possession.

"A few million?" she guessed, looking at Leslie. Leslie reached for a diamond ring off the table and said, "This ring alone is over a million."

"Oh for crying out loud," I said, sounding like my dad. "That's insane."

"What about this one?" Dee asked, sliding a chunky, ruby filigree statement ring onto her index finger. Let me guess . . . $80,000?"

"I'm guessing $95,000," Heather said.

"I'm gonna go higher, $125,000," Shawna chimed in.

"I agree with Shawna," I said.

Dee flipped her hand over and looked at the price on a tiny tag that hung from a piece of white thread. "I was wrong. But only by a little." She laughed. "It's $185,000. It almost looks like costume jewelry, don't ya think, like it could hang on a display in a department store?"

"Noooo," Leslie said. "No, it doesn't." By the look on Leslie's face, you'd think Dee had mistaken the ruby stunner for a ring pop.

"Take a picture. Someone please take a picture of this table," Dee said. She liked to take frequent reality checks. She never wanted to take anything for granted. "Always stop and take in the moment" was something she had learned from Jonathan Larson and was determined to remember.

We played "Guess How Much" and drank champagne while I tried on some dresses. We narrowed the dress choices down to a low-cut canary-yellow gown and a periwinkle tulle gown that crisscrossed over my chest and gathered together at a silver beaded broach at my mid-back.

"Nah, you know what," Leslie said, "the yellow's too Golden Globe. The periwinkle is Oscar." In my life away from Beverly Hills and its jewelry-delivery services, there weren't varying degrees of black-tie occasions. You either needed a gown or you didn't, and usually you didn't. Luckily, the vote for the periwinkle dress was unanimous so I didn't have to worry about showing up to the Oscars like I thought I was going to the Golden Globes. How embarrassing would that have been!

The following day, Saturday, I joined Dee and her posse—her managers, Burt and Heather; assistant, Daphne; and voice coach, Tanya—at rehearsal. We entered The Dolby Theatre through a private entrance a few steps behind Pink and her people. Pink would be performing "Somewhere Over the Rainbow" in honor of the seventy-fifth anniversary of *The Wizard of Oz*. We stopped at security on our way in, where I took a quick picture for my badge, then walked the hallways backstage and convened in Dee's dressing room. Dee always preferred the acoustics of bathrooms for her vocal warm-ups and had scouted out a good backstage bathroom the day before. So when Dee left, I took a walk with Burt and Daphne into the auditorium, where we sat for a little while and watched the rehearsal.

In the orchestra section many of the seats were occupied by large foam-board posters on which the name and portrait of each expected celebrity attendee was printed. From a distance they reminded me of oversize old west Wanted posters and I chuckled for a second, wondering what the reward would be for capturing all those celebrities.

Some of the orchestra seats were filled with unknown actors hired to play their more famous counterparts. While I waited for Dee to take the stage I took an empty seat in the dark. I watched celebrity presenters rehearse their lines off the teleprompter, then fumble with an envelope and say, "And the winner of the 2014 Fake Oscars for this night only is . . ." At that point, the fake winner of a category, that is, the actor playing the actor who might win the following night, would jump out of his or her seat and kiss those around him. He'd make his way onto the stage and proceed to ad lib an acceptance speech. (For some, pretending to be an Oscar-winning actor was a bigger stretch than for others.) Occasionally a whole group of people would "win" a category and they'd huddle up in front of the microphone, beaming, or jumping up and down, or whispering, "I can't believe it," with hands to their hearts, as if they'd really won. There was no half-assing it at the Fake Oscars.

Eventually, it was Dee's turn to rehearse. Earlier, I'd learned that Dee needed two dresses, one for the red carpet, the green one, and one for her performance onstage. It was a secret, but Dee would be performing in front of a backdrop of hundreds of thousands of cascading Swarovski crystals, and needed a gown that would work well with that set and lighting. She was still vacillating between two gowns and needed to make a final decision at rehearsal, where she could see how the colors would play on set.

Then, of course, there was the song to rehearse. By the second verse of "Let It Go" I knew Dee was holding back. She often did during rehearsals. I thought of the people listening, including the production staff, other celebrities, agents and managers, and how maybe they didn't know that Dee was "saving it" for the next night. Maybe they thought that was the best she could do. Part of me wanted her to belt out the chorus so no one would doubt her, which was silly because she gave a beautiful performance. I was reminded of the nitro button on the cars in street-racing movies, the extra propulsion, the next level of speed. I was eager for Dee's nitro button, for her to show the world the difference between super and supernova. I only needed to wait one more day.

Dee spent the morning of the Oscars in rehearsal at the theater again, while I spent the morning in the care of her hair and makeup guys. I wore a loose off-the-shoulder cotton shirt so that when it was time to get in my dress, I could pull it over my head without ruining all their hard work. Earlier, Dee's hair stylist, Roke, had raised his hands into the air, framed my face like a portrait, and said, "I'm seeing Linda Evangelista circa 1990." By the time

Dee returned from rehearsals, my short, curly hair was straightened, pulled back off my face into a wavy pompadour, and slicked back with a product so thick and greasy that it required special removal instructions. My makeup was straight out of a Coco Chanel ad—eyebrows dark and dramatic, eyes smoky, lips soft pink. When Dee walked in and saw me she was ecstatic.

"Oh my god. You should wear your hair like that all the time!"

I laughed. "Right, like Roke's gonna get me ready for Foothill Elementary every morning. By the way, those flowers arrived for you."

Dee sat on the couch and opened the card. "Holy shit!"

"What? What?" I asked.

"They're from Bono!" she squealed. " 'Idina, Wishing you the very best for this evening, proud to share the stage with you . . . sing your royal heart out.–Bono, Edge, Adam, and Larry.' " U2's "Ordinary Love" from the movie *Mandela: A Long Walk to Freedom* was nominated for best original song alongside "Let It Go," Pharrell's "Happy," "Alone Yet Not Alone," from the movie of the same name, and "The Moon Song" from *Her.* "Those guys are class acts," she said with a starstruck glow.

Dee and I switched places. I sat on the couch, picking at some scrambled eggs and strawberries, while she sat in the chair facing the natural light of the windows that lined the far wall of the hotel room. It was Dee's turn for hair and makeup. Roke trimmed Dee's split ends while her publicist talked us through the plan for the red carpet. We would take a short walk there instead of taking a car. She and Dee discussed what interviews Dee would do—only a select few they'd agreed on. Dee had to be careful not to strain her voice before her performance by doing interviews all along the red carpet. This is also when I was instructed to memorize the designer of my jewels, clutch, shoes, and dress just in case someone with a microphone asked me.

Dee interjected, "I want you to have fun, babe," and reached her hand out for a squeeze. "I don't want you to worry about speaking up. Say whatever you want. Just be yourself."

"Aw, thanks, Dee. I will." I'd already given myself the "just be yourself" pep talk. I'd thought it all through. I would take in my surroundings and try to make the surreal feel real. I'd remain poised and, I hoped—given the height of my heels—upright. Dee may have wanted me to enjoy myself, but I also had a job to do. I was her date. By her side I was determined to be the calm and steady version of myself, but when I slipped into my flowing periwinkle gown I couldn't help but feel like Eliza Doolittle on her way to the Embassy Ball.

As soon as we left the room, we started to see celebrities. First there was Kelly Ripa in the elevator. Then, Kristen Bell and Dax Shepard as we neared the official red carpet. Jessica Biel posed for photographers, and Dee and Kristen laughed as they encouraged each other to go next. "No, you follow Jessica. No, no, really, you should." There was a hello and a hug from Kerry Washington—I had no idea she and Dee knew each other. There was Charlize Theron, Sandra Bullock, Jennifer Lawrence, Amy Adams, and Lupita Nyong'o. Dee gave interviews to Michael Strahan, Ryan Seacrest, Kathie Lee Gifford, and nameless others, definitely more than the three originally planned. It seemed as difficult for Dee to ignore an eager microphone on the red carpet as it was for her to ignore a fan begging for an autograph at a stage door. Even when we entered The Dolby Theater and thought we'd cleared the masses, we passed Naomi Watts, who stopped Dee to wish her luck and tell her how jealous her children would be when they found out that she'd met Idina Menzel.

And while I knew Dee worried that sometimes I followed behind her on the red carpet, or that I was shrinking in her metaphorical shadow, I couldn't have felt less so. Idina Menzel had made it to the Academy Awards and I didn't care where I stood, if I was trailing behind her long train or taking a cute selfie with Burt while she smiled for "real" cameras. I was her sister and I was there.

Dee and I took our seats in the center of a row six rows back from the stage. We watched Julia Roberts, Brad and Angelina, Bradley Cooper, and others in front of us greet each other and chat, smile, and laugh like normal people do. In fact, if their tuxes had been from the local rental shop or their dresses from Nordstrom, it could have been a high school reunion or an office holiday party. I was watching friends catch up.

The theater filled and eventually celebrities convening in the aisles ended their conversations and took their seats. Portia de Rossi and Ellen DeGeneres's mom sat down right in front of us, and Bono took the seat at the end of our row. I'd almost forgotten that I was there for a show until the music started, the audience cheered, and Ellen, the host, made her entrance.

I'd sit next to Dee for only the first twenty minutes or so of the show. Even though "Let It Go" was scheduled as the last musical performance of the nominated songs, Dee needed to leave during one of the first commercials to warm up, change her dress, and adjust her hair and makeup. Heather would take Dee's primo seat next to me.

From the minute Dee left my side, through all the awards and performances that led up to hers, she was on my mind. I thought about how little rest she'd been getting. Back in New York, Walker woke her up early every day. *If/Then* rehearsals kept her up late; she was in nearly every scene of the show. Then she had to fly across the country for the Oscars and those rehearsals and that prep.

She'd often laughed about "Let It Go" and how she'd opted to sing it in a higher key because she thought it more fitting of Elsa and her youth. Dee was well aware of how old—or young—her voice sounded. Years earlier she'd auditioned for *Tangled,* but was told her voice was too old for Rapunzel and too young for Mother Gothel. In fact, that audition was how she ended up becoming Elsa. She recorded "Blackbird" for one of *Tangled*'s casting directors and the woman loved the recording so much she listened to it over the years. When it was time to cast for *Frozen,* she suggested Dee.

Dee worked with Kristen Bell and the creative team for *Frozen* over the course of two years. During that time, Robert Lopez and Kristen Anderson-Lopez's "Let It Go" helped inspire an unconventional Disney nemesis—not a powerful, evil ice queen with a cold heart but a powerful, complicated sister with a loving heart. Not so different from Elphaba. Not so different from Dee.

Dee loved Elsa. She always gravitated toward the misunderstood, powerful female characters. She enjoyed exploring the relationship between fear and sadness, insecurity and strength, anger and power in the context of formidable women. For the same reason, she also loved "Let It Go." Furthermore, as a veteran perfectionist and a relatively new mother, she understood the importance of letting go. She'd often been encouraged to lighten up on herself and to stop perseverating on minor missteps. But no matter how relatable Elsa and "Let It Go" were to Dee, even she couldn't have predicted the song's success. How could she have known that "the storm would rage *on*" and on and on with its demanding high note day and night for talk shows at 6 A.M. and 6 P.M. and performances—including the performance that very night—televised for millions? She didn't know, though that probably wouldn't have stopped her from changing the key and doing right by Elsa—high notes never bothered her, anyway.

Finally, it was time for Dee's performance. I watched her walk onto a dark stage and plant herself comfortably in the middle. I pictured the hardy platform heels hidden behind the hem of her dress. They weren't elegant, but it didn't matter because no one would see them. Dee preferred to feel sturdy and grounded when she sang, like she drew her power from the earth beneath her. John Travolta walked out to a small portion of the stage off to the left as the *Pulp Fiction* theme played, and I could feel the adrenaline in my body, the sudden awareness of my heartbeat, my breathing, and then the distracting sound of Mark's voice in my head: "Plugs, he's totally got plugs, right?" and I had my own private chuckle at Mark's fixation on celebrity hairlines. The lights and television cameras were squarely on Mr. Travolta as he read from the teleprompter about his love of the movie musical.

"Here to perform the Oscar-nominated, gorgeously empowering song "Let It Go," from the Oscar-winning animated movie *Frozen,* please welcome . . ." I waited in my seat and Dee waited, standing straight ahead of me in the dark to hear her name announced for the whole world, ". . . the wick-ed-ly talented, one and only, A-del Da-zeem."

Who? I leaned over to Heather. "Did he just . . ." I was going to say, "speak in tongues," but she cut me off.

"Shhh, not now," she said. The theater went dark except for a spotlight that shone down on Dee in her cream-colored lace dress and the blue light that lit up the sheets of crystals behind her. The first gentle piano notes of "Let It Go" began and an entire audience of furrowed brows and cocked heads set their confusion aside in deference to my sister, my sister who I'd later learn was clearing a mental path through about ten seconds of what-the-fuck, poor-me, did-that-just-happen, with a deep breath and a focus on Walker, to whom she'd earlier planned to sing.

Dee began. She started out soft and deep, taking her time, her voice like warm maple syrup. With the next verse she shifted into a more hopeful, bright sound, and as she neared the chorus, her intensity grew until there she was in all her glory, belting out that anthem like only she could, sending a shiver up my spine and emotions swirling through the theater. On and on she sang, her voice still building, not Elsa, but Idina. The Idina that doesn't fit in a box, that's neither Disney nor Broadway nor pop. Not exclusively fit for the screen, or the stage, or the radio. But Idina who is all of the above. Holding nothing back, she sent the final high note swiftly into the mezzanine, and after she claimed that the "cold never bothered me anyway," she let her arms drop to her sides. The audience rose to their feet and cheered. It was a drop-the-mic moment. There was a subtle look of satisfaction on her face, followed by a bow. She was poised, but I suspected—or maybe I hoped—that her inner truck driver had a few choice words for a certain actor whom I didn't remember seeing at the rehearsals the day before.

Heather grabbed my hand and said, "Let's go. I'm gonna kill John Travolta." We sidestepped our way past the neighbors in our row, but when I got to the end, I realized I was face-to-face with Bono and his rose-colored glasses. In the fever and haste that filled the minute after Dee's performance, and the stardust that filled the few inches between his face and mine, I forgot about being calm and steady and instead I blurted out, "Mysistersaysthankyoufortheflowers," as if the sentence was one long, multisyllabic word. I threw a wide uncomfortable grin across my face and then took off down the aisle, trying to keep up with Heather. I left Bono behind, probably wondering who the hell I was and why I felt it was appropriate to shout in his face.

Dee's dressing room was packed with people, and it wasn't long before we realized two things: One, John Travolta's flub might give Dee more exposure than performing at the Oscars alone. Social media was already busy trying to come to an agreement on exactly what Mr. Travolta had called Dee and how to spell it phonetically. I thought Twitter and Facebook were jumping the gun. I still entertained the possibility that he wasn't saying Dee's name at all but rather had been body-snatched by aliens trying to get a message to a compatriot in a nearby galaxy. And two, we realized that "Let It Go" had just won the 2014 Academy Award for Best Original Song. It was a good night!

Dee had to make a red-eye flight back to New York. The previews of *If/Then* were starting that week and she needed to be at tech rehearsal the following day. We had limited time to attend after-parties but managed to stop in to the *Vanity Fair* party for about an hour, just enough time to learn that Anne Hathaway is more beautiful in person than on screen and that celebrities really *are* just like us, because even the ever-so-elegant Jenna Dewan Tatum had to pump milk for her baby in a public restroom.

It was around 1 A.M. when Dee and I sat in our big black Escalade in front of the hotel and I helped her unclasp her diamond necklace. We had signed insurance documents for our diamonds the night before and been educated about their "chain of custody"—a term that sounded familiar to me only because of my addiction to poorly scripted television crime dramas. I signed what papers I was asked to without asking why. I did, however, pay close attention to the plan for the jewels' safe return, and unfortunately, the responsibility was largely mine. I was instructed to put Dee's jewels in my purse before she left for the airport and then take them, along with my own, back to the safe in my hotel room, where Leslie would pick them up from me the next morning.

Dee handed me her ring and then her earrings. When I went to put them in my purse we looked at each other quizzically. Now that the moment had arrived, putting the jewels in my purse seemed like a severely flawed plan. There was no zipper, no snug pocket inside, no way to ensure they wouldn't fall out. Dee and I started to laugh. What the hell were two sisters from a little townhouse in Woodbury doing on Oscar night in a million-dollar-diamond predicament? How had we gotten from there to here?

"Wear them!" she shouted, and I remembered the time she'd said, "Taste it!" back when I was three and she offered me dirt. This time she offered me diamonds, but we easily could have been in the leaves of that backyard in New Jersey because we were wide eyed, playful, and together.

After she put the necklace on me and I slid on her ring, she placed her earrings in my hand and I held them tightly in my fist. Dee was beaming. It made her happy to take care of me, to make me feel like a million bucks, to pull me into the spotlight with her. When Dee expressed concern that I wouldn't be able to undo the elaborate clasps of the necklace and bracelet on my own, I assured her that it didn't matter because I didn't plan to take them off.

"I'm no dummy," I told her. "I'm totally gonna sleep in them!"

She cackled.

Soon we stood next to the open car door to say our goodbyes. She'd taken her shoes off and I'd recently put mine back on. With my heels on and hers off, I felt like a giant. No one could tell who was the big sister and who was the little one.

I said thank you and she kissed me on my lips.

I said it had been one of the best nights of my life and she wrapped her arms around me.

I said I'm off to case the joint and return the jewels, and she laughed.

I said I love you, and she said I love you too.

And then she left and I was alone again.

Alone, but with a mission, and with the theme to *Mission Impossible* playing in my head—dun, dun, dah-dah, dun, dun, dah-dah, dunananaa . . ." I felt for the thick necklace around my neck and confirmed it was still there, then squeezed the earrings in my other fist. I walked over the slick marble floors of the lobby, past a conversation among a small cluster of people, and around a corner to the elevators. A young gentleman in a suit had already pressed the Up button. I smiled at him and then looked down at my feet until the elevator doors slid open. I could feel every diamond on my body as if each one held a weight equal to its worth. My droplet earrings hung heavily from my earlobes. The ring on my index finger felt like a boulder. The necklace resting on my clavicle like a medieval chest plate. The doors opened to my floor and I walked briskly to my room, where I changed my mind about sleeping in the diamonds. I went straight to the safe, removed the jewels, and carefully set each one on the velvet tray, reviewing the inventory to ensure nothing was missing and then locking them away with my favorite four-digit code, 8-0-0-8, or BOOB—I never forget it.

I put on some comfy clothes and lay on the bed with a full face of makeup and my journal. Then, as I often did, I imagined where Dee was at that very moment. Had she made it to the jet yet? It was a lot of work for me to leave my boys and my students in Colorado, but unlike Dee, I was in no hurry to get anywhere that night. Between then and my afternoon flight the next day, my biggest undertaking would be getting the product out of my hair.

If Dee had made it to the tarmac, I knew it was only a matter of minutes before she was asleep and miles away from me once again. But whether miles or that metaphorical centimeter, what did it matter? I always seemed to be aware of a distance between us: physical or emotional or some combination of the two. Was I just a glass-half-empty kind of girl? Always seeing what's missing instead of what's there? I hated to think of myself like that, but recalled that the last time my glass was completely full I didn't even want it; I abandoned it next to a puddle of vomit.

Walking the red carpet and attending the Academy Awards had to fit someone's ideal of something—glamour, stardom, success? Though I'd never take my experience that day for granted, even attending the Oscars wasn't perfect. Dee was stressed about staying healthy and skinny. She was working overtime, sleep deprived, and single-parenting a toddler. She was negotiating a divorce and just when she thought she knew what to expect, frickin' John Travolta happened. For my part, I'd had my dress taken in too much at the waist and could only take shallow breaths when seated, my shoes were tearing up my feet, I was other-than-charming with Bono, and I didn't get to spend a whole lot of time with my sister.

In my ideal world, Dee and I are neighbors. I pop over in the morning for coffee and we chat briefly about how one of the kids wants to quit martial arts, or painting, or college. She gets a call and realizes she has to be somewhere and I offer to take Walker to school, because I can, because I'm right there and I know where his school is and what time he needs to be there. And a couple of nights later, she swings by my place with a bottle of wine and says thank you and we plop ourselves down on the couch and fall asleep watching Rachel McAdams and Ryan Gosling kiss each other in the rain, until one of our husbands shows up with take-out Chinese. *Why can't life with Dee be that simple?*

Before Elsa's image was on tissue boxes, T-shirts, and waffle irons, I had a freckled first-grade girl in one of my reading groups who asked me about my sister. I played a YouTube video of "Let It Go" for her after group one day. She looked at me and said, "But I don't get it, Ms. Mentzel. What is she letting go of?" I didn't know how to respond. Should I lead her into existential waters; the song is about what it means to truly be yourself? Do I tell her that Elsa is letting go of anything and everything that was getting in the way of her being proud and confident? That she was letting go of perfectionism, of whatever it was that made her think she needed to hide, needed to conceal her power? She was letting go of fear? Fear of what other people might think of her, fear of her own strength? Or do I tell her that as we grow up we all have things we'd benefit from letting go of and they're different for each of us? I wasn't sure I even knew the answer—not exactly. But I was a teacher and good teachers know that having the answer isn't always the same as having the understanding, and deep understanding is usually earned through experience.

The answers I could propose to "What is she letting go of?" are the results of *my* experiences, of having spent my life identifying with strong and complicated women. Women on and off the screen. On and off the stage. Women whose relationships required work, who became better people for having known each other. Women who were similar and different, flawed and funny, but whose relationships compelled them to be their best. Women who were lovers, friends, enemies, sisters, or—like Liz and Beth—two facets of the same woman. Women like Maureen, Elphaba and Glinda, Anna and Elsa. Women like my grandmother. My mom.

Women like Dee and me.

My Gratitude

In the more than four years it took me to write this book I juggled three great loves: family, writing, and teaching. I was all kinds of crazy. To everyone and everything that offered support through that experience (whether you're called out in this section or not), I assure you that my gratitude is boundless.

To Dee for not only letting me write about us, but for suggesting it. For trusting me with our stories and honoring my point of view. For your time, energy, and your huge heart. But mostly, for being an inspiration.

To Jake and Avery, for letting Mom tell your stories. For letting me be self-centered sometimes and still growing into exceptional, loving, thoughtful human beings, and for continuing to snuggle with me even as you grew taller than me.

To Oscar, for accepting me into your life.

To Dad for crying in therapy with me all those years ago, for never being surprised when I succeed, and always calling me on your way home from the casino.

To Mom—Is it funny that I want to thank you for your memory! You might have three pairs of reading glasses on your head and not remember what you told me this morning, but without your vivid memories I couldn't have written this book. Thank you for your endless supply of pep talks, for putting the needs of your daughters and grandsons above all else, and for your genes—I'm still holding out hope that I age as well as you.

And to Mark, the fastest pun in the west, whose generosity and devotion make him the easiest man to love. Thank you for working twice as hard so that I could write, for keeping me laughing, and for falling asleep with your hand on my ass nearly every night—all women should be so lucky.

To Shannon, for always making time, for understanding the difference between a semicolon, an em-dash, and an en-dash (that's a thing, right?). For loving me in my ugliest moments, and even when I pee my pants.

To Lisa, for your irreverent sense of humor and thoughtfulness. For having the most infectious laugh and cutest sneeze (and not the other way around). And for listening—no matter what.

To Shari Caudron, for telling me I had a story and then giving me the courage and the wherewithal to write it.

To Jennifer Joel, my badass agent, a hero in my book (but too classy for a gold-trim bustier and red boots).

To Michael Flamini and his posse at St. Martin's Press, for a warm welcome, for your patience, and enthusiasm. And Michael, for incorporating comedy into your edits so they were easily digestible (even at a DAR luncheon).

To the following special people who gave me cozy places to write: my friends at Ozo coffee shop on Arapahoe, Diane and Jack Bazler, Kelly and Don Degnan, and Jeri and Erik Chapin.

To my many readers along the way for their helpful input including: Brittany Rocheleau-Unwin, Heather Glick, Julie Herman, Laura Jordan (thanks for nothin'), Lauren Ward-Larson, Lauren Szenina, Tim Hillmer, and Karyn Smith.

To Neil Rosini (my attorney and a calm voice of reason), Mary Jo Bode (my forever mentor and another calm voice of reason), Martin and Mason Balgach (because you're like family, but definitely not calm voices of reason). To the Idina Menzel posse: Burt Goldstein, Heather Reynolds, Bonnie Bernstein, and Ken Weinrib. And more family: Ron and Sylvia Phillips, Paul, Bets, and Ollie, Sarah, Kevin, Korynne and Kyler, Susie Mentzel, Aaron Lohr and the incomparable Walker Diggs.

To my community at Foothill Elementary, especially my students—past and present—from whom I often learn my greatest lessons (like opt for the skort on a windy day).

To the accommodating staff at the Boulder Valley School District, my principals over the years who have graciously been flexible with my schedule, and the Boulder Valley Education Association for taking what was probably the strangest call they've answered to date.

To my cheerleaders at HireEducation.

To my crutches: Zoloft, Buspar, coffee, red wine, and binge television.

To my dogs: Miss Adelaide, may you never be without a lap. Benny, may you never be without a ball (and thanks for keeping your balls out of my lap).

And finally, to anyone whose real name is in this book and isn't pissed.

Thank you. Truly.